ARMAGEDDON IN THE ARCTIC OCEAN

*Up the Hawse Pipe from Galley Boy to
Third Mate on a Legendary Liberty Ship
in the Biggest Convoy Battle of World War II*

PAUL G. GILL

EDITED BY PAUL G. GILL, JR.

HELLGATE PRESS   ASHLAND, OREGON

ARMEGEDDON IN THE ARCTIC OCEAN
Published by Hellgate Press
(An imprint of L&R Publishing, LLC)

Hellgate Press
PO Box 3531
Ashland, OR 97520
email: sales@hellgatepress.com

Cover & Interior Design: L. Redding
Cover Art: "The *Nathanael Greene* Rejoins the Convoy" by Herb Hewitt

ISBN: 978-1-954163-38-6

Printed and bound in the United States of America
First edition 10 9 8 7 6 5 4 3 2 1

To my mother, Sarah Welsh Gill,
and my father, Capt. William F. Gill,
my anchors and the stars I steer by.

In Praise of

ARMAGEDDON IN THE ARCTIC OCEAN

"A 20th-century tale of grit, seafaring, bravery and patriotism. Gill's book is full of adventure and determination, a terrific read. Many autobiographies aren't page-turners, but this one is."

—Capt. James Noone, Chairman,
National Maritime Historical Society

"The story laid out in this marvelous work of nautical combat is real, relevant, and deeply meaningful to anyone who has set sail and headed into harm's way."

—James Stavridis, PhD, Admiral, US Navy (Retired)
Vice Chair, Global Affairs, The Carlyle Group
Chair of the Board of Trustees, the Rockefeller Foundation
Supreme Allied Commander at NATO, 2009-2013
Dean, The Fletcher School of Law and Diplomacy (2013-2018)

"What a story, and how well told! Those of us who were brought up on Alistair MacLean's *H.M.S Ulysses* and its mesmerizing and yet so tragic odyssey in Arctic waters, will revere *Armageddon* as a gem among World War II memoirs. Its account of the fierce battle for Convoy PQ18 and the dismal circumstances in northern Russia at the time contributes richly to our knowledge of the sacrifices the free world was willing to make to keep a reluctant Soviet ally in the war."

—Eric C. Rust, Professor of History, Baylor University,
author of *Naval Officers under Hitler* and *U-Boat Commander*
Oskar Kusch: Anatomy of a Nazi-Era Betrayal and Judicial Murder

"The years 1930 to 1945 transformed both America and the world. They also transformed the life of a young man named Paul Gill who was ten years old in 1930 and twenty-five in 1945. This lively and compelling memoir of those years, completed and edited by his son Paul Gill, Jr., is a poignant portrait of the country in that critical epoch. It illuminates the hardscrabble existence of a Boston Irish Catholic family during the depth of the depression; it evokes the determination of a young man who had to lie about his age to obtain a berth as a merchant seaman; it draws back the curtain on a hobo's life in those Depression years after young Paul and his brother decide to ride the rails across the country; and, finally, it cap-tures the terror of a convoy battle at sea in the Arctic Ocean in 1942 when the ship carrying now-Third Mate Paul Gill was attacked by both planes and U-boats on the Archangel Run. It is, in short, a story of poverty, hope, determination, desperation, courage, and eventually triumph. It is, as well, an absolutely splendid read."

—Craig L. Symonds, Professor Emeritus of History,
U.S. Naval Academy

"Gill writes with a directness and simplicity that is endearing but also hard-hitting. He delivers an extraordinary American tale of overcoming adversity that starts at a tender age. The memoir is centered on his seafaring career which reaches its climax aboard a Liberty ship on a particularly hellish voyage to Archangel during World War II. It culminates with being torpedoed in the Mediterranean Sea. While the salty parts of his story will make engaging reading for mariners and armchair sailors alike, a big surprise is his vivid descriptions of riding the rails across the U.S. during the Great Depression. His unvarnished account of the harrowing life of a hobo is brought to life as few ever have done. Life in the Civilian Conservation Corp, the brutality of seafarer strikes in the 1930s, and wartime conditions in Russia are other unexpected gems embedded in this story. The authenticity of Gill's voice and the extraordinary first-hand details make the pages fly."

—Capt. Daniel Parrott, Professor of Marine Transportation,
Maine Maritime Academy

"I've read many memoirs and accounts of this era, centered on the Great Depression and moving through the war. But few of them held my attention as urgently as Paul Gill's recollection of his young life, what he calls with gusto, 'my "up the hawse pipe" story, ascending from hobo to Merchant Marine and Naval officer at a young age.' It's a tale of poverty and defiance, one that offers a wide-angle look at a country trying to find itself in the guise of a young man trying to find himself. At its white-hot center lies the tale of Gill's fraught passage in the Arctic Ocean on the Archangel run, when his ship sustained attacks from waves of Nazi torpedo bombers over eight astonishing days. The writing in this book is vivid, clear, and utterly absorbing. I recommend *Armageddon in the Arctic Ocean* to anyone who wants a good war story that is also, in every way, an American story of considerable freshness."

—Jay Parini, Professor of English and Creative Writing,
Middlebury College, author of *Borges and Me*

"Though memorable for its C.S. Forester-style account of the terror wrought on convoy PQ18 by U-Boats and the Luftwaffe, Paul Gill's narrative of life as an American merchant mariner during the Great Depression is Melville-like in capturing the rigor of life at sea. This page-turner should be a must-add to history curricula at the nation's maritime academies."

—**David F. Winkler, Ph.D., Naval Historical Foundation**

"*Armageddon in the Arctic Ocean* is a fascinating memoir of a merchant mariner's ordeal in the North Atlantic during World War II. Edited by Paul Gill Jr., and written by his father, Paul Gill, a native of South Boston, he recalls his Irish-American father's seafaring life in fishing schooners and the great coal schooners and then as a rigger, sailmaker and professional yacht captain; and the family's tough times during the Great Depression. He tells anecdotes of his teenage meandering from one job to the next as a matter of survival. He joined the CCC in Vermont, enlisted in the Merchant Marine as an ordinary seaman, and rode the rails across the country before returning to sea in 1938. Best of all are his hair-raising experiences as Third Mate on the SS *Nathanael Greene* on the run to Archangel in Convoy PQ18. Later joining the Navy as a commissioned officer, he recalls his experiences with the Sea Bees in the Pacific. In the postwar era, he completed his B.A. in three years, and earned an MBA from Harvard University. This is truly a mariner's success story."

—**William S. Dudley, Ph.D., Naval Historian**

"A fascinating memoir by a roughshod Boston boy who scrambled to help his family survive the Depression, rode the rails, joined the Merchant Marine, lived through the hellish experience of Convoy PQ 18 on the Archangel Run, and went on to graduate from Harvard Business School. If you want a first-hand account of travail, tenacity, and triumph, read *Armageddon in the Arctic Ocean.*"

—**Jeffrey L. Cruikshank,** author of *In Peace and War: A History of the U.S. Merchant Marine Academy at Kings Point*

"What a remarkable legacy my uncle Paul Gill has given us! His story takes the reader from the rough and tumble streets of South Boston during the Great Depression, to the Green Mountains with the Civilian Conservation Corps, off to ride the rails with hobos and tramps, and finally into the heart of one of the most significant convoy battles of WWII. Chronicling the deprivations of this unique chapter of American history, Armageddon in the Arctic Ocean is a testament to the power of brotherhood and the sacrifices men make for family and country.

For those who love maritime history, tales of war, characters of faith and determination, and life's meaningful journeys, this is a book not to be missed."

**—LCDR Roger Gill, Associate Professor of Marine Engineering,
Massachusetts Maritime Academy**

"An excellent first hand account of human endurance in the harshest of conditions. *Armageddon in The Arctic Ocean* is a five-star World War II read."

—John R. McKay

"It would be hard to imagine a more engaging and thrilling work of fiction. But this story is not fiction. It is the autobiographical account of a young man's life during the Great Depression and World War II. The writing style is straightforward, and one can almost hear the narrator speaking the words he writes. The description of Gill's (and his brothers') hardscrabble life of scavenging for food and fuel during the depths of the Depression in South Boston; working for pennies to provide food for his family; "biting the bullet" and heading off to Alaska for an opportunity that may or may not exist; riding the rails, again scavenging for food, dealing with the hobos and ne'er do wells sharing boxcars, and sleeping in "hobo jungles" – and all as a teenager. The young man's drive and determination to follow his family's heritage in the marine trades sees him going to sea at a time when unions were forming, merchant seamen were equally violent and caring, and winning his "ticket" and ultimately his mate's license. When World War II begins, young Gill ships on a Liberty Ship as Third Mate ,which will put him squarely in the midst of the biggest convoy battle – on the horrific Archangel run – the world has ever seen. The descriptions he writes – taken from his contemporaneous diary – are beyond vivid, and have the ability to put the reader squarely in the midst of the explosions, torpedo attacks, and strafing runs by German aircraft. The book disappears and we are participants in the mayhem and horror of freezing cold air and water as well as the heat of fires, noise of explosions, and utter devastation to men and materiel. I can unhesitatingly recommend this story to anyone with an appetite for adventure, history (in the first person), and a penetrating look into life during the Great Depression."

—William H. White, Maritime Historian and author

"*Armageddon in the Arctic Ocean* provides a compelling first-hand account of one man's experiences coming of age in Depression-era America to become a merchant marine officer involved in one of the deadliest convoy battles of World War II. An inspiring story of perseverance and character in the face of great adversity, the book provides a fitting testament to the heroism and service of Paul Gill as well as the multitude of unsung heroes who served with him."

—**Brian E. Walter, Historian**, author of *The Longest Campaign: Britain's Maritime Struggle in the Atlantic and Northwest Europe, 1939-1945*

CONTENTS

INTRODUCTION

M Y EARLIEST MEMORY OF THE SS *Nathanael Greene* is of the time in 1957 when my father loaded the family into our station wagon and drove us to the U.S. Merchant Marine Academy at Kings Point, just outside New York City. He said there was something he wanted to see there, a plaque honoring the Liberty Ship he served on in World War II. I remember being led into a room and looking at a bronze plaque describing the heroic actions of my dad's ship during her voyages to Russia and the Mediterranean, where she was destroyed by a German U-boat.

The plaque read:

> *During a long voyage to North Russia,* SS Nathaniel [sic]
> Greene *was under incessant and violent attack by enemy
> planes and submarines. In most gallant fashion, and in
> spite of many crew casualties, she consistently out-ma-
> neuvered and out-fought the enemy, finally discharging
> her vital cargo at the designated port. After effecting tem-
> porary repairs to her battered hull and rigging, she took
> part in the North African Campaign. Bound for her last
> port, with limited cargo, she was torpedoed, and in a
> sinking condition was successfully beached.*
>
> *The stark courage of her heroic crew in battle against
> overpowering odds caused her name to be perpetuated as
> a Gallant Ship.*

Unit Citation plaque for the SS *Nathanael Greene*. Reproduced with permission of the American Merchant Marine Museum.

We read the words on the plaque in awe, scanned the other eight plaques in the Gallant Ships collection, and left. We were very proud to see our father's ship enshrined in a place of honor at Kings Point.

Dad was quiet on the drive home. It was as though we had paid our respects at the grave of a departed family member. My sisters and I wanted to learn more about the *Nathanael Greene* and Dad's role in the story, but his somber mood discouraged conversation, and the topic did not come up again until years later.

In 1960, when I was twelve years old, my parents purchased an old farmhouse in Southold, on Long Island's North Fork. The house had been vacant for many years and had fallen into disrepair. As the only son, I was conscripted to help Dad renovate the structure and turn it into a habitable vacation home. Almost every Saturday that spring and summer, Dad and I made the long trek out to Southold to work on the house. We were driving through farm country one morning when a haunting melody came over the airwaves, sung in German by a woman with a lovely voice. I didn't know a word of German, but the singer repeated what sounded to me like "seaman." We listened to the song, and then Dad, who knew German, told me the song was titled "*Seeman, deine Heimat ist das Meer*," "Sailor, the Sea is Your Home" in English.

Sailor, Sailor
Your home is the deep blue sea
Your ship is your love
And the stars are your best friends

And though you find your thrills
In the places far away from me
Just remember I'm always waiting
When your journey ends

The poignant lament seemed to touch Dad's heart and unleash a flood of memories. He started to tell me about his voyages to Germany as a sixteen-year-old merchant seaman in 1937. He made eight passages that year, first on SS *Manhattan*, the ship that had brought the American Olympic team to Germany for the Berlin Olympic Games, and then on the SS *President Roosevelt*. He spoke of the fun he had dancing, singing and drinking beer with young Germans in Hamburg beer halls, of his beautiful German girlfriend, Heidi, and learning German from her and his German shipmates. On the ride home from Southold that afternoon, he spoke about the *Nathanael Greene* and her voyage to Archangel as part of Convoy PQ18 in 1942. He grew excited as he described the ferocious barrage of antiaircraft gunfire the *Nathanael Greene* threw up against the waves of Heinkel 111 and Ju 88 bombers that swept down the columns of merchant ships at masthead height. He described the cataclysmic explosion of the ammunition ship, SS *Mary Luckenbach*; the *Nathanael Greene* being singled out for praise by the convoy commodore for shooting down nine German aircraft; leading shipmates down into the ship's magazine to load rounds into ammunition belts in the heat of battle; a powerful gale in the White Sea; the horrible conditions in Archangel; getting lost far north of the Arctic Circle on the return voyage; and *Nathanael Greene* going down with all guns blazing after being attacked by U-boats and Heinkel 111s in the Mediterranean Sea.

I never enjoyed laboring on that old farmhouse, but I was riveted by Dad's storytelling, which became a regular feature of our long drives back and forth to Southold. I learned about Dad's tough childhood growing up in Depression-era Boston; leaving home to join the Civilian Conservation Corps at age fifteen; going to sea at age sixteen; his pre-war years in the Merchant Marine; manning picket lines on the New York waterfront; working as a steeplejack on Manhattan skyscrapers; riding the rails across the country with his brother, Steve; port calls in Honolulu, Rio de Janeiro, Buenos Aires, and Le Havre; attending officer training school and earning his Third Mate's ticket; his fourteen war-zone runs on the *Nathanael Greene*; joining the Navy; and attending college and graduate school after the war.

Dad rarely spoke of these matters with other family members, and never to anyone outside the family. On the rare occasion when someone brought up the topic of the *Nathanael*

Greene, you could almost see a mask descend over his countenance. He would become quiet and withdrawn. He was not fun to be around at these times, and the rest of the family learned to give him a wide berth until the dark mood dissipated. But when he and I were alone together he seemed to enjoy opening up to me about his youthful adventures and misadventures, his brushes with death, and his determination to overcome the many obstacles placed in his path as a young man and survive poverty, battles with violent men, and combat, to finally acquire a family, an education, and a secure place in society.

I sensed that Dad needed to share these stories with someone, and that I was the only person he felt he could confide in. He always said that he was going to write a book someday, to be titled *Red Waters*, based on the diary he kept on the voyage to Archangel.

In 1982, Dad retired after a long career in the shipbuilding industry and started to write *Red Waters*. He worked slavishly on the book for many years, and acquired a great deal of research material from the National Archives, the US Navy, the Coast Guard, and the Imperial War Museum in England.

The book project got a huge boost in 1990, when Dad tracked down his best friend on the *Nathanael Greene*, radioman John McNally, who lived in Swanton, Vermont. Dad and John had many wonderful reunions, usually at our home in nearby Middlebury. The two old shipmates would sit for hours on our front porch and exchange stories about the good and the bad times they experienced on the SS *Nathanael Greene*. Whenever I could, I would sit quietly and listen to their enthralling stories about their escapades in Glasgow and Edinburgh, Scotland; Sunderland and Middlesbrough, England; the convoy battle in the Arctic Ocean; the long overlay in Archangel; their return to Scotland; and the last days of the *Nathanael Greene* in Mostaganem, Algeria, before she steamed out into the Mediterranean on her last voyage.

At first, Dad seemed to make good progress on the manuscript. However, deteriorating vision and other health challenges prevented him from finishing the book. Shortly before he died in 2000, he asked me to edit the manuscript and find a publisher for the book. I promised him I would, but when I first looked at the manuscript and delved through the five boxes of notes and research material he left behind, I was overwhelmed. Many of the chapters were still in outline form, and I realized that finishing the project would require an enormous expenditure of time and energy, which at that time I could not commit to. I decided to put off editing the manuscript until I retired from medical practice. By the time I hung up my stethoscope in 2013, I had just started an ambitious boat-building project, and so I kept the book project on the proverbial back burner.

It stayed on the back burner until April, 2020, when I received a call from my twelve-year old granddaughter, Natalie Gill. Natalie's 6th-grade class was studying World War II, and she wanted to learn about my father's wartime experiences. I told her that Dad's ship, the SS *Nathanael Greene*, was part of a large convoy of ships that ran a ferocious gauntlet of U-boats and German warplanes in the Arctic Ocean in 1942 to deliver desperately-needed munitions to Archangel, Russia. I told her how the *Nathanael Greene* was briefly disabled when a nearby ammunition ship exploded, and was in mortal danger of being destroyed by German warplanes and U-boats as she fell behind the rest of the convoy. I had to fight back tears as I told my granddaughter that her great-grandfather and his shipmates got the *Greene* underway again and steamed back into convoy formation with the Stars and Stripes streaming proudly from her mast and the men in the other ships in the convoy cheering wildly. I ended by describing how the SS *Nathanael Greene* was torpedoed by a German U-boat off the coast of North Africa.

Talking to Natalie about the *Nathanael Greene* reminded me of my unfulfilled promise to my dying father. I realized that I had an obligation not only to my father, but also to my children and grandchildren, to get his story into print. I dug out Dad's unfinished manuscript, his diary, and the research material he had amassed. To my great surprise and delight, I found copious notes describing his childhood, his experiences in the Civilian Conservation Corps and the Merchant Marine, as well as the voyages of the SS *Nathanael Greene*. I also found several old floppy disks containing more notes. As I sifted through this fascinating material, I realized that I could not put off the editing of *Red Waters* any longer. I had to share Dad's incredible story with the world. And when I came across this sentence in the manuscript, "This was Armageddon, the decisive battle of good versus evil prophesied in the Book of Revelation," I decided to change the title of the book to *Armageddon in the Arctic Ocean*. Every challenge Dad faced as a boy and young man had prepared him for what would be the sternest test he would ever face in mortal combat against a ferocious and determined enemy in one of the most formidable environments on the planet. This is my father's story.

—Paul G. Gill, Jr., M.D.
Middlebury, Vermont
February, 2022

ONE

LAYING THE KEEL TIMBERS

Beachcombing for Driftwood

L IVING BY THE SEA, MY twin brother, Phil, and I had always
been beachcombers, roaming up and down the beaches
near our South Boston home with our eyes peeled for pretty
seashells, sea glass, or sea gull feathers. But now, in the winter of 1931, the second winter of the Great Depression, we
were no longer *recreational* beachcombers, but ten-year-old
subsistence beachcombers. Our quarry was driftwood. Driftwood of any size or shape. No matter if it was painted, coated
with tar, or full of nails, bolts or screws, if it would burn in
our mother's kitchen stove, we grabbed it and tossed it in
the rickety pull cart we dragged up and down Carson Beach.

The pickings were slim this winter of 1931. Other boys
were out scavenging firewood as well. Earlier that year, the
driftwood harvest had been plentiful, and we had usually
been able to load our cart with firewood in less than an
hour. But it had been a long, cold winter, with heavy snowfall,
and the beach had been nearly scoured of combustibles.
What driftwood remained was locked in icy tangles of frozen

Paul (*left*) and Philip Gill

seaweed, rope, cardboard, and other flotsam. Now we had to get down on our hands and knees and claw furiously at the buried treasure, slowly detaching the log or plank from the concrete-hard sand it was embedded in. Sometimes, the reward for our stubborn efforts was hardly worth the cuts on our hands or the throbbing pain in our frost-nipped fingertips. We wore gloves to protect our hands from the sharp barnacles that encrusted the driftwood, but digging and clawing in the frozen sand soon wore holes in them. As a result, the flesh on our palms and fingers became hardened with callus and tough as the leather in our dad's sail palm.

When we couldn't find enough driftwood to fill our cart on Carson Beach, we would drag it over to M Street beach and continue our search there. This cart, with two iron automobile wheels and no pneumatic tires, was not the envy of the other beachcombers scavenging for driftwood. It was ugly, but it served its purpose. Rolling over the granite cobblestone streets, the screech of the iron wheels grinding over the pavement stones could be heard blocks away. Every evening, as we hauled the full cartload of driftwood home under the gaslights, we were mortified to think that our neighbors were laughing at us as we passed by, peering from behind drawn curtains, thinking, "There, but for the grace of God, go our children."

Frigid arctic winds and subfreezing temperatures in the late winter of 1931 brought an end to that year's beachcombing when the driftwood became frozen solid in the debris that covered the beach. Try as we might, we could not dislodge the driftwood from the sand, stones, shells, and seaweed with which it was encased in the ice. Periods of intense cold alternated with warm, rainy periods, followed by a cold snap that would last for days. When this happened, the beaches along the southern shore of the South Boston peninsula became solid ice, and we had to give up our hunt for driftwood.

In normal times, most of the homes in our Irish-American enclave of South Boston burned coal, not driftwood, in their furnaces and kitchen stoves. But these were not normal times, and coal cost money. Economic calamity had struck the United States in late 1929 and now families across America found themselves in a desperate struggle to survive.

Only a year earlier, Phil and I, and most of the other boys now trudging stoop-backed across the bleak, snow- and ice-encrusted beach, would have spent the after-school hours playing ball, sledding, or fishing, according to the season. But the word "play" had vanished from our vocabulary.

The Coke Fields

Demoralizing as it was to lose our main source of firewood for our mother's kitchen stove, we now faced the additional problem of a nearly-depleted coal bin. Fortunately, we had collected enough driftwood to burn in the kitchen stove for several weeks, but driftwood was not a suitable replacement fuel for coal in the furnace that heated our house. Coal burned slower than wood, and was a far more efficient heat source than wood. We had to find a cheap or free source of coal.

Fortunately for us, the local electric power plant loaded the ashes from its coal-fired power generating plant into trucks and hauled them to the dump near the docks and shipyards on the north side of the peninsula. Deep ravines cut into the land at various places in the dump, and the utility company trucks backfilled these ravines with ashes. The trucks would back up to the rim of a ravine and discharge their loads of hot ashes, cinders and clinkers through their tailgates.

We discovered this coke-picking gold mine just as we were burning the last few chunks of coal in our bin. We hurried down to the coke fields after school every afternoon and waded ankle-deep into the ashes and probed for unburned chunks of coke, which we collected in a tin box. As word of this free source of coke spread, coke pickers started to swarm like flies around the ravines after each load of ash was dumped, and we gradually came to understand that coke picking was not without its dangers, for the pickers and truck drivers alike.

The ground under the trucks' wheels consisted largely of poorly-compacted ashes, and was unstable and susceptible to collapsing under the weight of the loaded truck. If that were to happen with the giant rear wheels close to the rim of the ravine, the truck, its load of oven-hot ashes, and the pickers who had swarmed around it could all go tumbling down the steep wall of the ravine to their destruction. We knew we were in danger of being caught and crushed beneath the truck's rear wheels, but we suppressed our fears in order to gather as much life-sustaining coke as we could. We fought to be "Kings of the coke hill," and for our family's survival. It was a desperate struggle on the best of days. On bitter cold winter days, with a cold north wind blasting the coke fields, we were often driven to our knees, shivering and shrinking from nature's fury. Wiping tears from our eyes, with our faces blackened and smudged, we groped through the ashes with gloved fingers for fragments of precious coke. Periodically, we would have to remove our gloves to pick off the razor-sharp clinker edges which had been burned into the fabric. Our hands were chronically cut, bleeding and blackened.

Coke picking was a nasty business. Soot saturated every piece of our clothing and infiltrated every pore and every wrinkle on our skin. Mom subjected us to endless hot tub baths with vigorous scalp-to-toes brush scrubbing, but we were still plagued by Staph infections on our hands and arms. Despite the soot and the staph infections, Phil and I continued mining the ash fields through the frigid winter, and the wet and stormy fall and spring. Picking coke after school each day, and on weekends, holidays and vacations, Phil and I together were usually able to fill a 100-pound potato sack with coal after digging through the ashes for an hour or two. We would rather have been playing ball or fishing with our neighborhood pals, but we took pride in the fact that we were able to keep the home fires burning all winter, and were doing our part to keep our family together.

During slack periods, when we had collected a large reserve of coke, Phil and I drifted from the coke fields over to the waterfront docks in search of discarded dunnage to replace our family's dwindling supply of firewood. The dunnage consisted of rough planking used to protect freight carried in ships' cargo holds. Stevedores discarded damaged dunnage, which we collected and brought home to burn in the kitchen stove. Some of the dunnage consisted of mahogany and other exotic tropical hardwoods, which Dad used in his model-making.

We liked to watch the dock workers load and unload cargoes. We were mesmerized by the ocean liners, freighters, and oil tankers, steel-hulled, steam-powered 10,000-ton Leviathans being pushed by squat, smoke-belching, whistle-blowing tugs in and out of berths in Charlestown or East Boston. Smaller vessels, colliers, pilot boats and ferries, plowed up and down the harbor. Smelly, storm-battered fishing schooners crowded T-Wharf, or sailed into or out of the harbor. Along the wharves, shrilling steam winches hoisted cargo from unbattened holds, and brawny longshoremen moved ant-like up and down the gangplanks. Looking across the channel, we could see excursion boats and coastwise steamers tied up at Atlantic Avenue piers.

The South Boston waterfront was almost exclusively devoted to maritime affairs. It was a discharge center for West Coast lumber, and berthed many deep-draft passenger liners and ocean-going freighters. Railroad cars nosed in and out of the piers, loading or unloading cargo of all kinds from all over the world.

One day Phil and I went down to the waterfront to watch as the British battlecruiser HMS *Hood* steamed into the harbor and tied up at Commonwealth Pier. The "Mighty *Hood*" was the largest warship in the world, the pride of the Royal Navy. There was a large crowd in attendance, including most of our friends. We looked on in awe as tugboats nudged the massive ship up to the pier and Limey sailors scurried over her decks securing mooring lines. We were proud that this magnificent symbol of the might of our mother's native country was visiting our city. But Phil and I were probably the only people in the crowd who harbored anything other than contempt for the 860-foot long dreadnaught. South Boston was an Irish American neighborhood, and most of its residents viewed Britain as the ancestral enemy. At first, the crowd looked on in silence, as though overawed by the sheer size of the vessel. But then something, perhaps the sight of the four, massive fifteen-inch gun turrets, triggered an

HMS *Hood*, circa 1924

explosive outpouring of taunts and jeers. Phil and I were proud of our Irish heritage, and had an instinctive under-standing of the crowd's hostility toward the *Hood*, but our mother was English, and we were equally proud of her native land and its people. We got into a brief scuffle with boys who were tossing rocks at the *Hood*, but we were greatly outnum-bered. We decided that discretion was the better part of valor, and walked away before blood was spilled.

On another occasion, Phil and I went over to the South Boston Dry Dock to see the North Atlantic passenger liner SS *Leviathan*, then the largest ship to ever fly the American flag. We thought *Leviathan* looked huge when we saw her steaming up the main shipping channel the day before, but now, resting on chocks and cradled in scaffolding in the dry dock, she was an awesome sight. It boggled the mind to see a 59,956 ton, 950-foot-long ship suspended high and dry, as if in mid-air.

Leviathan had been launched as *Vaterland* in Hamburg, Germany, in 1913, but was seized by the U.S. government in New York in 1914 with the outbreak of war in Europe. When the United States entered the war in 1917, she was converted to a troop ship and renamed *Leviathan*. After the war, she was acquired by the United States Lines and put into service once again as a North Atlantic passenger liner.

Among the vessels that docked at the Army base and Commonwealth piers were Black Diamond Line freighters that Phil would someday sail to northern European ports, and Luckenbach Line freighters which I would sail to Portland, Seattle and San Francisco. We could not imagine what the future held in store for us as we gazed out over the harbor on those afternoons long ago.

SS *Leviathan* in South Boston Dry Dock, 1930

Scavenging for Food

Fuel was not the only commodity in short supply during those dark Depression days. Food was no longer taken for granted in the Gill household either. Starting in the summer of 1933, Phil and I would go over to the South Boston freight yards every day or two and scavenge for fruit, ice and vegetables in the reefer (refrigerated) cars.

As in every other facet of life, we had plenty of competition in our search for food in the railyard. There was a hobo jungle on the fringe of the yard where drifters lived in makeshift cardboard and wood crate shelters. The denizens of this encampment were constantly prowling through reefers and boxcars in search of produce and damaged containers of canned food, and sometimes tempers flared and fights broke out over contested food items.

At first, Phil and I just stumbled through the boxcars hoping to find a bunch of bananas, a crate of oranges, or a carton of canned sardines. Over time, we developed a system. First, we ascertained where the railroad crews were in the process of unloading vegetables and fruits from the reefers. We would trail the crews at a safe distance, waiting for them to finish unloading a car, and then move on to the next one. Then, we moved in to salvage damaged and leftover produce. We usually worked as a team of four: Phil, me, and a couple of other streetwise kids who knew the drill. After lookouts were set, the hauling cart was positioned, and our tools were gathered, we pushed open the doors and entered the car. We quickly surveyed what the railroad crew had left behind and stuffed everything that looked edible into burlap bags before moving quickly on to the next car.

When the sacks were nearly full, we climbed the ladder to the roof of the reefer, opened the hatch cover to the ice compartment, and crawled down inside with ice picks and tongs to collect ice to keep our salvaged fruits and vegetables fresh. After filling a bag with chopped ice, we climbed out of the ice compartment and back onto the roof of the car, lowered the bag to the ground, divided the ice among the bags of produce, and returned home with our treasure.

We didn't always go right home. Railroad bulls (guards) continually patrolled the yards checking the empty cars for trespassers, and inspecting the seals on the reefer doors. The bulls had their hands full chasing drifters out of the boxcars and flushing hobos out of the hobo jungles near the tracks. Some would look the other way when they saw that the trespassers were only young boys trying to salvage a little produce for their families. However, there were other bulls, real pricks, who were not inclined to show mercy.

They would rather give chase to the student scavengers, beat them severely with their fists, and then lock them in the reefer cars or the ice compartments to "cool off" before taking them to the police station to be charged with trespassing and theft of railroad property.

To escape such brutal treatment, if we were sighted by the bulls, we ran off in different directions to confuse our pursuers. Sometimes the only avenue of escape was also the most dangerous one. We would race up the reefer ladder to the roof and then run as fast as we could down the full length of the train in opposite directions to confuse the bulls. Leaping from car to car as we ran, jumping down into the gondolas, then onto flatcars, and finally down to the ground. Fearful of the brutal beatings we knew we would receive from the bulls if they caught us, we would stash the bags in the bushes, flee the freight yards, and return to retrieve our contraband later in the day when the coast was clear.

If the pickings were slim in the freight yard, we would go over to the docks and offer to clean the holds of fishing trawlers in exchange for a few pounds of freshly-caught flounder, cod, or haddock. If the haul was good that day, we'd get enough fish for Mom to prepare one of her wonderful seafood dishes, such as baked stuffed flounder, broiled haddock or fish chowder.

Going to the Dump for Fun and Profit

One of the unexpected consequences of the passage of the Eighteenth Amendment to the Constitution of the United States, which prohibited the sale of alcoholic beverages, was an explosion in alcohol consumption. Bootleg whiskey was easy to find, speakeasies proliferated in cities and small towns throughout America, and many families became familiar with the formula for "bathtub gin." As a result, there was a great demand for recycled glass jars and bottles. Phil and I spent many afternoons at the town dump, collecting any glass vessel which could conceivably hold alcohol. When we had collected a couple of bags of bottles, we would take them to a redemption center and collect a penny a jar or bottle.

Sometimes we would get bored raking through the refuse for bottles and we would amuse ourselves, and practice our marksmanship, tossing empty whiskey bottles at the myriad gray-brown rats that darted in and out of the stinking piles of decaying refuse. I believe the marksmanship skills I cultivated in the South Boston dump as a boy contributed to my success in shooting down a Heinkel 111 torpedo-bomber in the Barents Sea a few years later. Southie rats helped America win the war!

On hot summer days, the stench from the nearby glue factory, where they slaughtered horses, drove us away from the dump and over to the swimming hole at Stetson's Coal Pier. We'd slip into our shoulder-to-knee, moth-eaten, wool swimsuits and jump in. Sometimes we would watch with morbid fascination as Boston police officers dragged the waters around the pier for the body of a drowned drunk. Typically, the corpse would break the surface of the water festooned with hundreds of feeding crabs. There were a lot of drunks in those dark days, and not a few of them ended up, accidentally or otherwise, falling off a wharf and drowning.

Dad, the Captain of Our Family

For our father, William Francis (Bill) Gill, the hard times we were experiencing were a painful recapitulation of family history. As the eldest of eight children, he was introduced to

Captain William Francis Gill

hard work at a young age. The Gills had been fishermen for untold generations on the Aran Islands off the west coast of Ireland. Dad's father, Roger Gill, had emigrated to America with his family in 1864 at the age of eleven, and went fishing and clamming in local waters with his father, Steven, before he was old enough to shave. As a young boy, Dad, in his turn, accompanied Roger when he went out at night fishing for flounder, fluke and other groundfish in Boston Harbor. On those nights, Dad would bait hooks and clean the catch for his father until, overcome by fatigue, he would fall asleep in the grimy, wet bottom of their Swampscott dory.

Those were the easy years for Dad. Fishing became a full-time job for him before his thirteenth birthday, when his father died and he became the main support for his mother, Sarah Foley Gill, and his seven younger siblings. He dropped out of school and signed on the *Lydia A. Harvey*, a two-masted fishing schooner captained by his cousin, also named William Gill. Dad spent the next three years fishing on shares on the Georges Bank and Grand Banks. Then, seeking steadier wages, he shipped on a series of coastal schooners, rising "up the hawse pipe" from Ordinary Seaman to Able Seaman, and finally to Second Mate and Bosun on many of the great four- and five-masted schooners, and the six-masted coal schooner, *Ruth E. Merrill*.

As Second Mate, Dad was third in command of the ship. He was responsible for managing the crew, supervising sail operations, servicing the standing and running rigging, making and mending of sails, maintaining the hull, topsides, deck, cabins and other superstructure, oiling or varnishing the steering wheels, spars and rails, and keeping the binnacle, portholes and other brass objects polished. The owners of these great schooners expected their vessels to not only make swift passages between the Chesapeake Bay coal terminals and Boston and Portland, but also to arrive in port in pristine condition.

Dad had survived hurricanes, shark attacks, yellow fever, typhoid fever, and near collisions at sea, but his luck ran out in May, 1909. He was Second Mate on the five-masted coal schooner *Dorothy Palmer* when the vessel docked in South Boston. After the vessel secured alongside to discharge a load of coal, Dad started to disembark by means of a long, wooden ladder. The ladder broke, and he fell more than twenty feet, landing hard on the concrete dock. He sustained

The *Ruth E. Merrill*

a concussion, fractures to his spine, and a fracture of his left thigh bone. He was hospitalized and his leg placed in traction. When he was discharged from the hospital several months later, his left leg was more than an inch shorter than his right, and he had to walk with a cane for the rest of his life.

Dad realized that his game leg would keep him off the quarterdeck of the great blue-water schooners. But, with the skills he had learned working in shipyards and rigging shops between voyages, he had no trouble finding work at the renowned George Lawley & Son boatyard in South Boston and at various other rigging and sail-making shops around Boston. In addition to his rigging and sail-making business, Dad was a professional captain on *Corinthia, Earthly Dawn, Northern Light, Carline, My Epiphany* and many other yachts and schooners.

In 1913, Dad met Sarah Welsh, a winsome young lady from Chester, England, who had just arrived in South Boston on RMS *Carpathia*, the ship that rescued the *Titanic* survivors, to visit her Uncle, Ned Foster.

After a whirlwind courtship, Bill and Sarah were married in St. Brigid's Roman Catholic church on March 19, 1913. After a brief honeymoon, the couple moved onto a small farm in Durham, Maine. Unable to adjust to the loneliness and hard physical demands of farm life, Dad and Sarah sold the farm a few weeks later and moved back to South Boston.

Sarah Welsh Gill

Dad Opens His Rigging and Sailmaking Loft

American victories in America's Cup competition and other international yacht races spurred a tremendous yachting boom, and the demand for yacht outfitters, sailmakers and riggers exploded. Dad opened his own rigging and sailmaking loft in South Boston, and outfitted it with reels of manila, hemp and wire rope, yards of light and heavy duck canvas, countless spools of sail twine, whipping thread and seizing wire, Stockholm tar, shackles, thimbles, turnbuckles, sheaves and blocks, and sail palms, fids, marlinespikes, serving mallets, serving boards, and other tools of the rigger's trade.

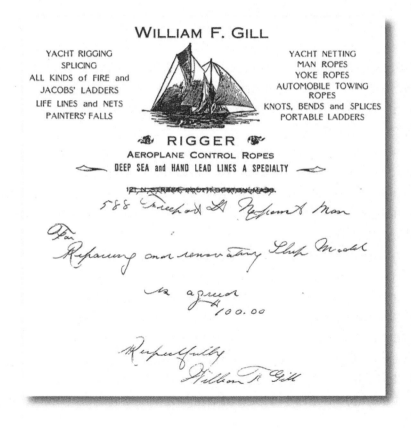

Dad had a wide circle of friends and associates in the yachting industry, including yacht brokers, marine insurers, ship chandlers, naval architects and port officials, so he never lacked for customers. In the winter months, when demand for his rigging services was at an ebb, he painted seascapes and famous clipper ships, Down Easters, and schooners, and carved half-hull and full-rigged ship models on commission or for sale on consignment in State Street ship's chandleries. It was the Roaring Twenties, and business was good and growing.

The Gill family grew as well. Our sister, Janet, was born in 1913, and five boys (Bill, Steve, John, Phil and I) followed over the next seven years. It was a full house, but we were a happy family, and optimistic about the future until economic calamity struck in the fall of 1929.

From our earliest years, we children found nothing so exciting as our frequent visits to Dad's rigging loft. In the wintertime, it resembled an artist's studio more than a rigger's shop, with its paintings of famous sailing ships mounted on easels and hanging on the walls and from ceiling braces, and with models of schooners and square-rigged clipper ships cradled in temporary berths on Dad's carving bench. We would watch, spellbound, as Dad used deft strokes of his brush to recreate on canvas the beautiful ships he had seen or sailed on as a young man.

The air in the loft was always redolent of the scent of hemp, manila, tarred marlin, rope yarn, cotton duck, and the fresh pine shavings which fell from the carving bench and piled ankle-deep on the shop's wooden floor boards. The smell of the oils drying on just-completed marine paintings added the perfect piquant spice to the loft's atmosphere.

It seemed every surface of the loft was covered with tools,

dies, fixtures, rope walks, blocks and tackles for making hemp and wire-rope rigging, rope yarns for seizings, burlap parcel, canvas strips, tarred marline, wooden fids, serving mallets and marlinespikes. Bolts of canvas and duck cloth, a sewing machine, twine, needles, beeswax, and a heavy leather palm were all on hand for Dad's next sail-making project.

While Dad made workbenches and equipment available for the boys to experiment and develop their wood-carving and painting skills, he required us to assist him in his rigging work occasionally so that he could tutor us in the basic marlinespike and palm-and-needle seamanship skills we might need one day.

Dad the Bonesetter

One day, when we were nine years old, Phil and I were tossing a ball back and forth in the street with some other boys. The ball fell into the gutter, and then rolled into the sewer opening and out of sight. We opened and raised the heavy iron lid, and then Phil climbed inside to retrieve the ball, keeping his left arm outside the opening to keep from falling into the sewer. Suddenly, we lost our grip on the lid, and it slammed down onto Phil's left upper arm with a sickening thud. Phil screamed out in pain as his humerus snapped with a loud "crack." The accident happened right in front of our house, so we lifted Phil out of the sewer opening and assisted him into the kitchen while someone called for a paddy wagon. While waiting for the ambulance, Dad took matters into his own hands and attempted to set the broken bone. Phil was then taken to the hospital, where his arm was placed in a cast without X-rays being taken. He was left with a permanently weak and crooked left arm.

Our (Brief) Foray into Commercial Fishing

A year or so after Phil's accident, Steve suffered even more serious injuries when he was struck by a truck while riding his bicycle. He suffered open fractures of his left leg that required multiple surgeries to repair. After a prolonged hospitalization, he was discharged to home, where he slowly recovered from his injuries. My parents reached a legal settlement with the moving company, and invested the proceeds in a double-ended wooden motorboat, which they christened *Jean*, after our sister. The plan was for my dad and his sons to use the boat to do a little commercial fishing in inshore waters to supplement the family's income. However, with the purported aim of acquiring boat-handling experience before venturing into the fishing business, my elder brothers would ride about the harbor in the boat, and ran it aground several times. The last such grounding resulted in the boat catching fire and burning to the waterline, thus putting an end to Dad's dreams of a glorious re-entry into the fishing industry. Bill joined the United States Coast Guard, but was given an early discharge and, after a short interval at home, left home for good to join the Merchant Marine.

Pipe the Quarterdeck

In his blue-water sailing days, Dad taught himself to play the fiddle to entertain himself and his shipmates during long port stays or when off watch. He had natural musical talent, and he found he could relieve the loneliness and monotony of shipboard life by taking out his fiddle and playing sea chanteys and sailors' ballads.

At home in South Boston, Dad would occasionally "pipe the quarterdeck," sending out word to old shipmates and their families to gather in the "quarterdeck" of his kitchen to sing, dance and relive the days of "iron men and wooden ships." There was nothing old sea dogs liked better than to share sea stories, recalling their rugged passages "rounding the Horn," brawls with bucko mates, the exotic women they dallied with in foreign ports, the scalawag seamen they had to put up with, and the mean and miserable masters they sometimes served under.

We kids would help prepare for these parties by assisting our parents in making home brew. We would wash a few bottles, and then combine Blue Ribbon Malt, yeast and sugar, and heat it on the kitchen stove. When Dad had determined that the brew was finished cooking, we'd help him and Ma to funnel the concoction into bottles, cap them, and stow them in the ice box or in the cellar.

Dad was a born entertainer. He would make sure every mug was filled with home brew or grog, then break out his fiddle and start in with the sea chanteys and sailor songs they all loved. With wind in their sails and grog in their gut, the old sea dogs, "three sheets to the wind," sang along as Dad played "Haul Away Joe," "Rolling Down to Old Maui," "Leave Her Johnny," "Drunken Sailor," "Shenandoah" and other sailor tunes. The tars would kick up their heels with a sailor's jig or two, twirling away with their former shipmates or wives or girlfriends.

The family dog, Teddy, hid under the table during these gatherings. He stayed there until the sound of the fiddle reached such an ear-piercing level that he could no longer stand it. He then crawled out from his hideaway to the center of the kitchen floor, sat on his haunches, raised his nose toward the ceiling, and let out a blood-curdling howl. The howl would continue until Dad put down his fiddle and escorted Teddy out of the house.

Everyone recognized that Teddy's howl was the canine equivalent of "All hands below!" to the quarters of their own homes. Everyone good-naturedly laughed and heeded the canine's signal to bring the evening's festivities to an end. With warm embraces, the guests bid each other goodnight and returned to their homes.

Dad's rigging business flourished through the 1920s. He had a steady stream of customers who hired him to make a suit of sails or install or tune the rigging on their yachts, and he served as professional captain on some of these vessels. The five older Gill boys learned marlinspike seamanship working in Dad's rigging shop. And we overcame our fear of heights. With his game leg, Dad could no longer climb the rigging to work in the top-hamper. Admonishing us to "keep one hand for the ship, and one hand for yourself," he sent us up the ratlines to replace the seizings on spar fittings, oil blocks, or reeve halyards through masthead sheaves. This was a skill that was to serve me in good stead in later years.

Middle Class Comfort

Our family had once enjoyed a comfortable lifestyle. Janet, the eldest child and the only girl, had demonstrated artistic talent at a young age, and she won a scholarship to the art training program at the Boston Museum of Fine Arts. John, the third son, also had artistic talent, and he received instruction in commercial art. All of us attended Catholic schools. We were well clothed, well groomed, and well fed, and we were each given a weekly allowance.

Every member of the family, except me, had an interest in developing both their artistic and musical skills. Dad could play a large repertoire of Irish reels and jigs on his fiddle, Mom had a wonderful singing voice, and the older boys all acquitted themselves well on the banjo, coronet, ukulele, and harmonica. Dad painted in oils and watercolors, as did Mom and all the boys except me. I was more interested in reading, and spent countless hours perusing random entries in the *Encyclopedia Britannica* and reading the Harvard Classics Dad had bought for us to supplement our school learning.

When I was eleven years old, I had to stay home from school for a couple of weeks to recuperate from an illness. I spent hours teaching myself mathematics, astronomy, and navigation, and reading books about America's naval history. I loved reading of the heroics of John Paul Jones in the USS *Ranger* and the USS *Bonhomme Richard*, the War of 1812 naval heroes Oliver Hazard Perry, Stephen Decatur, and James Lawrence, and Isaac Hull, commander of the USS *Constitution*, "Old Ironsides." I was proud to learn that one of Dad's uncles had been a gunner's mate on the USS *Kearsarge* when she sank the dreaded Confederate commerce raider CSS *Alabama* off Cherbourg, France, in 1864.

Janet was the artistic superstar of our family. She developed into a wonderful artist, specializing in fanciful renderings of gnomes, wood nymphs and fairies. Word of her skill even reached Walt Disney in California. The details are sketchy now, but the movie-maker flew her out to his studio in Los Angeles, where she spent several weeks sketching a variety of fanciful creatures under his direction. After she returned home to Boston she never heard from Disney again. When his movie *Snow White and the Seven Dwarfs* was released in 1937, Janet recognized her work in several of the characters. She was flattered, but felt cheated.

Losing Our Grip

As the American economy descended into the abyss, Dad's

rigging and sail-making business slowly evaporated. By 1931, only a few yachts remained in Boston Harbor, and he had to close his rigging loft. He was tormented by his inability to provide for his family. At times, he withdrew into an inner realm, and he consoled himself many evenings by playing melancholy tunes on his fiddle. He still sold an occasional ship model or a marine canvas, but sales dropped off precipitously.

Janet finished her art training at the Boston Museum of Fine arts, and procured a full-time, but low-paying, job with a Boston design firm. John was also able to contribute to the family's support with his commercial art.

Bill found work cleaning and repairing the nets on fishing trawlers after they returned from the Georges Bank with cargos of cod or haddock. Between arrivals, he picked and packed shellfish in the pier-side canneries, a tedious and mind-numbing job. The stench of the shellfish saturated his clothing and pervaded every room of the house.

Steve was good with machinery, and occasionally found work overhauling marine engines in one of the area boat yards, but those jobs were rare. He and John both spent more time performing menial labor, such as scraping barnacles off ship bottoms in the local graving dock, or unloading fish or loading ice and other supplies onto fishing trawlers

The earnings from these poorly-paid jobs only marginally improved the family's finances. The strain of trying to balance the competing demands of school and work slowly ground our brothers down. One after another, they dropped out of school to find full-time employment.

The prospects of finding meaningful work locally were dismal. Thousands of young men, many of them high school or even college graduates, walked the streets of Boston searching desperately for work. Teenage boys who had not finished high school could not compete with these older boys and men for the few available jobs. Much to the sorrow of our father, who had himself been forced down that pathway as a boy, they followed Gill family tradition and went to sea.

Phil and I were luckier than most of the kids of the Great Depression. Though Dad was out of work, with no income other than the meager odd-job earnings of us children, we felt that he was at the wheel of our future, and we would make it as long as we had his encouragement and that of our mother. We had a sense of direction, and knew that no matter how bad things were, we would survive.

Dad had been the master of many a schooner that could have gone down with all hands if not for his determination to survive any storm, no matter how fearsome the wind and waves. He was forever at the wheel of the family's fate, and his very presence gave us the strength we needed to survive the storm. If it was courage that was needed to survive the Depression, Dad bathed us in it. He made us believe that we were indestructible, and that we could survive the most terrible of ordeals, as long as we believed that we would do so.

Though physically weakened by the injuries he sustained in that terrible accident in 1909, in mind and spirit he still stood ten feet tall to his children. He was an inspirational father who gave each of us the feeling that, no matter what the problem, we could solve it with patience and determination.

Roger

In the fall of 1930, my brother, Roger, was born. He was diagnosed as having Down Syndrome. My parents were dismayed, and anguished over Roger's fate. What would become of this poor child, born during the depths of the Depression? From infancy, he failed to respond to normal parental care and training. He was, to use the language of the day, retarded in his physical and mental development.

After Roger was born, Mom found part-time work providing practical nursing services in patients' homes. She was already overworked and overburdened emotionally caring for her large family, but the family's financial state was now desperate.

I don't know where she found the time to work outside the home. She seemed doomed to never-ending cycles of soaking soiled laundry in heated copper cauldrons, scrubbing at the washboard in soapstone tubs, rinsing out the soap in clean water, wringing the articles out by passing the items through hand-turned rollers, and then hanging the laundry out to dry on the clothes line that spanned our backyard. After the laundry dried, she would take it in, heat her irons on the hot kitchen range, and then labor mightily, pushing the heavy implements back and forth over the ironing board, to press our shirts, blouses, and trousers. All of this work to keep us in clean, pressed clothing left her with red, chapped hands.

One day, because of wet weather, Mom left the laundry on the clothesline overnight to dry. Looking out her kitchen window the next morning, she was shocked to see the laundry gone. Every stitch of clothing, towels, linen, and even the clothes pins, had been stolen! It was shocking to think that there were people walking our streets who were so desperate they had to steal our laundry to clothe their family. Our family had now lost half its clothing and linen, and there was no money to replace it. Months passed before the stolen laundry could be replaced, mostly with donations by kindly neighbors and purchases from second hand stores. It would be a long time before any new clothing was purchased. Thanks to the palm-and-needle skills we learned from our father, we boys were able to mend and patch our trousers as needed, and we reversed the cuffs and collars on our shirts so that they always looked fresh and new.

That unusually cold winter, Mom occasionally escaped it all in the late evening when the children were all asleep. She would leave the house and walk the snow-covered streets, meandering with no sense of direction or care for where she was going or whether she would ever return. With his game leg and rheumatism, and unable to walk with our mother through the snow to comfort her, Dad roused Phil and me from bed and had us follow her to make sure she did not slip and fall on the ice-glazed cobblestone streets. And we made sure that no harm came to her at the hands of some hungry, impoverished wretch intent on robbing her of the few pennies in her purse. We would walk alongside her and talk to her in soothing tones, slowly calming her. She would soon start talking to us in her warm, loving, heartfelt way, and after a little while we would return home, walking hand in hand, one of us on each side of her.

Later that winter, Mom contracted pneumonia, and was at death's door for a time. We feared that she would die and leave us, and we gathered morning and night, day in and day out, in our candle-lit parlor, to kneel and pray the rosary. Our prayers were answered, as our beloved mother recovered and returned to full health.

All of the children, but especially Phil and I, loved Roger and were very protective of him. We would take him out for a stroll in his pram, giving Mom a break from her grinding routine. It didn't take more than a cursory examination of Roger's facial features to see that he was different. We knew that Roger was never going to be "normal," but he was our brother. The occasional boy who couldn't suppress a snicker or crude remark was immediately rewarded with a pummeling by either Phil or me, or both of us.

Before Roger was five years old, he was confined to Wrentham State School, some distance from our home. He would remain there for decades.

The *Ocean Queen*

On Saturday, August 19, 1933, Dad launched the *Ocean Queen* in our backyard. She was the latest and the largest of his ship models, a fourteen-foot-long replica of the famous clipper ship which was launched on the banks of the Mystic River in the early 1800s. Dad worked night and day for two months in his basement workshop to turn out the model for a Brookline customer, and decided to have a launching day and invite the public to view his creation. Phil and I helped him pack her in the sand in our backyard, and Mom helped him arrange floral decorations in the port and starboard railings and on the taffrail.

Hundreds of people gathered at our house to witness the event, including a reporter and a photographer from the *Boston Herald*. Phil and I beamed with pride as Dad stood before the majestic ship, and told the crowd how he had carved the model out of the dunnage that Phil and I had retrieved from the docks, and described how he had recreated every detail of the original ship's rigging in the three masts and twenty-one yards of the model. We stood seven-feet tall, as high as the masts on the model, as we posed with Dad for the photographer. It was a never-to-be-forgotten moment for the Gill family, and it came at a time when we desperately needed such an event to boost our spirits.

A few days later, the *Boston Herald* ran a feature story on the event in which they described Dad's seafaring career and his wood carvings of many famous American sailing ships. All this publicity led to Dad being asked to host a radio program featuring stories of New England seafarers. This had us all very excited, but the radio station could not come up with a commercial sponsor, and the show never went on the air.

Top: Feature story in the *Boston Herald*
Bottom: Model of SS *Ariel* by Capt. William F. Gill

Descent into the Abyss

As the economic situation deteriorated, the Gill family dropped down the socioeconomic ladder, from respectable middle class to the ranks of the near impoverished. Phil and I were taken out of private school and enrolled in public school. Soon, we were being snubbed by our former private-school classmates. Our family's diminished social status was obvious to the children from families with greater means. Our parents could no longer afford to send us to the barber shop for haircuts, so Dad became our barber. When he was done with his shears, it looked as though someone had put an upturned bowl on top of our heads and cut around it. To avoid this look, we boys preferred to have bald heads, at least during the summer months. A bald head was a telltale sign of poverty but, as far as we were concerned, it was preferable to a haircut that looked to have been performed with a meat ax.

Other stigmata of our straitened circumstances included the "welfare shoes" and clothing given to us by the welfare agency. The former were Victorian-style, button-up shoes that were so repulsive in appearance that we boys refused to wear them. The clothing clearly had its origin in another era and was unmarketable by the manufacturer. Rather than don such out-of-style apparel, we wore our own patched and ragged clothing until it was in tatters.

More than anything, it was the lean and haggard expressions on our faces that marked us as "poor kids." The line between the "haves" and the "have nots" was sharply drawn in South Boston. The distinction between the two classes of children was not lost on Phil and me.

In isolating ourselves from the "have" kids, we made our own way in the world of street gangs, emulating the tough young characters who now appeared in the movies and on the streets of Boston. "Southie" had its gangs, and was known as the toughest neighborhood in Boston. Boys gathered on tenement doorsteps and on waterfront piers to swap information about job openings, ways to get around the need for work permits, and what documents we would need to show sweat shop operators when applying for a job. We would walk for miles up and down the streets of Boston, doggedly looking for work, knocking on random shop or factory doors in the hope that we would stumble upon a willing employer. The fierce competition among the boys often led to fist fights, with the victor getting the job and the loser a bruised face and deflated self-esteem.

There were a few jobs available in the sweat shops scattered throughout the city, but the pay was pitiful and the working conditions intolerable to most boys. Rather than demean themselves working in such conditions for miserable pay, some boys swallowed their pride and turned to begging on street corners, in subway stations, in front of restaurants and movie houses, and on Boston Common and in other parks. Here too, the best locations for "bumming," as they preferred to call the practice, went to those boys who were handiest with their fists.

Other boys turned to crime to keep body and soul together. Success at petty larceny often led to more serious crimes: property break-ins, robbery, and auto theft, often carried out with handguns. Many of these boys landed in the penitentiary.

Shortly after the start of my freshman year of high school, I found work cleaning and painting dilapidated tenement housing for "slum lords" in densely-populated, low-income neighborhoods. This was the lowest-paying and most demeaning of sweat shop employment.

Rat-ridden and crawling with roaches, in endless need of repair and maintenance, the tenement units were also in continuous need of fumigation to free them of vermin. They were often occupied by two families who were forced to share a unit when one of the impoverished families was evicted for non-payment of rent.

Most of these slum tenements were three-story buildings of wooden construction. They were tinder boxes, and often erupted in flames in the winter months when a kerosene heater was accidentally knocked over. The loss of life in these conflagrations was appalling.

I found work on the weekends with the slum lords for the princely sum of $1 per day. I was to work eight hours a day, cleaning and painting dilapidated rental units in some of the worst sections of the city. It was miserable work for paltry pay, but I could find no other job that was compatible with my school schedule, so I signed on.

These tenements were an insult to human dignity. Maintenance was shoddy, and city fire and health codes were flagrantly disregarded. The landlords found it cheaper to "grease the palm" of fire and health inspectors than to properly outfit the buildings with fire alarms, fire escapes, and proper sanitary facilities.

The agreed eight-hour work day always stretched to ten or twelve hours, and I was often cajoled into performing personal services for the landlord, such as washing his car, or hauling ashes from the furnace room. I was constantly under the gun to hurry, hurry, hurry and get the job done so the new renters could move into the unit. The slum lords were obsessed with squeezing the last dollar of revenue out of their real estate investments, and cheap, pliable labor was a key ingredient in maintaining full occupancy.

I knew I was being exploited, but I didn't dare complain, because I knew there was an almost endless supply of desperate boys and young men who would gladly take my place if I were to quit.

By the end of my first year of high school, I realized that dedicated, hard study was nearly impossible with the long, tiring hours of work on the tenements on the weekends and the constant search for firewood, coal and food during the week. I had been near the top of my grade school graduating class, but now my grades were suffering. I longed to be able to play sports and to participate in the extracurricular activities that should have been part of daily life for a young boy. My dream of attending college to study aeronautical engineering was melting like a block of ice in the summer sun. Discouraged by my inability to both work part time and keep up with my schoolwork, I became bitter about my lot in life. I gave up all hope for continuing my education and quit school in the spring of 1935 at the age of fourteen in order to look for a full-time job.

Now that I had made the decision to "cut my moorings" to the family and find full-time employment, I encountered more problems than I had anticipated. For one thing, I was still too young to be legally hired; I had insufficient education to be a candidate for training for any kind of white-collar job; I did not have the requisite skills for factory or craftwork; and I was not physically mature enough to handle sustained hard labor. The fact that I had known nothing but hard work from the age of ten meant nothing to prospective employers. I wanted to ship out, but I didn't think I was ready for a life at sea.

I was too young to obtain a work permit, too puny, at 135 pounds, to be a laborer, and too little educated to qualify for any kind of white-collar job. My future prospects looked dismal.

TWO

OFF TO THE GREEN MOUNTAINS

Ma Bresnahan

D URING MY SEARCH FOR WORK, I learned about the Civilian Conservation Corps (CCC), which was enlisting unemployed men and boys to build roads and parks across the country. The CCC was the most popular of all the New Deal programs, and a particular favorite of President Roosevelt, who was an ardent conservationist. At its peak at the end of 1935, 500,000 men were enrolled in the CCC, in 2600 camps in every state. Seventy percent of the enrollees were malnourished and inadequately clothed on their induction into the program. Most of them left the program well-conditioned and a few pounds heavier. The CCC was a literal lifesaver for many of these impoverished boys and young men.

By the time the CCC was disbanded in June, 1942, it had left its mark on every state of the Union. The corps constructed state parks, dams, picnic grounds, airfields, drainage ditches, levees, bridges, roads, trails, and power lines. They also worked on flood and erosion control, planted billions of trees and shrubs, stocked streams and ponds with fish, helped control the spread of invasive insect species, fought forest fires, and even built ski trails.

The CCC appeared to be my only hope for employment, offering me an escape from my current hopeless situation, so I went over to the enrollment center in South Boston. Nervously, I joined a crowd of applicants milling around the enrollment center at the Army base. They were waiting to be interviewed by "Ma" Bresnahan, the administrator in charge of enrollment. Ma Bresnahan informed each applicant that they had to be single and out of work to qualify for the program. They would receive $30 a month, of which $25 would be sent to their parents and $5 was for themselves. They would be furnished meals, clothing, shelter, medical services, holidays, and other basic needs. Compared to the $1 a day I got from the slum lord, with no benefits and lots of unpaid overtime, this sounded like a wonderful opportunity. Warm and caring in her questioning, she asked me my age, education level, health status, work status, and the financial needs of my family.

The CCC seemed tailor-made for me, but there was one problem: at fourteen, I was four years younger than the minimum age of eighteen. My only option was to assume my brother John's identity, and doctor the figures on his birth certificate so that I would meet the minimum age requirement. I performed the forgery as artfully as I could, and discussed my plan to join the Corps with my parents. They wept bitter tears at the thought of their fourteen-year-old son, a promising student, quitting school and leaving home to help his family survive the economic storm. They feared for my safety, and the possible repercussions of my forging John's birth certificate and assuming his identity. But we all agreed that I had no alternative and, with their blessings, I reported back to the South Boston army base the next morning with the forged document.

I and the majority of the boys and men at the enrollment center received preliminary approval of our applications, but an anxious mood took hold as we were briefed on the processing we would undergo next. Those of us who had forged our birth certificates were especially ill at ease, as were the young men who were nattily dressed in homburg hats, with Chesterfield coats on their arms, and spats on their shoes. The sad truth was that behind their trim and stylish facades, they and their families were now among the hordes of needy and jobless Americans desperately struggling to survive. Many of the applicants weren't certain that this was what they really wanted to do, whether they could bear to leave their families and friends behind, and whether they could even pass the frightening battery of tests they would have to undergo before being accepted into the Corps.

Fort Devens

About 200 of us were herded onto buses that headed west in convoy formation to Fort Devens, forty miles west of Boston. On our arrival at the Fort, we climbed out of the trucks and joined hundreds of other applicants who were milling around like anxious cattle awaiting slaughter with a hammer blow to the skull. We were herded into giant washrooms, where we disrobed and showered in near-scalding water in preparation for thorough head-to-toe physical examinations. With the expertise and cold efficiency which one would expect of the U.S. Army Medical Corps, we were subjected to physical probing and prodding that the youngest and most naive among us had never imagined were a standard part of medical practice. We were assembled in long lines and ordered to "Bend over! Spread your cheeks!" after which the medics performed short-arm inspections with the command "Straighten up! Peel back your penises!" and finally "Turn your head! Cough! Again!" as they checked us for hernias.

After the physical examinations, we were vaccinated against smallpox and typhoid fever and then given lengthy aptitude tests. Those who met the enrollment requirements were mustered before the flag in the Fort Devens auditorium and sworn into the Civilian Conservation Corps by a U.S. Army officer. Our hair was quickly and expertly shorn by Army barbers, and then we were outfitted with handsome new olive drab Army dress uniforms and blue fatigue work uniforms. We also received two pairs of Army shoes, a pair of boots, foul weather gear, shoe kits, toilet kits, mess kits, canteens, service belts, hats, ties, and gloves. We recruits were overwhelmed by our spanking new outfits. Few of us had ever owned such a wardrobe of our very own before.

Camp Mansfield

Following my indoctrination and swearing in at Fort Devens, I was assigned to CCC Company #1135, Camp Mansfield, in Underhill Center, Vermont. We were replacements for enrollees who had completed their six-month enlistment and would restore the company to its full 200-man complement. Camp Manfield was situated on an Army reservation adjoining an artillery range where maneuvers were held by local Army Reserve units.

We piled into Army trucks and were taken to a nearby railroad station, where we boarded a train that took us to Essex Junction, Vermont, about a dozen miles from Camp Mansfield in Underhill Center. The young men traveling north with me to an unknown future came from cities such as Boston, Springfield, and New Bedford, dairy farms in the western part of the state, seaports and fishing villages along its eastern coast, small textile mill towns in the river valleys, and from Connecticut farm towns. The largest percentage of these men were of French-Canadian descent, followed by those of Irish, English, Portuguese, and Italian extraction. This was a significantly different ethnic brew than what I was exposed to in heavily Irish South Boston. Recognition and respect for the differences between these men of different ethnic backgrounds was a major factor in my staying at Camp Mansfield twice as long (fifteen months) as the average man.

We disembarked from the train in Essex Junction, boarded Army trucks, and headed east to Camp Mansfield. As the long line of trucks rolled over the winding roads toward the camp, the raw recruits joked about their future in the Army. To mask their anxiety, they broke out in Army field songs, such as "You're in the Army now, you're not behind a plow..."

* * * *

Camp Mansfield was nestled in the heart of the Green Mountains in northern Vermont, on the western slope of Mt. Mansfield, at 4,395 feet the highest peak in the state. The closest village was Underhill Center, a small farming community a few miles to the west, and the nearest city was Burlington, forty miles to the west.

The camp had a traditional military layout, with a rectangular parade ground and a flagpole in front of the mess hall. The officers' quarters, the mess hall, and the enrollees' recreation center were located at one end of the parade ground and the four barracks for enrollees and camp leaders at the opposite end. The long sides of the rectangle consisted

A postcard from Camp Mansfield, Vermont

of an education building, a lavatory and showers, a medical dispensary, and a supply building. These structures were of wood construction, with tin roofs.

Each of the four barracks housed fifty enrollees with two Camp Leaders in residence to advise and guide the young men while they were working in the forests and in day-to-day camp life. Many of our Camp Leaders had been infantrymen in the Great War, and had fought the Germans at the Second Battle of the Marne, Belleau Wood and Chateau Thierry. The Commanding Officer of our camp and his staff of advisors worked hard to develop desirable character traits in the enrollees and to improve their chances of finding work when they left the Corps. The enrollees were so impressed with the Army Officers leadership that a number of them signed up with the regular Army at Fort Ethan Allen, near Burlington, when their enlistments in the Corps were up.

Each enrollee's performance and conduct were reviewed and rated periodically by the Army officers, and suggestions were given on ways to improve their status. Emphasis was placed on building strong moral character, particularly in regard to leadership, initiative, adaptability, industry, perseverance, cooperation, courtesy, loyalty, ambition, and attitude. The enrollees had no fear of militarism being imposed on the Corps. There were no military drills of any kind; no close order drill and no weapons training. We were there to work on conservation projects, learn to work together, improve our moral character, and to earn a little money for our families.

Camp Routine

Immediately after piling out of the trucks at Camp Mansfield, we were divided into four groups of fifty men each, taken to our assigned barracks by an Army sergeant, assigned a cot, and shown where to stow our clothing and personal items. Then, we were given a quick tour of the camp, followed by dinner in the mess hall. After dinner, the commanding officer welcomed us to Camp Mansfield and described what daily life would be like. He laid down camp rules, and described the conservation work we would be doing in the forests around Mt. Mansfield over the next few months.

The first week at Camp Mansfield was devoted to physical training and KP (kitchen patrol) duty: cleaning the kitchen and mess hall, scrubbing floors, washing pots and pans and tableware, peeling vegetables, and digging latrine trenches.

Along with the physical training and KP and ground maintenance activities, we underwent a two-week indoctrination period during which we received intense instruction in the rules and regulations of the Corps, the role of the Army in the administration of the camps, the role of the Camp Leaders, the supervision of field work by engineers and foresters, and the services provided by the Army chaplain.

Reveille was sounded at six o'clock each morning, with the demanding "YA GOTTA GET UP, YA GOTTA GET UP!" blasted out by the bugler. Breakfast was served promptly fifteen minutes after reveille, so the sound of the bugle triggered a mad dash to jump into our work clothes, sprint to the lavatory to wash and shave, and then race over to the mess hall. With mess kits and utensils in hand, the men moved quickly down the long "chow line" where they had choices of fruit, juices, cereals, eggs cooked any way you could imagine, bacon, sausage, hot cakes, French toast, milk, and coffee. What a far cry this breakfast was from the handouts at the early morning breadlines in Boston, where you were issued black coffee and a biscuit before you started a long day's search for work!

Following breakfast, the enrollees would police their living quarters and the campgrounds, and then line up for roll call and the raising of the colors at 7:30 a.m. As the bugler sounded "To the Colors," we held our heads high and placed our right hands over our hearts while the Stars and Stripes was raised to the top of the flagpole. Then, on Monday through Friday, we went over to the supply building and broke out the tools and equipment we would need for road construction and forest conservation work and load them onto the waiting stake trucks. On getting the signal from our Camp Leaders, we climbed into canvas-covered field trucks. The trucks motored up the steep grade to that day's work site on Mt. Mansfield, where we would spend the day cutting roads through the forest, quarrying stone, topping trees, clearing brush, and creating a new ski trail.

The engineers and foresters who supervised our work and taught us how to clear trees, move boulders, and carve out roadbeds with bulldozers, excavators, graders, and other heavy equipment were real professionals. Many of them had honed their craft as combat field engineers on the battlefields of France during the Great War.

Building roads through the dense forests on Mt. Mansfield in our Army fatigues, we believed we were "citizen soldiers" in every sense of the term. Instead of bearing rifles on our shoulders to defend our country against enemy attack, we bore shovels, picks, axes, grub hoes, crowbars, sledge hammers, jack hammers, blasting caps, and explosion-ignition batteries on our shoulders. Instead of driving tanks and weapons carriers to fend off an enemy assault on our country, we drove gravel trucks, bulldozers, and earth graders to build roads, bridges, earth dams, and parks to earn a living and to support our government's efforts to conserve and protect the country's natural resources and rebuild the stricken economy. We were proud of the role we were playing in the struggle to restore the economic health of our country.

By far the most popular of the many jobs we performed in the forest was "stump jumping." Under the watchful eye of the forester, we would use an auger to drive holes in the stumps of a fallen tree and stuff the holes with sticks of dynamite. We then attached explosive caps to the explosive, packed mud around it, and wired it to the detonating battery, and, after taking cover, plunged the battery handle to ignite the dynamite. The explosion would blast the stump and its roots out of the ground, saving us many hours of sweat and toil. Logging trucks would move into place after the explosion to load and deliver the oak, maple or cherry trees to a lumber mill. Bulldozers then pushed the stumps into the closest ravine.

The more daring and athletic among us learned how to attach spikes to our boots and climb high into the tree tops to "top" a tree before it was felled with an ax and a bow saw. Those who mastered this skill felt like professional lumberjacks. With my experience working high in the rigging of sailing yachts in Boston Harbor, I was a natural for this job.

The work was hard, and "goldbricks" were not tolerated by their fellow Corpsmen. Every man had to do his fair share of the work, and the occasional loafer would suffer terrible harassment by his fellows until they either shaped up, and shared equally in the workload, or were mustered out of the CCC.

We were proud of the fact that none of the enrollees in our camp went "over the hill," deserting the Corps, as was rumored to be a common occurrence in other companies. No one threw in the towel, defied the firm CCC discipline, or shied away from the hard work we were asked to do. I was a lean, limber testament to the tenacity of the Aran Island culture I had been weaned on.

The work day ended at 4:30 in the afternoon and the young men, happy to see the end of another day of hard work, would climb aboard the trucks, find seats on the benches, engage in small talk and rib and jostle one another. As the Camp Mansfield-bound convoy of trucks crawled cautiously down the steep gravel road to the valley below, the men would start singing their favorite songs at the tops of their lungs, in what they were sure was perfect harmony. Some of the songs were sad, and reflected the hard times that their families and our country were going through, but others were more upbeat, such as "Red River Valley," "I've Been Working on the Railroad," and "She'll Be Coming Around the Mountain."

Road building in the CCC

The singing came to an abrupt halt when the trucks pulled into camp. Then, the men would leap from the trucks and race to the barracks to see if they had received mail from home. Sadly, there was little mail waiting for most of the men, except at the start of each month, when their families received their $25 allotment from the enrollee's CCC pay. What letters they did receive were brief and repetitive recountings of how hard things were for their families. Such sad tidings from home moved some men to send part or all of their monthly $5 stipend home rather than spend it on themselves.

After checking for mail, the next stop was always the showers. This was instinctual for most of us, but there were a few guys in the company to whom personal hygiene seemed an alien concept. But we had to sit next to these guys in the mess hall, and sleep in the same barracks with them, so those who did not shower after a hard day's work in the mountains were dragged and pushed under ice-cold showers, sprayed with soap powder, scrubbed with stiff-bristled brooms, and rinsed clean under steaming hot showers. We rarely had to repeat the procedure to inculcate a higher standard of cleanliness in the wayward enrollee.

These late afternoons were a time for reflection, refreshed as we were by the hot shower and the scrubbing off of the grit, grime and sweat accumulated in a day of hard work, and rejuvenated by the thought of how much better our lives were now, with three square meals a day, and laundered underclothing and outerwear to jump into after showering. We jobless and (many of us) homeless children of the streets, who had never had the regular meals and warm and clean shelter provided by the CCC, could now dare to dream of a future in which there was a place for us in American society.

Supper was served at six o'clock every evening. The Camp Leaders were served at the head table, while we enrollees picked up our meal trays at the serving counter and ate at sawbuck tables arranged in rows in the mess halls. After supper, we pursued various recreational, educational or social activities. For some, this meant writing letters home to assure worried parents that they were thriving in the CCC. For others, it might mean a game or two of ping pong in the recreation building, or a hand or two of poker. But, after working hard in the fresh mountain air all day, we were bone tired, and welcomed the sound of "Taps" echoing from the parade ground, the official end of camp activities for that day, and the signal for "lights out." It was the saddest of bugle calls for us young men, so far from our homes and loved ones, with only one wish in our hearts as we dropped off to sleep, to not be forgotten.

Day is done, gone the sun,
From the lake, from the hills, from the sky;
All is well, safely rest, God is nigh.

Establishing the Pecking Order

Enrolling in the Civilian Conservation Corps was a daring challenge, a means of escaping poverty, and maybe the only opportunity I would ever get. I was determined to face it head on.

Part of the sorting-out process after we arrived at Camp Mansfield was the establishment of a pecking order. I am sure that most of the other enrollees looked at me, four years younger and thirty pounds lighter than the average recruit, as an easy mark. I had not yet begun to shave, nor had

Camp Mansfield barracks

my voice yet taken on the deeper pitch of a post-pubertal teenager, so I was a natural target for bullies on the lookout for a patsy. Apparently, they took one look at me and, judging from my size and smooth cheeks, assumed that I was either much younger than eighteen, or a girl in disguise. I was in an awkward position. There was the repeated embarrassment of working under the assumed name of "John," and at times forgetting myself and expecting to be called "Paul," my real name. And then, being three to ten years younger than the other enrollees, I had to compete against muscular, grown men with the puny physique of an early teenager. They called me "Doris" to egg me on in the workplace or in the ring.

The "ring" was nothing more than a clearing or indoor space where the combatants had sufficient freedom of movement to conduct their pugilistic trial without interference from the spectators. It was where disputes and antagonisms between the young men were settled.

For the most part, the taunting came to a quick end when I outworked them in the field. But others weren't convinced, and so I had to prove that I could fight with my fists just as fiercely as I could wield an ax, swing a pick, drive a shovel, sledge a rock, blow a stump, or top a tree.

Impromptu fistfights behind the barracks gave way to boxing matches fought according to the Marquis of Queensbury rules. Fighting in the ring with boxing gloves on was a whole new experience for me, as I was strictly a bareknuckle street fighter. While I learned quickly and whipped a number of challengers, I was eventually singled out and put down by two unexpectedly fierce fighters who were also skilled boxers.

Roberto was a young Portuguese man from New Bedford. He was a freckle-faced mulatto with wild, curly, red hair, crossed eyes, a mean disposition, and a fiery temper. He was at least five years older than me, and a much savvier fighter. He was a dynamo in the boxing ring and, with a lightning-quick flurry of punches, he put me on my back. "Red" was an equally daunting force, and neither I nor anyone else in the company could handle this pair in the boxing ring. These tough "children of the streets" won my deep respect and friendship.

When I left the Corps after fifteen months in September, 1935, I was able to single-handedly load a 1½-ton dump

Sparring Partners. Paul Gill is on the left.

truck with gravel in less than twenty minutes, top off the highest trees and split quarry stones with a sledge hammer. All of these performances were at the top of the class. The work ethic whose seeds had been firmly planted at home had been solidly entrenched in my personality.

Fun and Games

During the long Vermont winters, sledding, ice skating, and cross country skiing were popular recreational pursuits for young people in the villages surrounding Camp Mansfield. I frequently joined them on long treks across farms and over logging trails in the forests. I wore primitive fir skis lashed to my boots with heavy leather thongs. They were a step above my previous ski equipment, barrel staves lashed to my boots with hemp yarn on which I would ski up and down the streets of South Boston after a winter storm dropped a few inches of snow on the area.

The young bucks of Camp Mansfield never overlooked an opportunity to break up the monotony and loneliness of camp life with weekend forays into neighboring towns to socialize with the girls who lived there. Underhill Center, the closest village, held festive events throughout the year, such as town fairs, corn-husking bees, and square dances, new experiences for those of us who hailed from Boston, Springfield and other cities. Even those of us who were not of French ancestry were soon speaking quasi-French after dating the gorgeous French-Canadian *filles* of these villages. A fun time was had by all, at least until we had to cope with our buddies who'd had a wee bit too much to drink.

The Camp Leaders understood their charges' needs. We Corpsmen worked hard and fought hard all week long, and come Saturday night, we were ready to party hard. As soon as supper was finished, the dishes washed, and the kitchen cleaned up, the Camp Leaders herded us into canvas-roofed troop carriers and drove us west toward the setting sun and the "big city" of Burlington for a "fun and sin" getaway from our mountain retreat.

Burlington, a beautiful town on the shores of Lake Champlain, offered all the glitter and excitement we young mountain men could ask for. The trucks disgorged us on Church Street, and from there we fanned out to explore the cabarets, taverns, dance halls, movie houses that seemed to dominate every block. Although the local boys and men didn't share their excitement at our arrival, Burlington's many attractive girls were welcoming and eager to show us their town. We reveled long past the legal hour with wine, women, beer and song every Saturday and holiday night.

When the curfew hour approached, we gradually straggled back to Church Street and climbed aboard the trucks for our ride back to Camp Mansfield. Those of us who were still conscious would break out in a raucous medley of French, country, and Army marching songs, serenading and awakening the villages in the convoy route back to our retreat in the mountains. Thoroughly enjoying the merriment, the veteran Camp Leaders in the cab up front would join in as we sang some of the popular songs of the Great War, including "Hinky Dinky, Parley-Voos!," "Mademoiselle from Armentieres" and "She Never Heard of Underwear."

It was easy to lose track of time on those Saturday night bacchanalias in Burlington when a young man was in the company of a ravishing young beauty, especially if a few drinks had passed his lips. If we missed our ride back to camp, we had few options. We would set out on foot on the road east toward Underhill Center but, with few vehicles on the road late on a Saturday night, and the lights long extinguished in the farm houses we passed, there was little hope of hitching a ride back to camp. We would walk as far as we could before sleep threatened to overtake us, and then seek shelter in the hayloft of a dairy farmer's barn. We were dimly aware that we were incurring the risk of being speared with a farmer's pitchfork, or even being blasted with his shotgun, but we put those unpleasant thoughts aside and burrowed deep into the warm hay to fall into a pleasant sleep, dreaming of the lovely maidens we had befriended and the good times we had enjoyed in Burlington.

Lost in the Mountains

November 26, 1935, the day after Thanksgiving, was a day I will never forget. While enjoying a delicious turkey dinner the day before, four of us came up with the idea of embarking on an overnight hike to the summit of Mt. Mansfield the next day. We had been living and working in the shadow of Mt. Mansfield for several months, and we thought we were fit and savvy enough to meet the challenge of a late-fall hike in the Green Mountains. We pored over maps; checked the radio for the weather forecast; selected appropriate clothing; made a list of our food and water requirements; collected compasses, flashlights, matches, candles, hatchets, and ropes; decided on which trails to take; and pinpointed the location of the cabin, Taft Lodge, we would spend the night in.

After a pre-dawn breakfast and double-checking our packs to make sure we had all the items necessary for an assault on Mt. Mansfield, we departed camp and made our way down to Underhill Center. We passed through the still-sleeping town and over country lanes and fields toward the western base of Mt. Mansfield. After climbing for a couple of hours, we took a break to reassess the weather situation. The sky had been clear when we started out, but sheets of thin, cirrostratus clouds were moving in now, and the wind had veered from the northwest to the north. These were disturbing signs, but they did not deter us, and we continued our slog up the mountain.

We reached the Halfway House at noon. We were famished, and wolfed down turkey sandwiches and cider while we considered our options. Blue-gray clouds now covered the entire sky, and all we could see of the sun was a dim disk over Mt. Mansfield. The wind was blowing harder now, and the spruce and fir trees creaked as they swayed with the gusts. Rested and sated, and with the confidence of youth, we decided to push on to Taft Lodge.

The trail we had decided to take to the ridge line atop Mt. Mansfield, the Halfway House Trail, was not well traveled, judging by the thick undergrowth that crowded the path. As we climbed higher, the trail grew steeper, and we found it necessary to grab tree branches to maintain our balance and to pull ourselves up the slope. We were working hard and sweating under our layers of underclothes and heavy jackets. The air temperature had dropped a few degrees since noon, but we were hot, so we stopped to remove a layer of clothing before resuming our climb.

We kept a close eye out for the blue blazes on the tree trunks that marked the trail. There was supposed to be one every seventy-five feet or so, but sometimes we would hike 200 feet or more before seeing the next blaze. Some stretches of the trail were so overgrown that we couldn't be certain that we hadn't wandered off of it. We would have to go back and retrace our steps until we were certain we were on the trail before moving on. With only a few hours of daylight remaining and the temperature steadily dropping, the fear of getting lost intruded on our thoughts like an unwelcome visitor.

After we emerged from the forest canopy and into the wide open landscape above the treeline, the blue blazes were replaced by cairns, piles of gray-white stones assembled to mark the way. We craned our necks to see the top of the mountain, but it was enshrouded in dark clouds. Looking to the west, we could faintly make out the silvery ribbon that was Lake Champlain, with the ripply contour of the Adirondack Mountains forming a backdrop that extended southward as far as the eye could see. Scattered tawny fields speckled the floor of the Champlain Valley far below us. Peregrine falcons, coasting on the brisk north wind, soared high over the cliffs immediately above us, alternately disappearing into and reemerging from the cloud cover.

After another half hour's climb, we were in the clouds, and could see only a few yards in any direction. The temperature had dropped to below freezing, the wind was blowing hard, and it had started to snow. We were no longer walking on a dirt trail, but rock, with sheer walls of granite looming up all around us. In places, the trail was just a narrow ledge, and we knew that a misplaced footstep could send us tumbling hundreds of feet down the mountain.

We wouldn't admit it, but we were scared. The snow was falling hard and accumulating fast, and the cairns were impossible to discern. The wind was blowing harder than ever, and was driving giant snowflakes into our eyes that almost blinded us. We knew we were close to the ridge trail that ran from the forehead to the chin of Mt. Mansfield, but snow had obliterated the trail. We were lost, but there was no turning back. The wind-driven snow had covered our tracks as well as the cairns. Snow and ice made the footing treacherous.

It was late afternoon, and nightfall was approaching rapidly. We moved slowly up the mountain, guided by our compasses and hoping that we were still on the marked path. We rejoiced when we rounded a sharp bend in the trail and came upon two large cairns, standing a few yards apart. They were covered with snow and ice, and barely visible, but they were as large as mail collection boxes, so we would have bumped into them even if we hadn't seen them. We pulled out our map and orientated ourselves. We found the twin cairns on the map, and shone a flashlight on the document in order to read the fine print next to each one. According to the map, the trail diverged at this point, with one cairn marking the trail that led to Taft Lodge, two miles to the north, and the other cairn indicating the trail to Smuggler's Notch, two miles to the east. Stowe was eight miles to the southeast.

We took out hatchets and chipped away the ice that covered the markings on the cairns, but were disappointed to see that the direction indicators on the cairns had been worn away by years of exposure to the elements. We were happy that we had ascertained our whereabouts, but we were unsure how to proceed. The lodge and Smuggler's notch were equidistant from the cairns. We could set out north for the lodge, but it might be hard to find in the near darkness. The alternative was to head east, hike down the mountain to State Route 108 in Smuggler's Notch, hitch a ride to Stowe, and call the camp and ask for a ride. We decided to break into two teams of two, with my partner and I heading north, hoping to find Taft Lodge before dark. The other two men headed east in the direction of Smuggler's Notch.

We set out on the ridge trail, our progress slowed by the uneven terrain and the frequent need to climb up or slide down a tall rock formation. After a few minutes, the trail meandered over to the west side of the mountain, and for half an hour we had to walk with our heads down into the full force of the wind and driving snow. Once or twice, I was rocked by sudden wind gusts and nearly blown off the mountain.

Just south of the "chin," we left the ridge trail and followed a sign pointing the way to the Profanity Trail and Taft Lodge. The last few hundred yards of our hike were downhill, over slippery rock slabs, and we thought we would wear out the seats of our pants sliding down the mountain on our rears. It was the only way to survive the descent.

At last, in the final minutes before darkness enveloped us, we came to a sign indicating the spur trail that led to Taft Lodge.

We were ecstatic! Taft Lodge was a simple log cabin, but to our weary eyes, it was Windsor Castle. We couldn't believe our good luck in finding shelter just as time was running out on us.

We opened the heavy wooden door, walked in, and scanned every nook and cranny of the interior with our flashlights to make sure the lodge wasn't harboring a bear, a mountain lion, or some other wild creature. On a board nailed to the back wall hung a sign saying:

TAFT LODGE
1920
WELCOME

The lodge consisted of one large room with six double bunks, three on each side of a cast-iron wood stove. We

Taft Lodge (Photo courtesy of the Old Stone House and Historic Village, Brownington, VT.)

peered into the stove and saw that some kind soul had arranged a pyramid of kindling over crumpled newspaper. There was a wooden box full of dry kindling on one side of the stove, and a pile of split hardwood logs on the other. The only other furniture in the cabin was a long table and two benches. There was no wash basin or cooking stove. A sign on one wall gave directions to a latrine and a water source in the woods behind the cabin.

Satisfied that we weren't going to be set upon by a black bear, we stacked our gear in a corner and rummaged through our packs for matches and candles. We lit two candles and set them on the table. Then, we got a fire going in the stove, laid our bedrolls out on bunks, and sat down to eat our supper of peanut butter and jam sandwiches and soda. It was a far cry from the delicious turkey dinner with all the trimmings we had enjoyed the day before, but it was all we had, and we were thankful we were enjoying our repast in a warm shelter, and not in some lonely cave on the mountainside!

We speculated on the fate of our teammates who had set out for Smuggler's Notch. We shuddered to think about all that might have gone wrong on the descent down the east side of Mt.Mansfield in the fading daylight: they might be lost; they might have fallen off a cliff; one of them might have broken an ankle and be lying immobilized on the trail. All of these horrible scenarios paraded before my eyes as I slipped into a deep sleep.

We awoke shortly after daybreak. The fire in the wood stove had gone out during the night, and the air in the lodge was so frigid that we emitted clouds of water vapor with each breath. We quickly pulled on our pants, shirts, sweaters, wool caps, and jackets to control our violent shivering. It was too cold to sit and eat breakfast, so we packed our bedrolls and prepared to break camp. We replenished the firewood supply, placed a pile of kindling in the stove for the next visitor, and bid adieu to Taft Lodge. We were determined to make our way back to Camp Mansfield without delay, retracing our steps of the day before. If our teammates hadn't returned to camp, we would have to organize a search party. There was no time to waste.

In stark contrast to the day before, the sky was clear, the sun bright and warm, and the snow soft underfoot. We hiked back up the Profanity Trail to where it intersected with the ridge trail, and then headed south. We had no trouble locating the cairns today, and we were confident that we would be back in Underhill Center before noon. We hoped and prayed that our buddies would be there to greet us.

A couple of miles down the trail, we found the turnoff for

the Halfway House Trail. The warming sun had not yet reached the west side of the mountain, and the trail was still a sheet of ice. The only way to negotiate it safely was on the seat of our pants. This technique worked well until we reached the treeline. Then we had to proceed carefully on foot, grabbing ice-laden fir and spruce branches to control our descent.

When we reached the Halfway House, we stopped to rest and eat peanut butter and jam sandwiches and soda for breakfast. Our diet was monotonous, but our exertions on the mountain had made us ravenous, and we relished every morsel.

We got back on the trail around ten o'clock. Anxious to learn the fate of our comrades, we picked up the pace. The trail was blanketed by an ankle-deep layer of fresh snow, and it was easy to pick out the fresh tracks of birds, rabbits, deer, and moose wandering helter-skelter in every direction across the forest floor. We never saw a single creature, but the evidence of their silent presence in the fir forest was all around us.

After a couple of hours, we were walking across the open fields of Underhill Center, and the tension mounted as we passed through the entrance to Camp Mansfield. Would our comrades be there? Would we have to lead a search party to look for them on the vast eastern slope of Mt. Mansfield? My heart pounded in my chest as I approached the Headquarters Building. When two men who were standing on the porch caught sight of us, they let out a loud yell and came running over and crushed us with powerful hugs.

It was our teammates! They had reached Smuggler's Notch the previous evening around the time we stumbled upon Taft Lodge. A dairy farmer came along and gave them a ride to Stowe in his horse-drawn sleigh. From the general store in Stowe they placed a call to Camp Mansfield, and a truck was sent to retrieve them.

Our expedition was the talk of the camp for a few days. What a thrill it had been to come so close to perishing on the mountain and yet survive! Every man in the camp wanted to join us on our next mountain-climbing adventure, and we promised to take anyone who wanted to go. But, in our heart of hearts, we knew the story could have had a tragic ending, and that we would never again venture out on that mountain in the winter time.

Leaving the CCC

Life in the beautiful Green Mountains of Vermont came to a close for me in early September, 1936, when my enlistment in the Corps ended and I boarded a train to return home to Boston. The average length of stay for CCC enrollees was nine months, and I had remained for fifteen months. When I left, I had just celebrated my sixteenth birthday, still two years younger than the minimum age for enlistment in the Corps.

The decision to leave the CCC was a difficult one. The Corps was a shelter from the ugly world I had left behind. I had found it impossible to excel in school and work under sweatshop conditions at the same time. Then, as a high school dropout, I could not get a decent job because I was underage and didn't have a high school diploma. It was a "Catch-22" situation. Time was wasting, and I had to get on with my life. I need to discard my false identity and return to being Paul Gill. Now that I had reached the age of sixteen, I could obtain a work permit. I had high hopes of finding full-time work close to home, putting an end to my wandering, and making a mark in life.

During the fifteen months I was in the CCC, the camp had become my home, and the commanding officers, the engineers, the foresters, and my fellow enrollees became my family. I will never forget them.

THREE

SHIPPING OUT

No Work at Home

I LOVED MY YEAR AT Camp Mansfield in the Green Mountains, but it was good to be home again with my family in South Boston. Sadly, though, the close friendships I had enjoyed with schoolmates and neighborhood pals had withered during my absence. They had remained in school and had matured, while I was on my own and looking for work again.

My wardrobe now consisted entirely of the olive drab shirts and trousers that I had been issued by the Civilian Conservation Corps. This was appropriate attire for camp life, but not conducive to a successful job search in the civilian world. So I applied black polish to my boots, dyed my uniform navy blue, and set out in search for employment.

It wasn't long before I realized that job opportunities were scarcer than they had been before I joined the Corps. Without a high school diploma, or a record of sustained employment, I had no hope of landing a remunerative job.

Looking for a Crimp

Facing such bleak employment prospects, I decided that I would give up the futile search for work ashore and make the Merchant Marine my career. Gills had been seafarers from time immemorial, so it seemed foreordained that I, too, would become a professional mariner.

With that in mind, I applied to the United States Shipping Board for the Seaman's Papers necessary for securing a shipboard berth. When I was told that I had to be eighteen years of age to obtain this credential, I again altered my birth certificate by ante-dating my birth year to 1918. This passed the scrutiny of the Board, and I was issued the all-important Seaman's Papers. The way was now clear for me to go to sea.

Inquiring at the various ship's chandlers that lined Boston's waterfront, I was told that a shipping agent by the name of Raymond was looking for crew on an oil tanker about to sail for Texas.

Raymond's on Fleet Street

Raymond's shipping hall, on old Fleet Street, was a non-union "crimp shop," and I was warned that Raymond and his staff did everything but shanghai sailors to meet a ship master's manning requirements to gain authorization to depart Boston Harbor.

Fleet Street was in the old North End of Boston, where my great-grandfather, Steven Gill, settled after immigrating from the Aran Islands around 1860. Steven, and later his son, my grandfather, Roger, sailed out of the old T-Wharf on Atlantic Avenue to fish on the Georges Bank and the Grand Banks of Newfoundland for cod, haddock and halibut.

The ancient thoroughfare was paved with smooth-worn

granite cobblestones and lined with granite curbstones. Red brick sidewalks, illuminated at night by gas lamps, ran past rows of red brick apartment buildings and rooming houses that lodged sailors on the beach looking for berths.

Fleet Street had been the home of Raymond's and other crimp shops for generations. In days of old, they catered to the captains of the great square-rigged packet ships, clipper ships, and Down Easters. Now they provided crews for the coal colliers, oil tankers, and general-cargo steamships that plied the trade routes of American coastal waters and all the oceans of the world.

Raymond's was a crimp shop in the old style, with beached sailors of all ages, colors, races and sizes lolling about the entranceway waiting for a berth to be called out from Raymond's inner office.

I pushed through the weather-beaten oaken doors and climbed the stairs to the shipping hall on the second floor. It was a dark, dingy, room, its still air rank with the mixed odors of tobacco smoke and the body odor of the dozen or so seamen sitting or stretched out on wooden benches, waiting for the next announcement of open berths. It was obvious to me, both from their accents and the Spanish-language newspaper *La Prensa* some of them were reading, that many of these men were Spaniards. I later learned that many Spanish seamen had sought asylum in America from the brutal civil war raging in their native land.

I found Raymond, a burly brute of a man, standing behind a counter at the back of the hall. Raymond had close-cropped iron-gray hair, no discernible neck, a massive barrel chest, doorway-wide shoulders, and arms thicker than my thighs. He looked like he could brawl with the toughest of sailors who might enter his crimp shop.

Shipping Out

Raymond was more approachable than his rough exterior had led me to expect. I introduced myself and told him I wanted to ship out. A faint smile crossed his flinty countenance as he examined my Seaman's Papers. He handed them back and told me that, with my lack of seafaring experience, the best position he could offer me would be as a galleyman, a cook's "man Friday" who helped him to prepare meals and cleaned up the galley after he had created his "culinary works of art."

The berth was mine if I wanted it, since no one else did. I immediately accepted the position, and Raymond told me it was on the SS *Halo*, a Cities Service oil tanker. The pay was $45 a month, and the ship was scheduled to depart the next morning from its dock at the Braintree refinery, on Boston's South Shore, for a three-week round-trip voyage to Aransas Pass, Texas. It would take on a cargo of fuel oil and deliver it to the Braintree refinery. My continuing employment on the *Halo* depended on my performance.

That afternoon, October 1, 1936, I sailed out of Boston Harbor on a ship's chandler's launch loaded with provisions and supplies for the *Halo*. I was to report to the ship's master and sign the ship's articles as galleyman.

Cook and Galley Description

After the launch secured alongside the *Halo* to unload its cargo, I went on board, met the captain, and signed the ship's articles. I was directed to report to the cook in the ship's galley aft on the main deck.

Dressed in a white chef's hat and uniform, the cook was easy to find. He welcomed me aboard in broken English, and told me his name was Pedro. He was a tall, lean man in his early thirties, and he needed a shave.

His accent reminded me of the Castilian Spanish I had studied in grammar school, and he told me he was a Spaniard. Later on in the voyage, after we had gotten more familiar with each other, he told me about his seafaring background and the reasons he had left Spain. Realizing that I had to go home to fetch clothing for the voyage, he gave me leave to do so, directing me to return that evening and report for duty in the galley at five o'clock the next morning.

Description of the SS *Halo*

Walking down the *Halo's* gangway to the dock, I turned and looked back for a better look at the first ship I would sail on in my newly-launched nautical career.

Discharging operations were underway for the ship's cargo of 65,000 barrels of crude oil, which was pouring through a bank of heavy pipes from the ship to the dock and to its shoreside storage tanks. There was a sense of urgency among the crew as it hastened to complete the discharge operations in order to meet the next morning's departure schedule.

The ship that lay before me was vastly longer, beamier, and faster than any of the square-rigged or fore-and-aft rigged sailing vessels my father had described to his children when he would gather us of an evening and regale us with sea stories. The clipper ships, Down Easters and schooners Dad described were beautiful fabrications, designed to cleanly and quietly harness nature's forces to propel man and vessel to seaports around the world, leaving only smokeless skies and bubbling, clean water in their wakes. None of us had ever sailed on such a majestic vessel, but our South Boston house was home port to many scale models of these beautiful wind ships. Gazing at Dad's creations, berthed in their oaken cradles on the sidebar in our

The SS *Halo*

dining room and on tables in the front parlor, it was easy to let our minds wander to times past when our forefathers had sailed on such vessels.

The SS *Halo*, like all modern steamships, was designed to earn money for her owners, and aesthetics be damned. She was a functional, 20th-century working ship, and her form followed her function. Her fore-and-aft catwalks stretched from the forecastle deck at the bow over the main deck's tank openings to reach the midships housing, and then aft to the poop deck at the stern.

Work-horse that the *Halo* was meant to be, she was nothing but an oversized oil tank for carrying "black gold" for her owners. Her hard years at sea hauling oil were betrayed by the rust stains bleeding from the surfaces of her decks and from the skin of her hull and housing above- and below-decks, from stem to stern.

Never did I foresee that this rust bucket, which would

carry me on my first sea voyage, would carry all but three of her forty-two crewmen to Fiddler's Green when she was sunk in the Gulf of Mexico by *U-506* on May 20, 1942.

Farewell, Family

That evening, with little time to dally, I shared my good fortune at finding a berth on an oil tanker with Phil and my parents. I then packed what little gear I had and, with their blessings, returned to the *Halo*.

At the gangway, the seaman on watch gave me directions to the sleeping quarters for the steward's department crew, which he called the "glory hole." They were aft, by the ship's stern, a deck level below the main deck.

Welcome Aboard...Bang!

I found my quarters without difficulty, but before I could enter I was suddenly hammered with hard-driving blows from a young sailor who cursed me, called me a "Goddamned flunky!" and knocked me to the deck, straddling me as he whaled away at me.

Blocking his blows with my forearms, and at a loss to understand why he was attacking me, I held back on returning his punches. I was the newcomer in the crew, and I was afraid that, while a couple of well-placed retaliatory blows might have given me the upper hand, they might also have caused his shipmates to come to his assistance. Soon, the others watching the set-to pulled him off of me.

From the odor of alcohol on my assailant's breath, it was evident that whisky had brought out the pugilist in him. The next day, he claimed that he was horrified by his actions, and had no memory whatsoever of what had happened.

I learned from this experience. From that time on, whenever

I was in unfamiliar surroundings, I tried to identify potential assailants who might be on the lookout for a human punching bag. There were people who would take a whack at you because your nose was out of joint, or for some other ridiculous reason. I would be wary, and let new friendships take their course. Welcome to the galleyman's Glory Hole!

Bound for Deep Waters

At six o'clock the next morning, the deck hands cast off *Halo's* docking lines and she steamed seaward to the open waters of the Atlantic Ocean. We were bound for Aransas Pass, Texas, to pick up another load of crude oil. At 5:00 a.m., the cook had me up and at it in the galley, washing pots and pans and utensils as fast as he finished with them. When he was in need of a pot, a pan, a ladling spoon, or some other item, he would call out, "*Pronto*, Pablo!" and I responded quickly with "*Si, si, senor!*"

Sea Watches

Sea watches were set for the *Halo's* deck hands and "Black Gang" before the ship left port. They worked four hours on and eight hours off, around the clock, a full eight hours every day the ship was at sea until the ship arrived at its port of destination.

To signal the ship's sea-watch time, the ship's bell was struck every half hour in the wheelhouse on the bridge, starting after midnight at 12:30 a.m. with one bell, then at 1:00 a.m.with two bells, on up to 4:00 a.m. when eight bells were struck.

At the end of every four-hour watch, the ship's bell would again sound each half-hour until the new watch had been completed. The ship's bell alerted those off watch to be ready to relieve those on watch in the engine room, at the wheel in the wheelhouse, and on lookout in the crow's nest or forward at the forecastle head.

Work in the galley for the cook and his galleyman went on day in and day out, seven days a week, from five in the morning until seven in the evening, with mid-morning and mid-afternoon breaks between meals.

Thanks to my "KP duty" in the CCC kitchen, which served hundreds of men at a sitting, the galleyman's work for a crew of forty was quickly dispatched with expertise, without pain or strain!

The Crew of the SS *Halo*

I slowly became acquainted with the *Halo's* crew and officers, their work, and how they lived aboard ship.

The deck hands included sailors who steered the ship in the wheelhouse on the bridge, served as lookouts in the crow's nest high up on the foremast, maintained the ship's rigging, and kept the lifeboats ready for emergency launching.

The Black Bang was made up of the oilers, wipers and firemen who manned and maintained the ship's engine room.

The steward's department consisted of a cook, a galleyman, messmen for the crew's and officers' mess rooms, and stewards for cleaning the officers' living quarters.

The master of the ship and his officers, the mates, engineers and the radio operator, were quartered in cabins in the ship's amidships housing. Here they had their washrooms and mess room separate from those of the unlicensed crew.

While in the CCC, there had been a close relationship between the officers and the men, with a strong informal dialogue and shared meals in the mess hall. Things were different aboard the *Halo*. There was a significant difference in the living conditions of the ship's officers and those of the unlicensed crewmen, and what little dialogue there was between them had strictly to do with the ship's operations and management.

The Crew's Quarters

The fo'c'sle and Glory Hole for the crew were aft, at the ship's stern. They were one level below the main deck, next to the noisy ship's steering room, where its engine over the rudder post grinded and groaned continuously with every turn of the ship's helm by the sailor in the wheelhouse.

The crew's living quarters were overcrowded, with double-tier bunks, and straw mattresses covered with blue linen to extend the time between launderings. In stormy weather with heavy seas, the portholes in the crew's living quarters were dogged to shut out the sea, leaving the fo'c'sle and Glory Hole with inadequate illumination. The lanterns on the walls were too dim to read by.

These cramped sleeping quarters were a breeding ground for tuberculosis, a disease with which I was soon to become familiar.

Heavy Weather

Three days out of Braintree, *Halo* was on a southerly course, bucking the Gulf Stream's northerly current flow, and we were soon enjoying warmer weather.

Cape Hatteras was on our starboard beam, marking the halfway point between Cape Cod and the Florida Keys. The vessel steamed far offshore of Hatteras, as the treacherous Cape waters had long been known as the "Graveyard of the Atlantic," where countless vessels had foundered on its unmarked shoals and gone down with all hands.

It was warm in the Glory Hole that night, so I moved my mattress to the open main deck at the ship's stern for my first night's sleep under the stars. The sailors had pointed out some of the constellations, and from where I lay I could make out the North Star, the Seven Sisters and Orion's Belt in the heavens above me. With the gentle vibration of the mattress caused by the propeller and the ship's steering engine below me, I was soon asleep.

Halfway through the night, I was rudely awakened by the ship struggling against a sudden head storm. Its bow was climbing and plunging wildly as its stern dragged in the trough of the giant waves.

Before I was fully awake, the deck around me was awash with sea water and my mattress, with me on top of it, was being dragged between the rails and over the stern to a point just above the giant thrashing propeller blades. I clutched desperately at the upper railing and climbed to safety on the poop deck housing as the mattress disappeared into the sea below.

Perilous moments were to be expected, I was learning, sailing merchant vessels with unknown shipmates, some of dubious character, and in unfamiliar waters, most of which were unpredictably treacherous. Few mariners could decide which of the two was more dangerous.

Poop Deck Musters

The off-watch crew held regular gab sessions on the poop deck at the ship's stern. With time, the old tars gradually started to accept the landlubber voyagers into the inner circle of seafarers.

On sailing ships, the poop deck was known as the quarter-deck. The captain's and the officers' accommodations were situated one deck below the quarterdeck, as was the chart room and the steering wheel. Modern day steamships, such as the *Halo*, located their chart room, wheelhouse and their master's and officers' quarters amidships, while the crew was quartered astern, below the poop deck.

Off-Watch Pastimes

As we continued on our southerly course, through calm seas and fine weather, some of the *Halo's* offwatch crew passed the time sunbathing, writing letters, or reading. Others were more interested in observing the interaction of the wind and water, gazing intently at the surface of the water as the ship skirted the edge of the seemingly boundless Sargasso Sea to port. The sea was engorged with seaweed, and teemed with marine life of all varieties. Whale spouts were sighted to port and starboard, and the forward lookout delighted in the play of porpoises surfing the *Halo's* bow wave. The thick mats of floating sargassum seaweed were peppered with myriads of small sea turtles that seemed to cling to their floating hotel like barnacles on a piling. Once or twice we spotted a funnel-shaped waterspout reaching down to the sea's surface from a cumulus cloud. The air grew steadily warmer and the northerly-flowing Gulf Stream quickened its pace as we plowed southward through the ever-thickening rafts of seaweed.

During the evening hours, and usually extending late into the night, several of the crew, gambling addicts all, played high-stakes poker in the crew mess room. These games were a nightly occurrence while we were at sea, but were suspended while the ship was in port, when the men focused their energy on more alluring, fleshly pursuits.

Other crew members were content to sit up on the open

poop deck, spinning tales of their travels to exotic lands and scanning the night sky, with its countless sparkling stars, planets and galaxies. Most wondrous of the heavenly objects were the meteors that flashed brilliantly across the black celestial dome for a few seconds before winking out.

We all were fascinated by the porpoises who raced alongside the ship, leaving streams of phosphorescent light in their wakes. Flying fish, attracted by the bright lights in the wash-room, leaped up from the sea, through the open portholes and landed in wash basins, urinals, and toilet bowls.

Bound for Port

Four days south of Cape Hatteras, *Halo* reached the southern tip of the Florida Keys and altered course to the westward to pass between the coast of Cuba and the Dry Tortugas Light. We were now in the Gulf of Mexico, and steering for the Aransas Pass in Texas. The hurricane season had passed, and prospects were good for continued fine weather for the remainder of the passage.

The night before our arrival, I lay restlessly awake, afflicted with Channel Fever, a malady that commonly afflicts sailors eager to reach port after a long sea voyage. I had been briefed by my shipmates on the many attractions on offer in this small seaport town, and I was anxious to see if the vaunted beauty of the southern belles would measure up to the standards of female pulchritude set by the French Canadian *filles* I had encountered in Vermont.

Sailor Town Frolics

At daybreak the next morning, *Halo* reached the outer waters of the Aransas Pass. As the sun started to peek above the eastern horizon, the pilot boarded, tugs came alongside, and we docked and prepared to load our crude oil cargo. In the next twenty-four hours, loading would be completed and *Halo* would be departing on its return voyage to Braintree.

That evening, I visited this sailor town with several shipmates to take in the sights, enjoy a little liquid refreshment at the local watering holes and, perhaps, enjoy the company of one of the southern belles the older men spoke so admiringly of.

We hired a cab, a dilapidated, canvas-roofed Model T Ford, to take us into town. The cabbie dropped us off on the edge of Port Aransas, in a neighborhood he thought would be a good starting point for our quest for fun and entertainment.

We were in a seedy section of this southern town, not all reminiscent of the quaint New England towns of similar size I knew. Apparently, the driver did not have a high regard for the tastes and proclivities of visiting sailors. But my shipmates were determined to make the best of the situation, and headed for the classiest-looking gin mill in the area, with sizteen-year-old me in tow.

The establishment we chose to patronize had fancy, swinging louvered entrance doors. As we settled into our seats around a large, stained, oaken table, we couldn't help but notice pedestrians passing by the entrance peeking over or under the doors to see which of their neighbors were imbibing that night.

After ordering a round of beers and toasting each other's good health and fortune, I took a long look around the establishment. The wooden floors were covered with sawdust, and ceiling fans spun just fast enough to keep the smoke-filled air circulating. Most of the other tables were occupied by customers too deeply absorbed in conversation to notice our presence.

Over the hum of conversation could be heard the then-popular jukebox music number "Put Another Nickel in the Nickelodeon," followed by "The Yellow Rose of Texas," and then "Mexicali Rose."

We were disappointed at the absence of Southern belles in this tavern. As we ordered and consumed more drinks and played more Southern tunes on the jukebox, we became ever more desirous of female company. We were reaching the point where, if we drank much more, we would not only forget our pain, but lose our aim as well, which was directed at finding attractive female company. We decided that if the ladies were not going to come to us, we would go to them. A quick consultation with the bartender yielded the address of a nearby whorehouse. We finished our drinks and left the gin mill. We had reason to suspect that he was the master of the establishment he had directed us to. If that were so, we reasoned, we had better be careful we were not rolled for the few dollars we had among us.

We located the bordello in a residential neighborhood, knocked on the front door, and told the attractive woman who answered that the bartender had sent us. That was all she needed to know, and she opened the door and ushered us into the front parlor. She invited us to sit down and enjoy a cold bottle of beer before we met the girls.

We did not want to get too comfortable in the madam's cozy parlor and forget our purpose in coming there but, after we finished our beer and the girls were brought in for us to review, we enjoyed another beer with the young lady we had selected.

Evidently, the house had a number of parlors, because as we sat in ours, the front door kept opening and closing as customers passed in and out. One of our more observant shipmates remarked that the place reminded him of an undertaker's home, with all the parlors available to its customers!

True to the assurances of the more experienced seamen in our group, these Southern belles were stunningly beautiful. One could not help asking one's chosen belle, "What's a nice girl like you doing in a place like this?" Very likely, the same question passed repeatedly through the minds of these girls. The obvious answer was, "What else was a girl to do in her hometown, when half the workforce was unemployed?" Without their socially unacceptable earnings, how would their families put food on the table, how would they clothe themselves, how would they pay the rent? The country's leaders had left their families hungry, jobless, and feeling hopeless. These girls were children of the Depression, children of the streets, like me, and many of them my age or even younger. The only difference between the likes of me and the likes of them was that I had scavenged for survival working the flesh off my fingers, while they were forfeiting their moral values to support their families. I didn't have the heart to take advantage of the young lady I had chosen. Rather than add to her shame, I pulled a dollar out of my pocket, gave it to her, wished her well, and left the house.

We arrived back at the dock well after midnight, with less than three hours remaining until I had to report for duty in the galley. Sleep eluded me as I lay on my straw mattress thinking of my visit ashore, my shipmates, the pretty girls in the house of ill repute, our return voyage to Braintree, and my coming reunion with my mother, father and siblings in South Boston.

Homeward Bound

No sooner had I dozed off than I felt Pedro's hand on my

shoulder, shaking me awake and telling me to hurry to the galley for work. The crew would want a hearty breakfast before going on sea watches and preparing the vessel for sea.

The return voyage north was more interesting than the trip south. Friendships between shipmates grew stronger with time. Our brief shore leave in Port Aransas had accelerated the formation of social bonds between men who had learned to work as a team to drive an 8,000-ton vessel from port to port.

The crew gathered on the poop deck more frequently to exchange sea stories and to discuss the state of the seamen's unions, the economy, the Spanish Civil War, girlfriends, and any number of other topics.

As we steamed north, aided by the powerful Gulf Stream current, the air temperature dropped steadily and stormy seas off Cape Hatteras provoked my first bout of seasickness. It caught me off guard, and I didn't want my older and saltier shipmates to know that I was suffering from a lubberly malady. But they weren't fooled. One of the older men told me I would be okay if I just stayed in the center of the ship, where there was less movement, and to keep my eyes focused on the horizon. Pedro agreed with that advice, but told me he had an infallible cure for *mal de mer*. He sat me down on a bench outside the galley entrance, opened a can of stewed tomatoes, handed me a plate of saltine crackers, and bade me eat. I did so, all the while keeping my gaze focused on the far horizon. Half an hour later, my stomach was calm and I was back at work in the galley.

Now a Mess Boy

After the *Halo* discharged her cargo in Braintree, I signed the ship's articles as mess boy for the crew's mess room. I made three more voyages to the Gulf of Mexico on *Halo*, round trip voyages from Braintree to Aransas Pass, Corpus Christi, and New Orleans.

My work hours as crew's messman revolved around the crew's morning, noon and evening meal hours, with time off dependent on how efficient I was at setting tables, serving food, washing and drying dishes, and sweeping and swabbing the mess room deck.

The mess room job was a plum assignment, and I was grateful to the gamblers among the crew for putting me forward for the job. In addition to my usual duties, I would be responsible for running the nightly poker games, and would be well-compensated for doing so.

Running the Poker Games

My wages as a messman were $45 a month, $1.50 a day, the same amount I earned as a galleyman. The earnings for running the poker games ran to $4.50 a day which, added to my base pay, gave me $6.00 a day, six times what I had earned in the CCC!

Immediately after supper each evening, after the mess tables had been cleaned and had I laid out hot coffee, cold cuts, and bread as late snacks for the players, the poker games commenced.

I furnished the cards, red and blue decks of Bicycle playing cards, nothing but the best for the players! I also placed a large white coffee cup in the center of the table, a receptacle for the nickel that went into the kitty for each hand played. As time went on, the number of players grew to six, the games became more heated, and the size of kitty grew proportionately. As sea watches changed, so did the players, and the games dragged on through the night, often until dawn.

After a while, the stagnant air in the mess room, pregnant with the rank smell of body odor and tobacco smoke, became almost unbearable. But the gamblers played on, retaining their "lucky places" at the table, determined to play on until they either won or lost the big pot.

The games were a choice of either stud or draw poker, and they were not exactly played "according to Hoyle." Especially not when tempers flared and dealer demands were made to switch to "Piss in the Ocean," "1492," or whatever other deviate variety of poker a losing player might think of. More often than not on such occasions, the cards would be torn to pieces and thrown in the air, with the infuriated loser either demanding a new deck of cards to change his luck, or exiting the game and storming out of the mess room in a rage.

Though I was not an expert card player, limited to the "backwoods knowledge" I had acquired at Camp Mansfield, I was frequently called on to settle disputes between hot-tempered players. This often led to a head bashing from the loser. The "referee" role I assumed during these unpleasant confrontations between shipmates would serve me well in shipboard disputes yet to come during my seafaring career.

Call to Strike Duty

In the late fall of 1936, I returned to Braintree to find a letter from my seldom-heard-from eldest brother, Bill, who had been sailing out of New York on foreign-bound freighters and passenger liners for several years. He told me that the rank-and-file members of the International Seafarers Union had called a general strike against East and West Coast shipowners. From previous strike experience, Bill knew that violence was sure to erupt on the piers between strikers and strike breakers. For my personal safety, Bill urged me to leave the *Halo* and join him for picket duty on the New York waterfront.

The strike was a revolt led by rank-and-file seamen against their corrupt union leaders and the ship owners. Their aim was the long-overdue settlement of grievances over low wages, unfair hiring practices, and the miserable living and working conditions on board American merchant ships.

A few days later, I signed off the *Halo* and took a train to New York City to join the striking union seamen on the picket lines.

FOUR

REVOLT ON THE WATERFRONT

Leaving the *Halo*

THE SEAFARING EXPERIENCE I HAD gained during my four voyages on the *Halo*, though limited, was very exciting for a sixteen-year-old boy with an inborn love of the sea and a deep respect for the men who go down to the sea in ships. Working fourteen hours a day, seven days a week, in a hot, windowless kitchen ashore would have numbed my mind and tortured my soul. Working alongside Pedro on a ship at sea, with the constantly changing moods of the wind and sea, the rhythmic movements of the ship, the constant thrum of the engine, the laughter of the sailors, and even their arguing and fighting during their long poker sessions, was thrilling. I was immersed in nature in its most elemental state, awestruck at night by the myriad stars strewn like glittering diamonds across the black celestial dome, and thrilled by day by the broaching whales and the porpoises cavorting in the *Halo's* bow wave. And listening to old salts tell sea stories on the poop deck at night calmed my soul, as I closed my eyes and imagined I was back home in Southie, and it was Dad who was spinning the yarn.

Reunion with Bill

When I went to New York City to find Bill and report for picket duty with the striking seamen, I was apprehensive. I had not seen him since he had dropped out of school at age sixteen and gone to sea four years ago. I was afraid we would not recognize each other, and that the bonds of brotherhood might have atrophied with the passage of time. I knew nothing of Bill's seafaring experiences, his union activities, his radical associates, or of his struggle, along with other rank-and-file members, to oust the corrupt leaders of the ISU (International Seamen's Union) and force the shipowners to settle many longstanding labor grievances.

Paul (*left*) and Bill Gill

By the time I had climbed the six flights of stairs to his apartment on 90th Street, I was seriously questioning the wisdom of giving up my berth on *Halo* to participate in a seamen's strike on the New York waterfront. But those fears melted away when Bill opened the door and welcomed me into the apartment. We hugged warmly and stepped back to take a good look at each other. We each had the markings of street-wise individuals who appeared older than our years. To Bill, I was a tall and gangly kid, still wet behind the ears. To me, Bill was a seaman to be reckoned with. The determined set of his jaw, his wide shoulders and massive chest, and the steadfast look in his eyes told anyone encountering him that he would not flinch from any challenge, at sea or ashore. Bill had an intimidating presence. He was not a man to be trifled with.

Bill had made several voyages to Germany as Able Seaman on the passenger liner SS *Washington*. During a brief sojourn in Hamburg in 1935, Bill got into a dustup with the Nazi authorities that was reported in the October 4, 1935, edition of *The New York Times*:

Nazi-Jailed Sailor Works Way Home

Seaman Who Threw Salty Slur about Hitler Told Never to Return.

GIRL IN PORT ADDS TO WOE

Off-Shore Remarks Made When Shaking Off Effects of Liberty, He Says

---

William Francis Gill, a young seaman formerly employed by the United States Lines, returned from Germany yesterday with some of his sails furled. He passed ten days in a Hamburg jail and returned yesterday on the liner Washington as a "workaway," a little bit bewildered by the German inability to understand that when he made a derogatory remark about Reichsfuehrer Hitler on a Hamburg ferry Sept. 12, he was just having some fun and shaking off the remnants of liberty ashore.

The worst feature to him is that when he left Germany, his sentence having been shortened by intervention of American authorities who appeared to understand a seaman's vocal prerogatives, he was told that he could never return. He also signed a paper in which he said that he loved the German people. Gill said that he did not love the two policemen who overheard him whistling a few bars of "The Internationale" and who asked him what he thought of Hitler, but there was, of course, his sweetheart in Hamburg.

Gets One Cent Pay

He wiped a cloth across another dish and put it on the stack representing a part of the chores which earned him the title of "workaway" and the remuneration of one cent. He put down the cloth and bared his chest where, nestling among nautical designs, was the tattooed writing of her name.

"Please don't mention her name," he hastened to implore. "I only show it to you to show how I feel about a part of the German people. But if you use her name it might make trouble. I have known her for six years and who knows, I may yet save enough money to bring her over here. But now I am flat broke, without a cent in my britches and only patches on the outside."

Says He Was Feeling Low

"How it happened was this: I was on the ferry that night between Hamburg and Rosshoft. I'd been on a bender for a couple of days and was feeling low. For some reason I whistled this Red song and two policemen came along and the tune seemed to upset them. Then they asked me about Hitler. That was when I made my classic remark. Boy, did I pay for it. They beat me up and put me in jail! I tried to explain how we say such things about Americans and it don't mean anything."

This, divested of Gill's more picturesque mode of expression, is his story. He turned over another dish, buttoned up his shirt and wiped away a tear with a generous swipe of the blue sleeve.

"I got to get to work," he added. "They might hold out my penny on me."

*****

During the ISU rank-and-file spring strike of 1936, Bill was the captain of a seaman's beef squad that was frequently called out to "neutralize" the shipowners' goons and the International Longshoremen's Union thugs that harassed and beat up seamen picketers on duty on the West Side waterfront.

To make ends meet during the spring strike, Bill worked as a bouncer and a "bouncer's bouncer" in waterfront gin mills, where the sailor clientele could get unruly. It was rough duty, but no rougher than strike duty. Bill's scalp rippled like a washboard from the clubbings he had received from goons, thugs and policemen, and his thick, calloused hands had been molded out of shape by the many fractures he had sustained in waterfront fights with opponents of the strikers.

With his powerful physique and the street-fighting skills Bill learned growing up in our tough South Boston neighborhood, he was well-prepared to take on any adversary. To hone his boxing skills and earn a few extra bucks, he spent time in the ring as a sparring partner for heavyweight contenders at Stillman's Gym and other West Side boxing clubs. Bill's motto was, "Hit 'em first and ask questions later!" He demonstrated this principle one morning when, as we were walking past a row of horse-drawn produce wagons, an ornery horse who didn't like the cut of Bill's jib reached out and bit him in the arm. Bill reflexively turned and threw a haymaker at the horse. He didn't score a knockdown with that punch, but I am certain the animal saw stars for a while.

Life in New York City

Bill invited me to live with him and his wife, Kitty Kelly Gill, in their apartment on the top floor of a red brick, seven-storey building on the upper West Side. This was an Irish neighborhood in those years, similar in its ethnic makeup to South Boston, our hometown, and Hell's Kitchen and Chelsea on the lower West Side.

The apartment was small, with barely enough room to accommodate Bill and Kitty, so I occasionally thumbed a ride home to Boston to give them more privacy. On returning to New York, I would often stay in a flop house near South Street on the East River in lower Manhattan. If I couldn't afford the twenty-five cent lodging fee, I would sleep on a cot in a public shelter provided for free to vagrants, like me, by the city.

A day or so after arriving in New York, Bill took me down to the West Street headquarters of the new union he and his fellow strikers were forming, the National Maritime Union, to replace the corrupt International Seamen's Union. He introduced me to Jerry King, the secretary of the union, who issued me Union Book Number 189. In a few short months, the membership in the new union would swell to over 50,000 seamen.

After giving a share of my *Halo* earnings to my parents, I set aside the remainder to cover living expenses while I was

National Maritime Union Book #189

"on the beach" during the strike and later, while looking for a berth on a merchant ship. Having signed off the *Halo* sooner than planned, I had insufficient funds to support myself for more than a few weeks. Being frugal was second nature to me. I had spent most of my young life in that frugal borderland between the "haves" and the "have nots." But I knew that I was going to make it. My survival instinct told me so!

I had gained a few pounds of lean muscle during my twelve months in the CCC in Vermont. All that hard physical labor and a steady diet of nutritious food had done wonders for my previously frail physique. But soon I started losing weight. This was due partly to my reduced diet, but also to the long daily walks from Bill's apartment to the picket lines on the West Side waterfront. I calculated that it was seventy blocks each way between Bill's apartment on 90th Street to Eleventh Avenue and 20th Street where I did picket duty. The bus or subway fare was cheap, but I couldn't afford to both ride and eat. By walking all the way down to the union hall I could save the cost of the subway token and spend that dime instead on a hot breakfast of fried eggs, bacon, home fries, buttered toast, and hot coffee. I would rather eat than ride.

When I was feeling flush, I took the Eight Avenue or IRT subway line between West 90th Street and 23rd Streets for a nickel, and then walked from Seventh or Eight Avenue down to the union headquarters at Eleventh Avenue and West Street, where I would be given my picket duty assignment for the day.

There was a seaman's YMCA on West Street, not far from the union hall, that offered a day's lodging for $1, which was much more than I could afford. From time to time, however, Bill's former shipmates would chip in and give me a dollar to stay at this "luxury" hotel where I could avail myself of regular meals, laundry services, a lounge, recreational facilities, counseling services, and a library. A stay at the "Y, no matter how brief, always boosted my spirits.

West Street Gin Mills

New York was a great "sailor town." Before the strike, the first thing sailors did when they came into port and hit the docks was to head to nearby bars and saloons to call girl friends, wives, lovers, families, or drinking buddies to announce their arrival home and to arrange get-togethers. There were secondary concerns, of course, such as haircuts; taking clothing to the laundry or to a tailor shop; checking for mail at the West Street YMCA; replenishing or replacing sea gear at an outfitter; or seeking medical care at a clinic or doctor's office. But mostly the Jack Tars wanted to "belly up" to the bar in a waterfront gin mill with their shipmates to celebrate their safe return from another perilous voyage in their rust-bottomed vessels.

Picket Duty on the Docks

But now, in the winter of 1937, the ships tied up at the docks were empty and most of the seamen were deployed in picket lines all up and down the waterfront to prevent scabs hired by the ship owners from boarding the vessels.

It was a seamen's waterfront revolt against the shipowners who denied them their fundamental rights as workers. It was a bitter struggle between seamen who were fighting for better shipboard working conditions and the avaricious shipowners who were willing to use any means, including violence, to preserve the gaudy profits they reaped through their government-subsidized shipping operations.

Riotous battles broke out between the striking seamen and horse-mounted policemen, strikebreakers, and finks who tried to bull their way through the picket lines. When sheer human numbers couldn't breach the line, the strike breakers would pile into a taxi and attempt to plow their way through the strikers and onto the piers. The strikers responded by gathering on one side of the invading taxi and lifting it onto its side with its shocked occupants still inside. Police on horseback would wade into the strikers and flail them with long clubs. In self-defense, the strikers would grab the horse's legs and flip the animal over onto its side. Sometimes the strikers would hold a scab's legs or forearms across a curb and fracture the man's legs or forearms with a Louisville slugger baseball bat.

Meanwhile, the company goons were always lurking on the sidelines, armed with leather-covered lead "persuaders" (black jacks) and concealed "gats" (hand guns), ready to identify the strike leaders and administer special, often lethal treatment. It was all too common to find a striking sailor, who had been assigned to picket duty on some far-flung pier, lying dead in an alley, his head split open by a baseball bat. By the time the strike ended in May, twenty-seven striking sailors had died in the violent struggle, and hundreds had been injured.

Once, in the early days of the strike, I was asked to board a ship docked at the pier we were picketing and retrieve some personal belongings for one of the older strikers. I found the crew's quarters in the fo'c'sle and was rummaging through a sea bag in search of the item I was sent to fetch. Suddenly, I sensed a presence behind me, and turned around to find a massive hulk of a man pointing a pistol at my head. Without hesitating, I scrambled between the man's legs, came up behind him and put him in a chokehold. I squeezed with all my might as the man staggered, shook violently, and tried to wriggle out of my hold. He sputtered and wheezed until finally, after what seemed an eternity, he dropped the pistol. I released him from the chokehold, reached down and picked up the gun, and ran out of the room. The shipowners were playing for keeps, and so were we.

Steeplejacking

One day, Bill pulled me aside and asked me if I wanted to

join him in a new part-time job he had lined up waterproofing the windows in a skyscraper in lower Manhattan. He looked me squarely in the eye as he posed the question, looking for signs of fear, I am sure. I had none. I was hungry, the pay would be good, and we'd get plenty of fresh air. I didn't hesitate to say "yes." I was down to the last of my savings and had no other job prospects. We could work as steeplejacks by day and man the picket lines during the evenings or nights.

Bill had done a lot of steeplejack work prior to this, and had no fear of heights. All of us Gill boys had gone aloft in a bosun's chair for Dad to repair or install rigging on the yachts he serviced in Boston Harbor, and were used to working at heights of up to 100 feet. The building we were going to work on, the New York Telephone Building was thirty-two storeys tall. I was sure I could handle it.

And I did. Not that Bill didn't do his best to rattle me. My main job was to hand him caulking guns, scrapers and other items as he called for them, and to keep the ropes neatly coiled and running through heavy blocks as we slowly worked our way down from the top of the building to the street, squeezing caulking compound into the window frames of the building. Aside from these tasks, I didn't have much to do other than to look around and enjoy the bird's eye view of Manhattan.

Every half hour or so, Bill would send me on an errand. "Paul, go get me a Coke!" he would say, and hand me some coins. I'd grab hold of one of the heavy ropes that stretched from the roof down to the street and slide all the way down to the ground. When I returned with Bill's Coke, I would take the elevator up to the 32nd floor, walk out onto the roof, and slide down the rope to the scaffolding. It was a fun exercise, if hard on the skin of my palms. Bill would repeat this game once every couple of hours, sending me for cigarettes, a sandwich, or another Coke, until he realized that I actually enjoyed sliding down the rope and getting off the scaffolding for a few minutes. Then he stopped.

We worked on this water-proofing job weekdays until the strike ended in May. Without the income from that job I don't know how I would have kept body and soul together that spring.

Thumbing to Boston

Whenever I could that winter and spring of 1937, I would go home for a few days to visit my family. When I had the money, I traveled by bus. When I didn't, I hitchhiked and walked.

On one of those trips thumbing across the Worcester Turnpike, returning to Bill's home in New York, I was feeling "down and out" with a miserable cold I had caught while thumbing and tramping northward through a heavy snowstorm. The winter weather heading southbound a few days later was even worse. I had left home in mid-afternoon, thumbing for rides in tractor-trailers. The highways were slick with ice and traffic was at a near-standstill. Halfway down the Pike, driving conditions became dangerous and the traffic came to a complete stop. Too sick and weak to continue trudging through the deep, wet snow, I determined to find shelter of some sort in which to ride out the storm. I came upon a used truck lot, picked out a truck, crawled into the cab, stretched out on the seat and closed my eyes.

But sleep never came. I was hungry, I couldn't stop shivering, and I couldn't find a comfortable position. I tossed and turned until I was startled by the blinding glare of a powerful flashlight shoved in my face. I was frightened until I recognized the uniform and gun holster of a Massachusetts State Police officer. He quickly put me at my ease and expressed concern for my safety. After asking me a few questions and examining my government seaman's credentials, which included a photo, my fingerprints, and personal data, he drove me to his barracks. There, he warmed me up with food and coffee, and let me sleep in an empty cell for the balance of the night. Early the next morning, another trooper served me breakfast and sent me on my way with best wishes for a safe journey back to New York City.

The Dust Settles

At the age of sixteen, I had passed through a veil of violence into the raging battles between the seaman and the shipowners when I joined the strike. After this experience, I turned cynically against what I perceived to be the warped virtues of the great American capitalist society. The seeds of hatred were fermenting within me against anything and everything that the capitalist system stood for. Under the lily-white banners of the National Association of Manufacturers, the capitalists branded all organized seamen as being nothing more than a bunch of "Reds," communists and revolutionaries. But all we seamen wanted was what was rightfully ours under the United States Constitution: the right as workers to bargain with management.

The shipowners finally yielded to most of the strikers' demands, and the East Coast shipping strike ended in May, 1937. Thirty-thousand seamen left the moribund International Seamen's Union and joined the new National Maritime Union. Armed with my new NMU book and more worldly wise, I started looking for my next ship.

FIVE

ON THE NORTH ATLANTIC RUN

O N FEBRUARY 20, 1937, AT the age of sixteen, I signed on the United States Lines luxury liner SS *Manhattan* as an Ordinary Seaman. The *Manhattan* made regularly-scheduled round trips from New York to Hamburg, Germany. On eastbound voyages, the *Manhattan* made brief stops in Plymouth, England, Le Havre, France, and Bremerhaven en route to Hamburg, her final destination. On the return voyage westbound, the ship made brief calls in Le Havre, Southampton, England, and Cobh, Ireland.

The *Manhattan* was the biggest and fastest passenger liner built in the United States at the time of her launching in 1931. She displaced 24,289 tons, was 705 feet long, and had a beam (breadth) of eighty-six feet. The *Manhattan* and her sister ship, SS *Washington*, were the fastest passenger liners in the world, and could cruise at 20 knots. She had a crew of 478, and could accommodate 1239 passengers. She had three passenger decks: a Sun Deck, a Boat Deck and a Promenade Deck. There was a tennis court on the sun deck between the two funnels. Public rooms open to cabin class passengers included a grand salon, a library, a palm court, a verandah cafe, and an open recreational/dance space aft on the promenade deck.

Shipping out on the SS *Manhattan* was a big step up for me. I had made four voyages on the SS *Halo*, but they were inter-coastal voyages and, as a galleyman, I had not gotten much of an education in seamanship. Now I was in the Deck Department of one of the newest and biggest passenger liners in the world. As an Ordinary Seaman, I would start my apprenticeship in what I intended to be my life's work as a professional mariner. And I would be sailing the stormy waters of the North Atlantic, which had tested the mettle of mariners since the time of the Vikings. But I was game, and excited to be continuing the Gill family seafaring tradition on the big stage. My father had sailed to Hamburg on the Hamburg America liner *Markomannia* as a seventeen-year old. He loved Hamburg, and enjoyed reminiscing about his experiences in Germany and the many fine German sailors he had shipped with. I wanted to see the famous port for myself.

Ordinary Seaman

An Ordinary Seaman (OS) is an apprentice sailor in the Deck Department of a ship (the other departments are the Steward's Department and the Engine Department). An OS has to accrue a year or two of sea time before he is eligible to take an examination to become an Able Seaman (AB). The duties of an Ordinary Seaman include:

- Standing two four-hour watches a day, seven days a week.
- Maintaining the physical structure of the ship. This includes cleaning, scraping rust, painting the

Shipping Wonders of the World magazine, featuring an article on the SS *Manhattan* and SS *Washington*.

superstructure, polishing brass instruments and fittings, and keeping brightwork in good condition.

• Collecting and disposing of refuse.

• Lookout duty at the bow and in the crow's nest.

• Taking "tricks" at the wheel and becoming familiar with the ship's binnacle and other bridge equipment.

• Sweeping, buffing, painting and washing the decks.

• Handling of ropes and wire and learning marlin-spike seamanship skills, including a wide range of knots, hitches and splices.

• Launching and recovering launches and lifeboats.

• Participating in docking maneuvers and other ship movements at the direction of Able Seamen, mates or the captain.

First Crossing

My first transoceanic crossing was uneventful, other than for some rough mid-ocean weather. But that was to be expected on a winter passage on the North Atlantic. I got my "sea legs" quickly. The old salts on the *Halo* had taught me to stay topsides in the fresh air and to keep my gaze fixed on the horizon whenever I experienced the first twinges of sea-sickness. It always worked for me but, judging by the green-faced forms clutching the railing on the Promenade Deck, not all the *Manhattan's* passengers were familiar with this tactic. These unfortunates soon learned to avoid the windward side of the ship when *mal de mer* had its grip on them.

Eight days after leaving Pier 60 on the North River in New York, the *Manhattan* stopped in Plymouth, England, long enough to disembark a few passengers and unload thousands of bags of mail. Then, after a quick run across the English Channel, she pulled into Le Havre, France, for an overnight stay. I was eagerly anticipating my first foray into a foreign port, but I was warned by the older seamen that I had better be on my guard. They said the Le Havre waterfront was crawling with thieves and murderers who wouldn't think twice about cutting a sailor's throat for the few dollars he might have in his pockets. I tagged along with a group of ABs who had visited Le Havre on previous trips and assured

Ordinary Seaman Paul Gill, far right.

me they knew where to go and where not to go to have some fun and live to tell about it.

My bunkmate, Steve, an Ordinary Seaman a year or two older than me, had other ideas. He'd heard all the stories about the amorous French girls, and he figured he'd have better luck finding love in Le Havre operating as a lone wolf than as part of a pack, so we parted ways when the taxi disgorged us in the center of town. We entered the first gin mill we came to, and Steve walked off into the night.

When I awoke the next morning, I noticed that Steve's bunk was empty, and it didn't look as though it had been slept in. None of my watch mates had seen him, and we reported his absence to the captain, who sent the Third Mate to the local police station to make inquiries. The police told him that the body of a young man had been found floating in the River Seine that morning. His throat had been slit and his wallet was missing. The mate went to the morgue and identified Steve's corpse. He made arrangements for disposal of the body, and returned to the *Manhattan* just minutes before we cast off the docking lines and headed back out to sea, en route to the North Sea and the port of Hamburg.

I learned my lesson. I never again ventured into a seaport town without a knife secreted in one of my socks.

Hamburg Harbor

When the *Manhattan* entered the broad Elbe estuary, we picked up a river pilot and steamed seventy miles upstream to Hamburg. I was not prepared for the spectacle that greeted my eyes! I had been told that Hamburg was one of the busiest seaports in the world, but I was stunned by the incredible array of vessels of every size and description in the vast harbor, flying the flags of every maritime nation. Tugs, barges, jolly boats, ferries, passenger liners, freighters, and tankers were docked or bustling about like worker bees in a hive. There were even a few square-riggers docked in various parts of the harbor, including the famous Flying-P Line four-masted bark *Padua*, which had just arrived in Hamburg with a load of grain from Australia. I wished Dad could have been there to see her.

Assisted by four harbor tugs, *Manhattan* came alongside a dock in the Wilhelmsburg section of Hamburg and prepared to tie up. I was sent forward to join the forward mooring party. Our job was to secure the bow of the ship to the dock with four hawsers, each as thick as my thigh. One of the ABs taught me how to make a "monkey's fist," a large knot in manila rope, and tie it to a heaving line whose other end was tied to the eye of a hawser. I threw the monkey's fist to a couple of men on the dock below, who pulled on the heaving line until the hawser was pulled from the mooring bitt on our bow, through a chock, and down to the dock, where it was secured to a bollard. Then, a mooring winch on the *Manhattan* took up the slack in the hawser until the line was taut. We repeated this procedure three times. The stern mooring party carried out the same maneuvers aft, and then two spring lines and two breast lines were run from the ship to bollards on the dock below. When we were done, the *Manhattan* was secured to the dock by a total of twelve hawsers.

Once the ship was tied up, we installed passenger and crew gangways and started disembarking passengers and discharging cargo from the forward and stern cargo holds. Spirits were high among the crew, and we worked at a feverish pace. Hamburg was one of the world's great "sailor towns," and we were champing at the bit to get ashore and partake of all that the town had to offer.

As soon as I was dismissed from duty that afternoon, I rushed to the fo'c'sle, donned my best clothes, and headed for the crew gangway. Five minutes later, I boarded a jolly boat that took me across the busy waterway to the north bank of the Elbe. There I found a *U-Bahn* (train) station, jumped onto an eastbound train, and got off at Die Reeperbahn in St. Pauli.

Die Reeperbahn

St. Pauli is the waterfront district of Hamburg, home of the Landungsbrücken, a series of floating docks connected to the river bank by five bridges (*Brücken*), and the main landing place in Hamburg. Die Reeperbahn, a street running parallel

The "Landungsbrücken" in the St. Pauli district of Hamburg, Germany

to the Elbe a few blocks north of the waterfront, is the red light district of Hamburg. The Germans refer to it as *"die sündigste Meile,"* the most sinful mile. It is a fitting sobriquet.

When I emerged from the U-Bahn onto Die Reeperbahn, my eyes and ears were assaulted by a barrage of bright neon lights and a cacophony of sounds emanating from the many cafes, bars, beer gardens, dance halls, and cabarets that lined both sides of the street. A river of humanity drifted up and down the cobblestoned thoroughfare, laughing, singing, and shouting, most with no obvious destination in mind and no apparent purpose other than to celebrate life. Neon signs in both German and English invited me to enter various establishments, where they promised to satisfy whatever bodily needs or urges I might have: "DOLL HOUSE," SEX HOUSE-GIRLS 24H," "SEXY DEVIL," "LOVE PARADISE."

My head was on a swivel as I walked up and down Die Reeperbahn. Here I was, a callow youth of sixteen, in the red light district in Hamburg, Germany, when, by all rights, I should have been at home in South Boston doing my geometry homework. But, when in Rome...

I entered a cabaret on Grosse Freiheit, a cross street near one end of Die Reeperbahn. It was a wild and rollicking place. Just inside the front door was a shooting gallery, where men and women, some in military uniform, were shooting at human silhouettes with rifles or pistols. The air was hazy with cigarette smoke and filled with the raucous sounds of hundreds of men and women laughing, shouting, or singing along with a man decked out in sailor garb who was belting out salty tunes in a deep baritone and accompanying himself on an accordion. Waitresses carrying trays loaded with drinks were shuttling back and forth between the bar and the packed tables that surrounded a central hippodrome. I had never seen anything like this...a riding ring in the center of a cabaret! A half-dozen or so horses and a mule, most carrying humans in various stages of intoxication, were walking around and around a circular sand pit. I assumed that the sand was there to minimize injuries, as few of the riders seemed capable of remaining on their mounts for more than a few seconds.

I spent the next few hours wandering in and out of bars and cabarets on Die Reeperbahn, enjoying the excellent German beer and dancing with pretty fräuleins. Sadly, neither I nor the fräuleins could speak the other's language, and that proved to be a barrier to strengthening social ties. I would fill that gap in my education over the next few voyages to Deutschland.

Some of the most shocking scenes in St. Pauli, to my innocent young eyes, were the storefronts on Herbertstrasse, known to the locals as *Zwei Mark Allee* (Two Mark Alley) where comely (or not-so-comely), scantily-clad young women sat on stools and displayed their charms to prospective customers. These fräuleins left nothing to the imagination! Some of them actively marketed their services, slipping out of what little clothing they wore and assuming different poses to accentuate the most pleasing aspects of their anatomy. Others, often the older and presumably more jaded among them, seemed to have a "take-it-or-leave-it" attitude, and simply sat there reading a novel or filing their nails while passersby gawked. There were small portholes in the windows through which the lady and her prospective customers could conduct negotiations.

I will never forget my first night in Hamburg. I was smitten with the spirited, fun-loving people! I loved the *sauerbraten,* the *kartoffelpuffer,* and the *spätzle*; the *hefeweizen* and Kölsch beer; the pretty blonde fräuleins; the oompah bands; and the dancing. I would return the next night, and on many other occasions on subsequent voyages to Hamburg.

I Learn German

Once I had been exposed to Germany and its alluring culture, I became obsessed with learning *Deutsch*. I wanted to be able to enjoy Hamburg without struggling to translate street signs, menus and the like. More than anything, I wanted to be able to converse with the lovely German girls that seemed to be everywhere in Hamburg. Few of my fellow seamen spoke German, so I befriended several of the German-speaking waiters and bartenders onboard the ship and asked them to teach me the language. About 70% of the *Manhattan's* crew, and virtually all of the men in the Stewards

Department, were German or of German descent. About half of these Germans were Jewish refugees.They were more than happy to oblige.

The first thing they told me was that the people from around Hamburg spoke *Plattdeutsch*, or Low German, and the Germans from the south of Germany spoke *Hochdeutsch*, or High German. In my desire to learn the language I did not care who taught me the language. To me, German was German, no matter whom I learned it from. It just so happened that the individuals who were interested in teaching me conversational German were of Jewish extraction and, without realizing it, I ended up speaking German with a Jewish accent! Because of my built-in Jewish accent, and the rising anti-Jewish sentiment in Nazi Germany, when I made new friends I was routinely asked *"Bist du Jüdish, Junge?* (Are you Jewish, young one?). I learned to reply, "*Ich bin* Irish-American!"

On the voyage back to New York, and on subsequent trips to Hamburg, I practiced my German language skills religiously. Every time I was around a German-speaking crew member, I would utter a few sentences *auf Deutsch*, and they would correct me, or demonstrate proper pronunciation of the German words I was learning. With excellent tutoring and regular practice, I picked up the language quickly. By the time the *Manhattan* tied up at the dock in Wilhelmsburg again, I was ready to try out my German on the people of Hamburg.

Das Bierhaus Zillertal

On my second foray into St. Pauli, I got off the U-Bahn and started walking west on the Reeperbahn. I passed the police station and stopped in front of a large, three-storey building whose facade was brilliantly illuminated in blue and white lights. Huge letters spelled out:

ZILLERTAL
BLEIBT
ZILLERTAL

"Zillertal Remains Zillertal"? I was mystified until I saw a sign over the entranceway that said: *"Zillertal ist die älteste Taverne der Welt."*

Using my newly-acquired German, I translated this into English: "Zillertal is the oldest tavern in the world." That was all the enticement I needed. I pushed through the heavy oak doors and entered into what was, if not the oldest tavern in the world, then certainly the biggest and the most lively. The first floor was one huge, open room, crammed with dozens of large, oaken tables and matching chairs. Massive beams supported lofts on the second floor that stretched from the front to back of the room. Every wall was covered by seascapes or skillfully painted bucolic scenes depicting life in the countryside surrounding Hamburg. At the back of the room was a large stage on which an oompah band was playing a spirited German drinking song, and over the stage the words *"Schau das'd in Schwung Kimmst!"* (See That You Get Going!) were emblazoned in large, gothic letters.

The crowd, a mixture of people of all ages, did not seem to need any prodding to get going. People were laughing, singing, and drinking beer from huge steins. Couples were dancing in the space in front of the stage, in the lofts, and even on the tabletops! *Barmädchen* (bar maids) were bustling back and forth from the bar to the tables, carrying as many as seven steins in each hand! I took a mug from one of them and found a seat at one of the tables.

I was soon talking with two young shipyard workers from

the Blohm & Voss yard in Hamburg. They told me they were building a battleship, the *Bismarck*, that would be *"das mächtigste Schlachtschiff"* (the most powerful battleship) in the world. These young Germans were proud of their country, and believed that Adolf Hitler was restoring Germany to its rightful place among the great industrial and military powers of the world. They told me about the *Hitlerjugend* (Hitler Youth), which they had been members of, and I told them about my experience in the Civilian Conservation Corps. The *Hitlerjugend* was a paramilitary organization designed to indoctrinate young German boys with Nazi ideology and to prepare them for military service. I told them the CCC was a non-political organization that put young men to work on conservation projects across the United States. We agreed that the two organizations had very little in common. But the Reich Labor Service (*Reichsarbeitsdienst*; RAD), which one of them had served in, sounded similar to the CCC. The RAD recruited young German men and women to work as laborers on a number of different projects, often military in nature, but sometimes having to do with civilian and agricultural construction projects. The workers were usually sent far away from home; wore military-style uniforms; lived in barracks; and received a modest monthly salary. They also received a heavy daily dose of political indoctrination, which we never were exposed to in the CCC.

After a while, the oompah band left the stage and was replaced by a polka band. Then things really started to liven up in the old Zillertal! The whole crowd got into it, and me with them, singing at the tops of our lungs, or dancing on the dance floor, or on the table tops when we couldn't find space on the dance floor.

I had been eyeing a pretty blonde fräulein at the next

table the whole time I was conversing with the Blohm & Voss men, and when the polka band started playing a lively number, I excused myself and approached the young lady.

"*Wirst du mit mir tanzen?*" I asked her. (Will you dance with me?) I had practiced the phrase the past few days on the ship, hoping that I would have a chance to use it during our layover in Hamburg.

She looked up at me for a moment or two before responding. I was afraid my attempt at German had failed. Then she asked, "*Hast du jüdisches Blut, Junge?* (Have you Jewish blood, young one?)

Surprised and puzzled by her question, I immediately replied, "*Nein! Ich bin* Irish-American!" She broke into a relieved smile, and said, "*Dann werde ich ja mit dir tanzen!*" (Then I will dance with you!) I was relieved that my Jewish-accented German didn't sabotage my chance to meet this fetching girl.

Heidi was her name. She had azure eyes, sparkling white teeth, and a radiant smile and happy demeanor that I found irresistible. She was the prettiest girl I had ever seen, on either side of the Atlantic, and she laughed self-consciously when I told her so. We danced polka after polka, and between dances, she gave me lessons *auf Deutsch*. I told her "*Ich bin ein seemann auf einem Amerikaner ocean liner.*" I didn't know the German for ocean liner.

"Ah, *der Überseedampfer*," she replied. I struggled with that before finally pronouncing the word to her satisfaction. Then, she told me she had just graduated from *gymnasium* and was studying to be an *apothekerin* (pharmacist) at Universität Hamburg. She didn't seem to mind that I was two years her junior and a ninth-grade dropout. "*Auch viele junge Deutsche mussten die Schule verlassen, um arbeiten zu können.*" (Many young Germans have had to leave school to work, too.)

When it was time for me to head back to the ship, I told her I had had a lot of *spass* (fun) dancing and talking with her. I told her there was an *Elektrizität* between us, and that I hoped we could meet again the next day.

"Ah, Paul, *willst du ein Date mit mir haben?*" (Ah, Paul, do you want to have a date with me?) She told me she would love to spend an afternoon showing me her favorite part of Hamburg, and we agreed to meet the next day outside the Jungfernstieg U-Bahn station.

Das Binnenalster

Heidi and I met outside the Jungfernstieg U-Bahn station the next afternoon. She looked even prettier in the daylight than she had in the Zillertal the night before. How fortunate I was to have such a lovely tour guide!

"Hallo, Paul, *ich möchte dir den schönsten Teil Hamburgs zeigen,*" she said. Luckily for me, Heidi had studied English in school, so she was able to repeat the sentence in English: "Hello, Paul! I want to show you the most beautiful part of Hamburg." She told me that the Alster was a river that flowed into the Elbe from the north. In medieval times, it was dammed to form a reservoir for a corn mill, and this created a large artificial lake. Later, two bridges were built across the river, dividing the Alster into Das Aussenalster (Outer Alster) and Das Binnenalster (Inner Alster). The Jungfernstieg, a broad promenade with many fashionable shops, ran along the southern edge of the Inner Alster. Heidi explained that Jungfern was the German word for maiden, and that in earlier times wealthy Hamburg families would take their young, unmarried daughters for a stroll on the Jungfernstieg on Sundays, a sort of Hanseatic coming-out tradition.

We crossed the Jungsfernstieg and looked northward over Das Binnenalster. It was a medium-sized lake, about the size of the Central Park reservoir in New York City. People were walking or riding bicycles on the terraces or promenades that bordered the lake on three sides, and tour boats were tied up at a dock along the Jungfernstieg side of the lake. Heidi suggested a tour of the lake, so we bought tickets at a dockside kiosk and were directed to board a boat named *Ammersbek*.

Ammersbek took us on a forty-five-minute tour around the Binnenalster. The captain doubled as a tour guide, pointing out luxury hotels, the Hamburger Rathaus (city hall), the tower of Hauptkirche St. Petri (St. Peter's Church), the Alster Pavilion, and other points of interest. It was an interesting tour, but we were getting hungry. Heidi pointed in the direction of the Alster Pavilion. *"Es ist das beste Café in Hamburg. Dorthin bringe ich dich als nächstes.* It's the best cafe in Hamburg, Paul. That's where I'm taking you next!" When *Ammersbek* returned to the dock, we hopped off the boat and within minutes were sitting at a window table in the Alster Pavilion. We had a wonderful view of the Binnenalster, the terraces and promenades that surrounded it on three sides, and the Jungfernstieg. It was a beautiful, sunny evening in Hamburg, Germany, I was in the company of *ein schönes Mädchen* (a beautiful girl), and I could not have been happier.

Abendessen (Dinner) at the Alster Pavilion

Heidi poked me kiddingly in the ribs and told me that I needed to put some meat on my bones, and she was going to help me do it. The menu was long and impenetrable to someone with my meager German language skills. It may as well have been written in Sanskrit. We ordered two glasses of Beck's, and started scrutinizing the offerings. Heidi suggested we start with *vorspeisen* (appetizers). I ordered *apfelwurstring* (apple sausage ring) and Heidi selected *rollmops* (a kind of herring-fillet jelly roll). The *vorspeisen* was followed by a bowl of *sauerkrautsuppe* (sauerkraut soup), for Heidi, and *bayerische Linsensuppe* (Bavarian lentil soup) for me. With Heidi's help, I selected *schwäbischer Schmorbraten* (Swabian Pot Roast) with *spaetzle*, while she had *sauerbraten* (oven-roasted beef). For dessert, we each had *Deutscher apfelkuchen* (German apple cake). We capped this epic meal with schnapps, and then headed out into the night.

Violence in Die Reeperbahn

Heidi and I left the Alster Pavilion and took the U-Bahn to Reeperbahn. The *Manhattan* was leaving for America on the outgoing tide the following morning, but that night we were determined to have fun. And we did. We went from bar to *biergarten* to cabaret, and danced and sang as though there were no tomorrow. It was a night to celebrate being young and free. But not for all Germans.

Later in the evening, we were sitting at a table in a cabaret on the Grosse Freiheit, drinking schnapps and enjoying the music of a jazz trio consisting of a drummer, a bassist, and a pianist. We were just a few feet from the stage where they were playing. Suddenly, there was a commotion at the entrance to the cabaret. There was an eruption of loud banging, shouting, and cursing as a phalanx of brownshirted soldiers wielding long clubs started to shove their way through the crowd. They were a tough-looking bunch.

There were six of them, and they wore identical uniforms: brimmed caps with chin straps, long-sleeved, brown shirts with brown ties, Sam Browne belts, brown riding breeches, and jackboots. On their left arms they wore red armbands with a black swastika in a white circle.

"Sie sind S.A., braune Hemden! (These are the S.A., Brown-shirts!) Heidi whispered. Afterwards, she told me that the S.A., the *Sturmabteilung,* were Hitler's storm troopers. The Nazis used them to terrorize communists, Gypsies, and Jews. The Nuremberg Race Laws, promulgated in 1935, had made it illegal for Jewish musicians to perform in public in Germany. Evidently, someone had tipped off the S.A. that Jews were performing in Die Reeperbahn that night.

The Brownshirts stormed the stage and started swinging their clubs wildly, smashing instruments and landing punishing blows on the cowering musicians. The drummer was struck full in the face with a club. His glasses went flying into the air and blood started streaming from his nose and mouth. He collapsed onto the floor, unconscious or dead. A Brownshirt picked up the bass, smashed it over the head of the bassist, and then started beating the man with his fists. Two other S.A. men jerked the piano player off his bench and pushed and bullied him out the front door of the cabaret and into the back of a waiting unmarked van. The bassist and the drummer were then tossed in with him, the doors of the van slammed shut, and the vehicle drove off into the night with its klaxon blaring loudly.

We walked out of the quickly emptying cabaret in a daze. Bill had told me how the Nazis dealt with perceived enemies of the regime, but I was shocked by the suddenness and ferocity of the Brownshirts' attack on the Jewish musicians. Heidi was embarrassed that a visitor to her country had witnessed such a vile act. As I walked her back to her apartment, we wondered aloud what the future held for Germany, for America, and for us. There was no way to know, of course, but we had enjoyed our date, and agreed to get together again when I returned to Hamburg in a couple of weeks.

Stapleton Marine Hospital

The voyage back to New York was not a pleasant one for me. I started feeling sick before we lost sight of land. It started with night sweats, fevers, chills, and a nagging cough. I felt as weak as a kitten, and went to see the ship's doctor. He listened to my chest, and told me I had pneumonia. He put me in sick bay for the rest of the voyage, and told me to report to the Stapleton Marine Hospital on Staten Island as soon as we docked in New York. He put my medical records in an envelope and instructed me to give them to the doctors at the hospital.

The nurse at the Marine Hospital put me into an examining room and had me change out of my clothes and into a hospital gown. She checked my temperature, blood pressure and pulse, and then weighed me. She said I had a slight fever, and was a few pounds underweight. When the doctor, a Dr. Boone, came in, I handed him the envelope given to me by the ship's doctor. He quickly read the other doctor's notes, and then reviewed my medical history and examined me. He frowned when he listened to my chest. I became alarmed when he told me he was sending me to get a chest x-ray.

When I returned from the x-ray department, Dr. Boone took the films and put them on a lighted box on the wall and scrutinized them for a minute or two. He had me come closer to the viewing box and pointed to a couple of spots on my right lung. He told me I had pulmonary tuberculosis.

He said there was no medical therapy for tuberculosis, but he recommended a few days rest in the hospital. When I was feeling better, he advised me to check into a federal tuberculosis sanitorium in Fort Stanton, New Mexico, for a few months. He said that rest, good nutrition, and the high altitude at the sanitorium would help my body's natural defenses "wall off" the tuberculosis infection. I agreed to a short hospital stay, but told him the sanatorium was not an option. I needed to work so that I could continue to help support my family back in Boston. Besides, I wanted to go back to sea and return to Hamburg.

I felt much better after a week in the hospital. My fever and cough had resolved, and I was eating better and gaining weight. I thanked the nurses and Dr. Boone for their excellent care, signed out of the Marine Hospital, and took the Staten Island Ferry to Lower Manhattan.

I got off the ferry at the Battery, the park at the tip of Manhattan Island, and took the subway up to 90th Street. I hadn't seen Bill in more than two months, and I was eager to tell him about my first two Atlantic crossings on the *Manhattan*. And I knew he would want to hear all about my adventures in St. Pauli and on Die Reeperbahn. I had more self-confidence now, and I knew he would be proud of his little brother, a veteran of the North Atlantic Ocean at the age sixteen!

There was no answer when I knocked on the apartment door, so I scribbled a note to Bill, slipped it under the door, and left. When I returned later that evening, Bill's wife, Kitty, opened the door and invited me in. I had missed Bill by two days, she said. He had just shipped out as AB on an American Line passenger liner, the SS *Virginia*, for a six week trip to South America. I slept on Kitty's couch that night, and left early the next morning for Boston.

Homecoming

It was wonderful to spend a few days at home with my mother and father. Phil wasn't at home. He had shipped out as an Ordinary Seaman on a coal collier in January, carrying coal to ports up and down the New England coast. Dad told me, with a wink, that Phil was jealous of me, sailing to Le Havre, Hamburg, and Southampton on a transatlantic liner, while he was delivering coal to New London, Portsmouth, and Portland!

Dad and I spent hours talking about Hamburg. Forty years had passed since he had shipped out as a seventeen-year-old fireman on a Hamburg-bound steamship, but his memories of the experience were still vivid.

"I wanted to go to Europe, so I shipped on the Hamburg American steamship *Markomannia*," he said. "I was there for the opening of the Kiel Canal, which connected the Baltic Sea with the North Sea. As we were going up the Elbe River to Hamburg, the *Hohenzollern*, the Kaiser's private yacht, passed by us. I saw the Kaiser on the bridge and we had to salute him.

"We carried about five-hundred Polish and Russian passengers from Hamburg to Baltimore and Philadelphia. We would load flour and other cargo at Newport News, Virginia, and take it to London, England. While we were in London, the Queen's Jubilee was going on, and there was plenty of excitement."

Dad smiled when I told him about Die Reeperbahn. "Some things never change, Paul. Sailors will always be sailors! But there weren't any storm troopers going around beating people up back in '95."

By May, 1937, the American economy had rebounded from

the depths of the Depression, and activity was picking up in the local shipyards. I had no difficulty finding a job as a scaler at a South Boston graving yard. The graving yard was a large basin at the water's edge that was filled with water. The ship would be moved into the drydock, supports placed under its keel and sides, and the water pumped out. Then, men armed with large scrapers and wire brushes would move in and scrape the barnacles and other marine growth off the ship's bottom so that it could be painted. It was nasty work, and I had no intention of making a career of it. I just wanted to earn a few bucks while I fattened up on Mom's cooking before I went back to sea.

In early June I quit the graving yard, bade farewell to my parents, and returned to New York to find a ship. I wanted to return to the *Manhattan*, but she was at sea. Instead, I shipped as OS on another United States Lines passenger liner, the S.S. *President Roosevelt*. The *President Roosevelt* was smaller and older than the *Manhattan*, but she made the same regularly-scheduled trips from New York to Le Havre, Hamburg, Southampton, and back.

It was good to be back in the saddle again. I was now a professional mariner, and the next step on my career ladder was to accrue enough sea time to take the US Coast Guard Able Seaman exam. Once I became an AB, I planned to move all the way up to the bridge as an officer.

Most merchant marine officers are graduates of one of the maritime academies. If they pass the Coast Guard qualifying examination, they can earn a Third Mate's license without spending a single day as an Ordinary Seaman or Able Seaman. But there is another pathway to the bridge for an unlicensed seaman. After acquiring the required sea time, taking appropriate courses, and achieving satisfactory onboard assessments of his skills and knowledge, he can sit for the same licensing examination and earn a Third Mate's "ticket." A seaman who ascends to the bridge this way is called a "hawsepiper." The hawse pipe is the opening in the bow of a ship through which the anchor chain passes. When an unlicensed seaman ascends to the bridge without the benefit of a formal education, he has metaphorically climbed "up the hawse pipe." That is what I intended to do.

Before the *President Roosevelt* left New York, I visited a ship's chandlery on South Street in lower Manhattan and bought a copy of Bowditch's *American Practical Navigator*. Over the next four years, I became thoroughly familiar with the contents of this classic marine text. I studied in my bunk when I was off watch, and brought sky charts with me into the crow's nest at night and memorized the locations of the constellations. I wrote down the rules of the nautical road (of which there were an almost unending number) on slips of paper, tucked the slips into my shirt pocket, and referred to them whenever I had a spare moment. By this means I was able to commit an enormous amount of useful nautical information to memory. To round out my education, I taught myself algebra, plane geometry, and trigonometry, and read as many of the classics of literature as I could get my hands on. I was an autodidact.

Six More Crossings To Germany

Between June 9 and October 23, 1937, I made six more North Atlantic crossings. My duties, as on the *Manhattan*, included participating in docking procedures, standing watch, lookout duty, taking tricks at the wheel, ship maintenance (chipping and painting rusty surfaces everywhere on the ship—a never-ending chore), and maintaining the decks. A

UNITED STATES LINES   S.S. PRESIDENT ROOSEVELT   14,187 TONS

couple of the old hands taught me the intricacies of marlinespike seamanship. I mastered a wide variety of knots, hitches and splices, and learned how to make Turk's Heads, bell ropes, becket handles, and lanyards. Dad had initiated me into the mysteries of ropework in his rigging shop, but I took my skills to an advanced level during my time aboard the *President Roosevelt.*

Just as on the *Manhattan,* the crew of the *President Roosevelt* was made up largely of Germans and German-Americans. I was surrounded by German speakers and I was learning the language by osmosis. I learned the German word for everything I could think of: parts of the ship, rigging, tools, food items, articles of clothing, body parts, the clouds, weather conditions, points of the compass, and so on.

The most helpful tutors were the waiters and busboys in the Stewards Department. At first, I was very receptive to their offers to assist me in my quest to master their native tongue. But after a couple of trips on the *President Roosevelt* it became clear to me that some of these characters had a *quid pro quo* in mind when they offered me their linguistic services. A large fraction of these men were gay, which didn't bother me. My attitude was "live and let live." Their sexual preferences were none of my concern. But, as a fresh-faced seventeen-year old, I apparently was seen by some of them as pogey bait. Once I accepted their offer of pedagogical assistance, some of these men seemed to feel they had the right to try to seduce me. Most of them would back off when they saw that I wasn't receptive to their advances. But a couple of these guys were blind to the unambiguously negative signals I had been sending out. The situation was getting out of hand, and I was starting to hear snickers and suppressed laughter from the other men in the fo'c'sle. I had to do something to demonstrate to these men that I was a confirmed heterosexual and would not tolerate their unwanted advances.

The bars on the ship were open around the clock. Sometimes, after I knocked off from my 8:00 p.m. to midnight watch, I would poke my face into the second-class passenger bar at the stern of the ship on my way to the crew quarters. If there were no passengers at the bar, I would ask the bartender for a glass of beer. He would always oblige, and I would linger at the bar for a few minutes, savoring the beer and chatting with the bartender and whatever waitstaff happened to be around. One night, one of my more ardent pursuers happened to be present. I had warned this fellow off before, but he didn't get the message. When he invited me to come out on the boat deck with him for a stroll, I nodded and finished my beer. We left the bar and started to walk aft on the boat deck. When we reached the taffrail at the stern, he snuggled up next to me. I suddenly grabbed him by the collar, lifted him bodily over the rail, and held him there, suspended between the star-studded sky and eternity. The thrashing of the propellers far below could be heard over his screams. I made him swear to stay away from me, and to tell his gay friends to leave me alone. Between sobs he swore he would comply with my demands. I hauled him back over the rail and stood him back up on his feet. When he had regained his composure, I went to the fo'c'sle and turned in. I had no more problems with the Stewards Department.

Inside the Third Reich

I was a politically naive teenager, but even I could feel the undercurrent of tension and fear in Germany, or at least in Hamburg. The Nazi flag, which featured a black swastika in a white circle on a red field, adorned every bus and streetcar and flew from flagstaffs on almost every building. The police were everywhere. They, and the Brownshirts, patrolled the streets and infiltrated the cabarets and bars, watching for any sign of resistance to the Nazi regime. They would pounce at the slightest sign of dissent, using clubs, fists and jackboots to crush anyone daring or foolish enough to voice opposition to the Nazi Party.

There were many Nazis among our crew. So many, in fact, that it was considered dangerous to openly disagree with them in any discussion of politics or race. We were constantly reminded of the glories of the Third Reich, and instructed on how to comport ourselves when in Hamburg. I was told that I had to salute when someone said *"Heil Hitler,"* and that if I did not, I could expect trouble. I took that warning to heart, especially in light of what had happened to Bill in Hamburg in 1935. If they could beat up Bill, the toughest man I knew, I shuddered to think of what they could do to me with their clubs and jackboots.

Even though there was a pall of fear hanging over German society, not all Germans had swallowed the Nazi line. I remember the day some dock workers showed us wood carvings of Hitler and Mussolini standing nude in a wooden beer barrel. With a flick of the thumb, the two dictators popped up out of the barrel locked in a lovers' embrace! There was plenty of pornographic material of this kind floating around Hamburg. German dock workers found it very amusing, and did not conceal their irreverent views of the Führer. But the police and the Brownshirts did not spend much time hanging around the docks. They apparently found the streets of Hamburg and St. Pauli to be more fertile hunting grounds. Jewish musicians were easier prey than dock workers.

Back to Die Reeperbahn

There were sections of Hamburg I liked to visit during the daylight hours. When the weather was nice, Heidi and I sometimes rented a small sailboat and went sailing on the Aussenalster. If there wasn't much of a breeze, we would rent a rowboat and explore the shorelines of both the inner and outer Alster. If we were feeling lazy, we might take a long ride around Hamburg Harbor on a *bierboot* (beer boat), enjoying the good German beer, delicious buffet, and lively music.

But once the sun went down, sailors like me were drawn to Die Reeperbahn like bears to honey. The Zillertal was one of my favorite haunts. It was always lively, and it was a magnet for people from every walk of life. I found the Germans I met there to be highly sociable, especially when the oompah band was playing drinking songs and the beer was flowing. I met men from every branch of the German military: the *Luftwaffe* (air force), *Kriegsmarine* (navy), and

Heer (army). Most of them had been in the Hitler Youth and, while few of them were ardent Nazis, they all endorsed Hitler's rapid expansion of the military. They claimed that morale was high in the German armed forces, and that there was a steady infusion of bigger and better weapons of every kind. Luftwaffe men bragged about the Messerschmitt 109, a single-engine fighter that they claimed was the best fighter aircraft in the world. The soldiers I met at Zillertal and other beer gardens in St. Pauli loved to talk about the new armored formations Hitler was creating, with over 500 tanks in each division! And the Kriegsmarine men said the *Bismarck* would outclass every battleship in the Royal Navy, including HMS *Hood*. I found this hard to credit. *Hood* was the pride of the Royal Navy, the largest warship in the world. I had been in awe of her when she docked in Boston when I was twelve years old, and I couldn't imagine a bigger or more intimidating warship. I grew to like these young German patriots, and sensed that they would be formidable foes if our two countries ever went to war with each other.

When Heidi could take time off from her studies, we would meet up on Die Reeperbahn and sing and dance the night away in the bars and cabarets. But when she couldn't join me, I found other fraüleins to sing and dance with. They were as sociable and friendly as the young men, once I got past "*Bist du ein jüdischer, Junge?*"

My sojourns in Hamburg were always brief, usually only a couple of days. When she was able, Heidi would come to the Wilhelmsburg dock to bid me adieu when the *President Roosevelt* was leaving to return to America. On one of these occasions, I was part of the stern mooring party, working with a mixed crew of Ordinary Seamen and Able Seamen. They all knew that my *schatz* (sweetheart) was down on the dock to see me off. Being young men, they couldn't help casting an appraising glance her way. Then, they would look my way and flash me a "thumbs up."

All except Horst. Horst was a German AB of about thirty. He was a big guy, an intimidating brute whom the men steered clear of as much as possible. He outweighed me by 100 pounds. Horst had no respect for anyone, not even a lovely *Mädchen* (girl) who had come to see her young man off as he headed out to sea. Horst walked over to the rail, looked down at Heidi on the dock far below, and said, in a voice loud enough for Heidi and all the men in the party to hear: "Gill, *Deine Hure weint um dich*! (Gill, your whore is crying for you!)

I ran over to Horst and punched him in the face as hard as I could. I expected that would be my last living act. I was prepared to die to defend the honor of my sweetheart. But, to my utter astonishment, Horst just stood there and cried. He looked at me through tear-filled eyes and blubbered, "*Warum hast du das getan*? (What did you do that for?)

I looked over the rail and blew a final kiss to Heidi. She had tears running down her cheeks, but a huge smile on her face as she waved goodbye. I waved back until I couldn't see her any more. *Aüf wiedersehen, liebe* Heidi!

SIX

ON THE BEACH, S.S. *GULFWAVE*, AND BACK ON THE BEACH

Forebodings

I REMEMBER STANDING ON THE afterdeck of the SS *President Roosevelt*, watching the Old Head of Kinsale fade from view as the ship headed into the open Atlantic. We had picked up a load of mail and a few passengers in Cobh, Ireland, and were now on a course for New York. Willy, one of the older ABs on my watch, and I were chipping and scraping paint from the taffrail. Willy looked pensively down at the blue-green waters of the Celtic Sea as they rushed by the black hull. He took a drag on his cigarette, turned to me, and said, "You know, Paul, we may be passing directly over the bones of the *Lusitania*." The British passenger liner RMS *Lusitania* was torpedoed and sunk by a German submarine eleven miles off the coast of Ireland on May 7, 1915. I hadn't been born yet, but everyone knew that the sinking of the *Lusitania* had pushed the United States into the Great War on the side of the Allies. I also knew that the great ship went down in eighteen minutes, and took over one thousand passengers with her to the bottom. I shuddered at the thought of the poor souls who spent the last few minutes of their lives in the frigid waters of the North Atlantic.

Willy shifted his gaze shoreward, where only a thin, green sliver of land remained visible above the horizon, and said, "And did ya know, what we're lookin' at now is the same last bit of land seen by the poor folks who went down on the *Titanic*?" Cobh had been the last port of call for the *Titanic* before heading seaward on her maiden and final voyage on April 11, 1912.

"No, Willy, I didn't know that," I replied. I kept my eyes fixed on the last visible remnant of land until it vanished from view. I was always excited at the start of an ocean crossing, but Willy's comments on the two great maritime disasters of the early twentieth century had an unsettling effect on me. The leaden skies to the east and the sound of the wind whistling through the ship's rigging added to my feeling of foreboding. It was late October and, as I picked up my chipping hammer and went back to work, my sailor's intuition told me we were in for a rough passage.

The Fury of the North Atlantic

My intuition proved correct. Over the next seven days, the *President Roosevelt* was subjected to a terrific beating as she plowed through a succession of violent storms that put her physical structure and the endurance and seamanship skills of her crew to the severest test. The western North Atlantic Ocean is a nursery for violent storms in the fall and winter, and these storm systems are propelled eastward by the prevailing southwesterly winds. We were steaming westward, right into the teeth of these eastward-moving storms. The wind velocity never fell below 30 knots during the voyage, and the effective wind velocity, the speed of the vessel plus the wind speed, often exceeded 50 knots. I overheard the bosun describe the sea state as "boisterous." "Berserk" might have been a more fitting adjective. It was as though Neptune had unlocked the gates of maritime hell, unleashing howling winds and an unending procession of mountainous waves that battered our 14,000-ton ship, sending shivers through her structure each time we plunged down into the trough of a wave and the bow burrowed into the next onrushing wave. The wind blew the tops off the wave crests, sending dense streaks off to leeward.

Port, starboard, and crow's nest lookouts were maintained as usual, but this was cruel duty under these hellish conditions. With each roll of the ship, the port and starboard lookouts were inundated by frigid seawater that soaked them to the skin, and the constant barrage of spray and horizontally-driven rainwater made it impossible for them to keep their eyes open for any length of time. Only safety harnesses secured to fore-and-aft lifelines kept the lookouts from being tossed into the sea.

The man in the crow's nest was subjected to a different kind of torture. The crow's nest was a kind of cylinder or barrel welded to the foremast about forty feet above the foredeck, sixty-five feet above the waterline. It had a roof, which provided the lookout some protection from the driving rain and spray. But crow's-nest duty in gale conditions was no picnic. With each roll of the ship from port to starboard and back again, the crow's nest swung like an upside-down pendulum through an arc of 60 degrees or more. Each time the pendulum reached the end of its excursion, the lookout was slammed hard against the inner wall of the barrel. Before he could recover from the shock of the impact, the ship started to roll back the other way, and he had to brace himself for the next impact. It was hard to maintain a lookout when you were being thrown around like a rag doll. In the days of sail, being sent to the masthead in a storm was a form of punishment. Personally, I would prefer to be flogged. It was the rare seaman who could tolerate more than a few minutes of this nausea-inducing, organ-grinding abuse. But there were a few among the crew who preferred to be dry and seasick rather than wet and cold, so I was usually able to swap the crow's nest for a deck-level lookout post.

Paul Gill in the crow's nest

Each time I came off lookout duty, I quickly stripped off my soaked clothing, took a hot shower, and made my way to the galley to down a mug of hot coffee. Then, I took my wet clothing down into the engine room and hung it up to dry. It was pleasantly hot down there, and I usually stayed until I stopped shivering.

The storm intensified, and the captain ordered all outer decks closed. The conditions were hardly conducive to strolls around the promenade deck or games of shuffleboard, so I don't imagine there were many complaints from the passengers. Most people stayed in their cabins, praying presumably. The adventurous few who dared to make their way to the public rooms were clustered around the windows, "oohing" and "ahhing" over the massive waves. As the ship started to roll more violently, the furniture slipped its moorings and started to slide back and forth across the parquet floor, from port to starboard, threatening to flatten anyone who dared to walk across the room.

The Third Mate organized a team of seamen to secure the suddenly itinerant furniture. It was like being in the rodeo, but instead of roping steers, we were roping and restraining couches, tables, chairs, and settles! It was dangerous work, but a fun diversion from lookout duty, and the passengers got into the spirit of the thing, clapping and cheered wildly as we lassoed and secured the last of the vagabond furnishings, a grand piano!

The *President Roosevelt* battled wind and waves all the way across the North Atlantic. By the time we passed Lightship Ambrose at the mouth of New York Harbor, I was exhausted and ready for a break. I decided to spend a couple of weeks ashore on terra firma before looking for a berth on a ship sailing to sunny climes.

Picket Duty

The *President Roosevelt* nosed into her slip at Pier 60 on the Hudson River on the morning of October 23, 1937. After helping to secure the docking lines and discharge cargo, I stowed my belongings in a sea bag, bade farewell to my shipmates, and went straight to Grand Central Station, where I boarded a train for Boston. During the trip, I picked up a copy of the *Boston Herald* and was surprised to read that the National Maritime Union had just gone on strike against the Eastern Steamship Lines. This was big news. The Eastern Steamship Lines consisted of a number of small ocean liners that made regular runs between Boston and Yarmouth, Nova Scotia, and between New York and Norfolk, Virginia. I knew I would be called upon to do picket duty until the strike ended. I had planned to spend a couple of weeks "on the beach." If the strike was prolonged, I could be shorebound a lot longer, and it might be hard to find my next ship. After several years of improving economic conditions, the United States was now experiencing a slump, and the unemployment rate was climbing again. I discarded the newspaper and put all that worrisome news out of my mind as I looked forward to being back home again.

Catching Up with Phil

When I arrived at the family home in South Boston, I let myself in quietly and walked stealthily across the dining room toward the kitchen at the back of the house, hoping to surprise Mom and Dad. Instead, I was the one who was surprised. I expected to see Dad seated at the table, hunched over one of his ship models, making fine adjustments to the rigging, or installing a miniature deck house on the afterdeck. And Mom would probably be bent over the kitchen counter, kneading dough, or peeling apples to put in one of her delicious apple pies. Instead, I saw Mom, Dad and my twin seated at the table, each with a glass of beer in their hands, laughing as though they had just shared a hilarious joke.

After a round of hugs and kisses, I poured myself a glass of beer and joined them at the table. I hadn't seen Phil in almost a year, and I was amazed at how much older and more mature he looked. I suddenly realized that we were no longer boys, but seventeen-year-old grown men who had seen more of the world than most men twice our age. We spent the rest of the evening catching up and sharing sea stories.

Phil was jealous after hearing about my adventures on the *Manhattan* and *President Roosevelt,* and the fun times I had had in Hamburg. He joined the CCC a few months after I did, but his falsified birth certificate did not stand up to scrutiny, and he was dismissed from the service after a brief stint. He returned to Boston and went back to school until he was sixteen, when he shipped out as an OS on an ancient oil tanker, making regular runs between Boston and Mobile, Alabama.

"Those winter months at sea on that old scow were miserable, Paul," said Phil. "She waddled along at 7 knots, maximum. She was more of a submersible than a ship. She plowed into, rather than over, the oncoming seas. With every pitch and roll, she'd creak and groan, and expel a cloud of fumes from her cargo. And she was infested with roaches and bedbugs."

Phil then joined our brother Steve on the S.S. *Black Tern*, a freighter that sailed out of Weehawken, New Jersey. This vessel made regular runs to Rotterdam and Bremerhaven. "She was a Hog Islander, built at Hog Island, Pennsylvania, during World War I. She was 400 feet long, had a beam of forty-five feet, a blunt, perpendicular stem, and a stern like an elephant. She had a coal-burning, reciprocating steam engine and, under favorable conditions, with fair winds and a following sea, she could make 9 knots.

"The ship was a bucket of rust. The old man had a closet-like state room about four feet by eight feet in size, and the mate's quarters were glorified pigeon holes. We in the deck gang had a crumb corner on the port side of the midship house and the engine room gang had theirs on the starboard side. The ship's officers ate their meals in the midships house forward. The unlicensed crew slept aft on the main deck, with the deck gang on the starboard side of the steering engine and the Black Gang on the port side. Bunks were tiered two-high against the insulated steel hull, with a single unshaded light bulb suspended from the ceiling.

"It was a hectic place to sleep, what with the constant

huffing and puffing of the steering engine and the clanking of the chains feeding in and out of the quadrant of the steering post.

"We had our own washing machine, too. A fourteen-quart galvanized bucket. First, you washed your clothes in salt water, and then rinsed them in fresh water when it was available. For our troubles, we were paid the princely wage of $25 a month."

Philip Gill

Phil signed off the *Black Tern* in August, 1937, and then got a job as a rigger at the Bethlehem Steel shipyard in Quincy, south of Boston. He was laid off after a few weeks, however, and had just signed on to a molasses tanker running between New England ports, Puerto Rico, and Havana. "She's another Hog Islander, Paul, a freighter converted to cargo tanker. Seems I can't escape these old barges. But jobs are scarce, and we'll be in the Caribbean, which is a good place to be in the winter time, so I took it. We'll be slipping our mooring in the morning."

Picket Duty

Phil and I rose at dawn the next morning, enjoyed a hearty breakfast, and then headed out, Phil to board his ship and me to find a job. I was fortunate to find work at the South Boston Naval Annex, and was instructed to report the next morning to work as a scaler in the graving dock. It was nasty work, but I was glad to get it.

My next stop was at the Boston local of the NMU. I knew they would be looking for volunteers to do picket duty during the strike against the Eastern Steamship Lines, and I was happy to do my part to improve the pay and working conditions for American merchant seamen. The NMU membership had grown tremendously since its founding the previous year, and now had more than 50,000 dues-paying members. I was optimistic that the walkout would be brief. Picket duty at Rowes Wharf was not fun. I had seen enough violence on the New York waterfront the year before during the East Coast shipping strike, and I hoped they wouldn't need a beef squad this time around.

I scraped ship bottoms at the Naval Annex Monday through Friday for the next several weeks, and walked the picket lines on Atlantic Avenue on the weekends and most afternoons. I was rewarded for my loyalty to the union with an OS berth on the S.S. *Gulfwave*, a new Gulf Oil tanker that was slated to make regular runs between Boston and Port Aransas, Texas. It wasn't an ideal gig, but at least I would be sailing in warm waters half the time, and I would be accruing sea time to qualify for my Able Seaman ticket. Also, I'd get to spend a night at home with Mom and Dad every three weeks.

S.S. *Gulfwave*

S.S. *Gulfwave* was a brand-new ship, launched on October 9, 1937, and delivered to Gulf Oil Corporation on December 1. She was about the same size as S.S. *Halo*, 441 feet long and 7,100 tons displacement, and slightly faster, with a speed of 12 knots. After completing her sea trials, she berthed at Mystic Pier in Charlestown. That's where I boarded her and signed the ship's articles on the last day of 1937. The next morning, *Gulfwave* cast off her docking lines, steamed slowly past the U.S.S. *Constitution* ("Old Ironsides"), which was berthed in the Boston Navy Yard, and departed on her maiden voyage, bound for Port Aransas, Texas, 2,215 nautical miles distant.

As we steamed past President Roads, with Deer Isle to port and Long Island to starboard, I couldn't suppress some vague misgivings. I was happy to have steady employment, and I would much rather be at sea doing sailor work than scraping barnacles off a ship's bottom on shore. But I had been to Port Aransas four times before, and the little oil port on the Gulf of Mexico held little allure for me. I missed Heidi, and would have much preferred to be sailing for Hamburg, but I had no stomach for another winter crossing of the North Atlantic. I decided I would make a few runs on

Gulfwave, get my Able Seaman ticket, and then get back on one of the transatlantic passenger liners in the late spring.

Between January 1 and May 26, 1938, I made seven round trips between Boston and Port Aransas. These were unremarkable passages, with only the occasional patch of stormy weather to contend with. Because *Gulfwave* was a new ship, we didn't spend any time chipping and painting the superstructure the first few months I was on her, but the bosun kept the deck crew busy with lifeboat drills, fire drills, lubricating the deck machinery, inspecting the myriad pipe fittings, and practicing loading and off-loading procedures. I devoted most of my offwatch hours to studying, whether in my bunk in the fo'c'sle or in the crow's nest. It could be boring up there, and I found that it was easier to keep a sharp lookout for ships and other navigational hazards if my mind was occupied. I'd bring lists of items to memorize, such as the nautical rules of the road, aids to navigation, cargo equipment, emergency procedures, lifeboat handling, damage control, fire fighting, and so on.

I also brought star charts with me at night so I could become familiar with the various constellations and their component stars. This knowledge would be indispensable when I started learning celestial navigation. In addition to the sun and the moon, a seaman can use a planet or one of the fifty-eight navigational stars to take a sighting and compute his position. Using star charts, I quickly learned the locations of the major constellations, and the names of the navigational stars in those constellations. The night sky is much brighter at sea, away from the lights of civilization, and that made the learning process easier. Once I found the constellation Auriga, "the charioteer," for example, it was easy to locate Capella, one of the brightest of the northern stars. I was thrilled one night in early April when I spotted Gacrux, the star at the top of the Southern Cross, as we rounded Key West. By mid-May, I was able to see the whole constellation. Southern Cross had a mystical allure for me. I had an intuition that I would be seeing more of it in the future.

I was self-conscious about my status as a high-school dropout. I regretted not having the opportunity to finish high school and go on to study engineering in college. But I was determined to acquire an education, so I became an autodidact. I taught myself algebra, geometry and trigonometry, and read history and classical literature. Whenever the ship was back in Boston, I would visit the Public Library in Copley Square and stock up on books to read on my next voyage. My favorite author was Mark Twain. His biting humor agreed with my own somewhat sardonic view of the world.

Growing up, my brothers teased me because I always had my nose in a book. They called me "Egghead," and "the Professor." My shipmates on the *Gulfwave* gave me a little good-natured ribbing, but respected me because I was conscientious and I was a hard worker. Or maybe they left me alone because they were high as a kite half the time. Marijuana smoking was rampant aboard *Gulfwave*, so much so that I couldn't lie in my upper berth without getting high from the fumes. Normally, a ship's fo'c'sle is a hotbed of petty grievances, perceived slights, and barely bridled hostility among a group of men lodged in tight quarters with little privacy and few healthy outlets for their anxieties and frustrations. Fist fights were a necessary outlet for the pent-up aggressive instincts of young sailors. At least that's the way it was on every ship I had sailed on. Things were different on *Gulfwave*. She was a "love boat" in comparison to those other vessels. There was very little scrapping, but a lot of silly, downright ridiculous behavior. Because I was the sober one in the group, I was often asked to act as arbitrator when differences did arise. I am not sure how marijuana affected the work performance of those who partook, but it certainly fostered an atmosphere of peace and harmony in the fo'c'sle and in the messroom. It put me in mind of Odysseus and his crew in the land of the Lotus eaters.

Not every member of the crew availed himself of the calming effects of marijuana. Snuffy Smith was a querulous, twenty-seven-year-old AB who sported question mark tattoos on each earlobe. He had a chip on his shoulder, and he was quick to pick a fight, usually with a smaller man. He singled out Joe Pringle, an ordinary seaman from New Hampshire, for particular abuse. Snuffy never missed an opportunity to make fun of Joe, a little guy with minimal seafaring experience. Snuffy made him the butt of his crude jokes, and constantly criticized his work habits and seamanship skills. Joe ignored the taunts at first, but when the verbal assaults turned to threats of physical violence, Joe turned to me for help, offering to pay me protection money to keep Snuffy from beating him. I refused Joe's money, but I took Snuffy aside one night and told him how much I despised bullies. Snuffy got the message, and Joe and I became fast friends.

On the Beach

On May 26, 1938, I signed off *Gulfwave* in Boston and a few days later, after a short visit with my family, packed my seabag and went to South Station and boarded a train for New York. My intent was to find a berth on a North Atlantic passenger liner and return to Hamburg. After seven round trips over five months, the Boston to Port Aransas run had gotten monotonous. I wanted to sail in deep waters again, and I was confident that, with the sailing experience I had acquired, I would have no difficulty securing a berth on a transatlantic liner. I would soon be disabused of that notion.

I went directly from Grand Central Station to the NMU headquarters on West Street. There were a few men loitering around the entrance, smoking and talking quietly in groups of two or three. Not a smile was in evidence. I entered the building with a sense of foreboding.

The large hiring hall was packed with men waiting for the union steward to come out of the back office to announce open positions on ships docked in New York Harbor. Many of the men were sitting on benches or folding chairs and intently studying newspapers. The *New York Times* published daily ship arrivals and departures, and a sailor could get a good idea of how many jobs would be available by studying this section of the paper. Jobs were allotted by seniority, and judging by the apparent age of the men around me, I knew I wasn't going to be in the running for the choicest berths.

The men put aside their newspapers and moved to the front of the hall when the steward entered the room carrying a sheaf of papers and approached a large blackboard mounted on the back wall. In the first column on the left side of the blackboard, he wrote the name of a ship, her destination, and her sailing date. In the columns to the right of the vessel's name, he listed the jobs available in the Deck, Engine, and Steward Departments of that vessel. He listed eight ships, but only a small number of open berths on any of them. As he announced each of the jobs, it was quickly claimed by a man who had likely spent more years at sea than I had been alive.

It took the union steward less than fifteen minutes to allocate the available jobs. When he gathered up his papers and left the room, the men stood around in small groups, complaining loudly and bitterly about the terrible employment prospects. I hung around the hiring hall for the rest of the day, and looked on despairingly as the union steward doled out a mere handful of jobs each time he sallied forth from the back office. By mid-afternoon, most of the younger men had left the hall. I went outside and talked to a few of these fellows. They told me that the employment situation had gotten steadily worse over the past few months, and that a kid like me would be lucky to land a berth on a New York City garbage scow. I left the hall that afternoon feeling deeply discouraged.

I would have gone to see my brother Bill on the upper west side, but Phil had told me he was somewhere in the Pacific on an American Presidents Lines passenger ship. Instead, I found lodging in a flop house in Hell's Kitchen, the West Side Irish neighborhood. I turned in early that night, and hit the streets before dawn the next morning, determined to find work.

I picked up a copy of the *New York Daily News* and scanned the Help Wanted section while I ate breakfast at a greasy spoon diner on Ninth Avenue. I circled a dozen notices, and when I finished eating, sat down in the phone booth at the back of the diner and started calling prospective employers. It didn't take long for me to realize I was wasting my nickels. Every single job had been taken! Jobs were snapped up as soon as they were posted.

I took another look at the Help Wanted listings. Most of the jobs I had not circled required a high school diploma or a driver's license, neither of which I possessed. I skipped over the listings for sewer worker, grave digger, and morgue attendant. Those were dead end jobs, so to speak. I wasn't that desperate, at least not yet.

I threw away the newspaper and decided to focus my efforts on finding work at one of the many shipyards in New York. I rode the subway to Brooklyn and walked into the employment office at Todd's Shipyard on the Erie Basin in the Red Hook section of Brooklyn. Todd's had the biggest drydock on the East Coast, and I was hopeful that my OS license and my experience working in South Boston shipyards would help me land a job there.

And they did. The shipyard was in a rush to complete construction of a Navy destroyer, and they desperately needed riggers to finish fitting out the ship. I had never worked as a rigger, but I convinced the man in the hiring office that my seafaring experience and working in my dad's rigging shop qualified me for the job. He offered to take me on as a temporary employee if I could start right away. I could, of course, and fifteen minutes later I was part of a crew installing a four-inch forward gun mount on the destroyer.

Over the next couple of weeks, I helped install every kind of ship's equipment above the decks: stays, shrouds, booms, masts, lifeboats, rafts, hatchways, funnels, winches, anchors, steering gear, machine gun mounts, beams and plates, magazines and ready boxes. I also helped to test hoists, ammunition lifts, and lifeboat launching mechanisms. It was enjoyable work, and I was learning new skills. When I worked the day shift and knocked off at 3:30 p.m., I would go to one of the taverns outside the yard for a few beers with the boys, and enjoy the free meal of cold cuts, sandwiches, cheese, cookies, biscuits, bread, salad and vegetables set out by the barkeeper.

As expected, I was laid off when the work on the destroyer was completed. But I was able to find occasional work washing windows on midtown skyscrapers, and a full-time job as a barboy at the Hotel Astor in Times Square. The pay was paltry, but the unemployment rate in New York City in 1938 was high, and I felt lucky to get the job, even if I had had to bribe the employment agent to secure it.

I was also lucky to find a room in the French Quarter, a boarding house in nearby Hell's Kitchen. Located on 346 West 46th Street, close to the heart of Manhattan nightlife, the brownstone building was on a tree-lined street in an attractive old neighborhood. It was early summer, and each apartment house on the street had a beautiful flower garden at its entrance. Largely hidden from passersby were the ivy-covered red brick tunnels that led from the street to cafes and bistros in the atria behind the buildings.

My new neighborhood was just a few blocks from the Hudson River waterfront, where majestic ocean liners from the United States, Britain, Germany, France, and other countries docked. Once these vessels tied up to the pier and cleared customs, there was always a mad rush by passengers and crew to race down the gangway and set out on foot or by taxi to visit legendary Broadway and Times Square in the heart of New York City. On their way, they would pass through my West Side neighborhood, and on their way back to the ship they would often stop for coffee, a drink, or a meal at one of the many charming cafes and cozy restaurants on Restaurant Row.

This was just the place for a young sailor, far from his home port, to hang out while waiting for his next ship. I was too busy to be lonesome. There was action around the clock, entertainment and excitement within easy reach, provided you had two bucks to rub together. When I finished work at the Astor Hotel, the night was just beginning for me. I was a regular at some of the private and unauthorized nightclubs in the side streets off Broadway that never closed. Some nights I would go up to Yorkville, the German neighborhood on the upper East Side, and whoop it up there, drinking Beck's beer and dancing with girls from Barnard or City College. It was almost like being back on the Reeperbahn with Heidi. Other nights I would go over to the Leitrim Castle Bar and drink Guiness Stout and dance jigs and reels with Irish-American lasses.

Some nights, I didn't even have to leave the Astor Hotel to find excitement. The hotel had an open-air cafe on its roof, called the Skywalk Cafe. It was in a garden setting with dramatic views of the Chrysler Building and the Empire State Building, and small tables arranged among lush foliage. It was a place New Yorkers went to be seen, and a magnet for visiting celebrities. While working there, I met, among other notables, Douglas "Wrong Way" Corrigan, who became world famous for "mistakenly" flying non-stop from New York to Dublin, Ireland; Canadian-American actress Norma Shearer; and the Ritz Brothers comedy team.

But life on the beach wasn't all fun and games. I kept a close eye on the shipping news in the *Times*, and walked down to the union hiring hall every morning in hopes of finding a ship. All I ever got out of those walks was exercise.

Phil visited me over the Fourth of July holiday. He had signed off the molasses carrier and was now sailing out of New York on an intercoastal freighter, making regular trips between New York and Charleston, New Orleans, and Corpus Christi. He needed just a few more months of sea time to qualify for the Coast Guard AB examination. I took him out to some of my favorite night spots, and on July 3 we celebrated our birthday with a swim in the Hudson River at 42nd Street. We had been through hard times together as boys, but we had emerged from that crucible with the confidence that we could endure any hardship and overcome any obstacle that fate might place in our paths.

Shortly after Phil sailed for Charleston, I had a reunion with another brother, Steve, who was three years my senior. Steve had been on the *Black Tern* with Phil for a few months in 1937, but had spent the winter and spring months working as a rigger in a shipyard in New Jersey. He had been laid off in June, and now he was struggling to get by on his meager earnings from day-labor and steeplejack jobs. He wanted to try something new, and mentioned a new federal homesteading project he had heard about in Alaska. Apparently, there was a need for loggers, carpenters, and tradesmen to support a new community the government was helping to establish there. I was in a rut in New York, and was open to any opportunity. We tossed around the idea of joining the Marine Corps, but neither of us liked the idea of a long enlistment.

I went to the New York Public Library near Bryant Park to see what I could find out about this Alaska homesteading project. I read in the *New York Times, Time* magazine, and other publications that the federal government had devised a scheme to help struggling farm families by moving them from the Dust Bowl to an experimental farming community in the Matanuska Valley in South Central Alaska. The goal was to remove the families from the relief rolls by making them self-sufficient, and to increase the population of the Alaska Territory. Two hundred families from Minnesota, Michigan and Wisconsin were selected and given forty acres of land to farm and a loan of $3,000 to buy equipment, seed, livestock, and furnishings. The government recruited men from Federal Transient Camps to help clear the land and build log cabins, barns, stores, and a hospital. The colonists had gotten a toehold on their land, but according to the *Times*, New Deal authorities were looking for more men to come to the Valley to cut timber, clear land, and build roads and infrastructure.

My heart leaped in my chest when I read this. My 15 months in the CCC had prepared me for this kind of work, and mid-summer seemed like a good time to make the break and head for Alaska. What an adventure it would be! I met with Steve that night, and we decided to go for it. We would ride the rails across the continent, find berths on an Anchorage-bound ship in Portland or Seattle, and then make our way to the promised land, the Matanuska Valley.

We vowed to stick together, no matter what happened during the long journey. To seal the pledge, the next day we went over to a tattoo parlor on Sand Street, near the Brooklyn Navy Yard, and got tattoos. I had an anchor with a red star on the shank tattooed on my left arm. The anchor represented hope; the star, faith. Despite everything, I had abundant quantities of each. There would be times in the coming months when I would have little else to fall back on.

Making Preparations

Having made the decision to head for the Matanuska Valley, Steve and I started to lay plans for the 5,000 mile journey. We had limited funds to underwrite such an ambitious venture, but we knew money would be our least important asset. Far more essential to the success of our undertaking would be our intangible assets: courage, determination, resourcefulness, stamina, and an ability to think clearly and act quickly in the face of danger. And we had no illusions about the dangers we would face riding the rails across the continent. We had heard stories of railroad bulls shooting hoboes, or throwing them off moving trains; men having their legs cut off when they slipped and fell under the wheels of a train; men being locked into refrigerated cars and freezing to

Steven (*left*) and Paul Gill

death; men being arrested and put to work on farms as slave labor; women being gang raped; and boys being preyed on by perverted older men.

We should have been intimidated by the prospect of hopping freights across thousands of miles of the American landscape with unknown fellow travelers; not knowing where or with whom we would bed down at night; where or when we would eat our next meal; whom we could trust not to murder us for the change in our pockets or the clothes on our backs; how to get on and off trains; or even how to determine which trains to board. But we weren't. Neither Steve nor I had ridden the rails before, but we had traveled the world as merchant mariners, boys among men, and had survived. We had negotiated the dangerous waterfronts of Le Havre, Southampton, St. Pauli, Bremerhaven, Rotterdam, and New York. There was nothing in the interior of America that could intimidate us. We were survivors. We knew how to defend ourselves, and we knew how to work the breadlines and soup kitchens for food, the missions for shelter, and the church outlets for used clothing. We had no money, but neither did we have any fear. We were streetwise. We knew how to grab what we needed from a world that offered us nothing.

We anticipated it would take us three or four months to travel across the continent to Alaska, and planned accordingly. We were going to be bindlestiffs, so our first purchase was two small canvas satchels with shoulder straps. Then, we bought clothing that we would live and sleep in: army field shoes; corduroy pants; woolen shirts; heavy army leather belts; leather jackets with zipped linings; leather gloves; scarves; and watch caps. We sliced open the inside of the leather belts to create a place to cache our paper currency.

There was enough room in the satchels for extra clothing, bags for toiletries, and, most important, a Marine Band harmonica! Steve was a laconic soul, and the harmonica was an extension of his personality. He would use it to lift our spirits and soothe our souls as we voyaged by boxcar across the country.

We knew our money would run out at some point in the journey. But we were prepared to work for food or shelter, to panhandle, and even to scavenge for food scraps if necessary. We were children of the Great Depression, and had long since lost our innocence. We had earned our master's degrees in the School of Hard Knocks over the past nine years.

Mrs. Higgins

Once we had selected our traveling wardrobe, we turned to the task of mapping out a route. As sailors, we were accustomed to the idea of laying out a course on a nautical chart, and then relying on a compass, a sextant, the stars, and dead reckoning to navigate our way across the sea. A steamship generally traveled in a straight line across open water until it reached its destination. There was no need to pull onto a siding to let a ship going in the opposite direction pass; no need to stop at a water tower to replenish the water supply for the steam engine; no need to change crews in the middle of a voyage; and no need for a brakeman to throw track switches. Sea travel was a straightforward proposition compared to railroad travel. Neither Steve nor I had any knowledge of the American railroad system, so we went to the New York Public Library to look at some railroad route maps.

Not sure how to begin our search, we approached the reference librarian, a kindly-looking lady about our mother's age, who was sitting at an oak desk in a corner of the main reading room. She had gray-streaked red hair pulled back into a bun, prominent cheekbones, and azure eyes that peered out at us through wire-rimmed glasses. Her face seemed to be set in a perpetual smile, and the name tag on her blouse identified her as "Mrs. Mary Higgins, Reference Librarian." She put down a book she had been reading, looked up at us, and said, "How can I help you gentlemen?"

I introduced myself, and explained that my brother and I had decided to travel by train to Portland, Oregon, or Seattle, and had come to the library for information to help plan our trip. She hesitated for a moment while she gave us a quick once-over. Then she said, "I see. Well, I think I can help you with that, but I'm curious. Why did you come to the library instead of a travel agency?"

I explained that we were at the very beginning of the planning process, and just wanted some general information about which railroads we should consider taking. We wanted to consider all of our options before making firm plans, and didn't want to be pressured into buying tickets by a travel agent before we were sure of our itinerary.

She considered that for a moment or two, and then asked "Are you planning on traveling straight through to the West

Coast, or do you want to stop on the way to do a little sight-seeing, say in Cleveland or Chicago? And do you want to reserve a sleeper compartment? Not all the trains have Pullman cars, but you could sleep in a regular seat. I think the conductor will give you a pillow and a blanket, if you ask for them." There was a twinkle in her eyes now. She was onto us, I was sure. But we kept up our pretense of being conventional travelers. We didn't want to come right out and say we were planning to become hobos and ride trains across the country without paying for tickets.

Steve cleared his throat, and said, "We intend to travel straight through, Ma'am. We expect we'll have to change trains at some point, but we don't plan to do any sightseeing. As for sleeping arrangements, we'd prefer to sleep on the train whenever possible, but we can't afford tickets for a Pullman coach. We'll be riding Third Class."

"I understand," she said. "Will you have much luggage?" Now I was certain she knew what we were about.

"Not much, Ma'am," I replied. "We'll each carry a small bag. We like to travel light."

The twinkle in her eyes had blossomed into a mirthful expression. "Well, let's see what I can do to help you plan your trip. Follow me." She got up from her desk and led us to another part of the library. The shelves there contained binders, folders, and pamphlets in a variety of sizes and colors. She pulled a handful of them off a shelf and took them over to a table. She opened one to a map of the United States overlaid with all the railroad routes. It was a dense spider web of color-coded routes, with the greatest concentration around the big cities, especially on the East Coast.

Steve and I gawked at the map. We had no idea there were so many railroads in the United States, or that the system was so complicated. A wave of despair came over me. How could we navigate 3,000 miles over such a vast, confusing network all the way to Seattle and not get lost? I found navigating the New York City subway system a challenge. This was a maze comparable to the labyrinth King Minos had built on Crete to hold the Minotaur. We might disappear into this tangle of railroads and never escape!

Mrs. Higgins bookmarked the page, put the pamphlet aside, and opened another one to a page displaying a different railroad route map. "This is the Nickel Plate Road. It runs along the southern shores of the Great Lakes from Buffalo to Chicago, and then on to St. Louis. I've taken it myself when I traveled to Chicago to visit relatives. You can take the Erie Railroad from Grand Central Station and switch

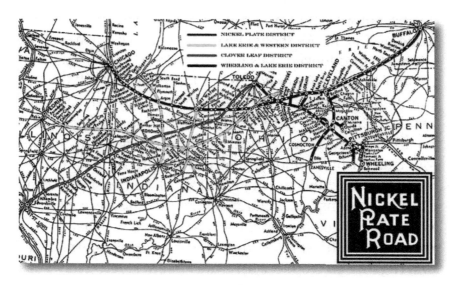

Map of the Nickel Plate Road (Image courtesy of the Nickel Plate Road Historical and Technical Society, used with permission.)

to the Nickel Plate Road in Cleveland. I think it's the best train to take to Chicago, and from there you could catch a Burlington Northern train to Portland or Seattle. You could take the 20th Century Limited, of course. That's the New York Central overnight express. But it's expensive. It mostly caters to rich people and businessmen, and I imagine you'll be on a budget." She gave us a playful look as she said this.

"Yes, Mrs. Higgins," Steve replied. "We'll be on a pretty tight budget alright. Maybe we'll ride the 20th Century Limited on the return trip, if things work out for us in Alaska."

She looked startled. "Alaska? I thought you were going to Portland or Seattle?" She looked genuinely confused, and a little concerned.

"Well, we're considering a side trip to Alaska," I said. "It depends on how things work out in Portland or Seattle. We're going out there to find work. Steve and I are in the Merchant Marine, but we can't find a ship right now, what with the bad economy and all. We thought we'd try our luck out West."

Mrs. Higgins looked at us for a few moments. She made no attempt to conceal her concern. I felt embarrassed. I didn't want her or anyone else to feel sorry for us, but it was comforting to know that here, in the middle of this huge, anonymous city, was a stranger who had genuine empathy for two young men who should have meant nothing to her. I had no way of knowing, and I wasn't about to ask her, but I suspected that Mrs. Higgins had children of her own, maybe even a son our age. I glanced over at Steve, and I could see that he was experiencing the same surprised sense of wonderment at Mrs. Higgins' concern for us. It was like we were stray dogs that a kindly stranger had taken the time to pet and rub under the ears. It was a strange but wonderful feeling.

"Well, boys," she said. "I'll mimeograph these and some

other maps for you. You can come by tomorrow afternoon and pick them up. Once you decide what trains you want to take, you can go to Grand Central Station and pick up schedules." And then she added, with a twinkle in her eye, "And buy your tickets, of course." We thanked her for her help, and left the library.

When I returned to the library the next day, Mrs. Higgins greeted me with her usual sparkling smile and handed me a large manila envelope. I noticed that it was sealed. "I made copies of a bunch of different route maps, Paul," she said. "There are several ways to travel by train from Chicago to Portland and Seattle. It looks rather confusing to me, so study those maps carefully and try not to get lost."

She handed me the envelope, and I thanked her. I couldn't resist giving this wonderful woman a warm hug. I was touched by her kindness, her motherly concern for two young men who were neither kith nor kin. I pretended not to see the tears wending their way down her cheeks as I turned and walked away. I waited until I had exited the library and was headed up Fifth Avenue before I wiped away my own tears.

Steve and I got together in my room at the French Quarter that evening. We opened Mrs. Higgins' envelope and removed its contents. There were mimeographed copies of route maps for all of the railroads servicing the western part of the United States, including the Burlington Northern, the Union Pacific, the Southern Pacific, and others. The last item was a Salvation Army pamphlet, titled "Salvation Army Homeless Shelter Directory for the United States." We were stunned. Our jaws dropped when we opened the directory and found two, five-dollar bills and a hand-written note. The note read:

Paul and Steve:

You are embarking on a very dangerous journey. I admire your pluck, but I am concerned for your safety, just as I would be for my own sons, if I had been blessed with sons. Please be careful, for your mother's sake, if not for your own. Save the money for an emergency. I am sure you will have occasion to use it to secure food or shelter. I will pray for you. Please write to tell me you have arrived safely when you reach your final destination.

—Mary Higgins

SEVEN

RIDING THE RAILS

The Journey Begins

I ROSE EARLY ON THE MORNING of August 15, 1938, dressed and shaved, and laid out all my earthly possessions on my bed. I packed my canvas satchel with the items I intended to take on the trip, and placed a few items of clothing and my *American Practical Navigator* in a paper bag. I looked around the room for the last time, turned out the light, and left for Penn Station, a few blocks south on Eighth Avenue, where Steve and I had agreed to meet.

At the station, we stored the items we weren't taking with us in a locker, and then went to a diner to eat breakfast and review our strategy. We had already decided to take Mrs. Higgins' advice and ride the Erie Railroad to Cleveland, and then board a westbound Nickel Plate Road freight train and ride it all the way to Chicago. I had discussed our plans with friends who had hoboing experience, and they warned me not to try to hop a freight train in the Erie rail yard in Jersey City. The railroad bulls were thick as thieves in that yard, they said, and mean as Hell. They recommended boarding a train in Port Jervis, a rail junction some eighty miles northwest of Manhattan on the New York-Pennsylvania border. We decided to hitchhike to Port Jervis, scout out the yard, and hop a fast westbound freight.

We boarded the 8th Avenue subway, rode it uptown to 181st Street, walked a few blocks south, and started across the George Washington Bridge. Halfway across the bridge, we stopped to enjoy the view from our perch 200 feet above the Hudson River. It was a clear day, and the panorama laid out before us was breathtaking. It was a typically busy day in New York Harbor.

The George Washington Bridge

We could see barges being towed up or down the river; sailboats tacking in the southerly breeze off Governor's Island; commuter ferries shuttling back and forth between

Hoboken and the Battery in lower Manhattan; and a row of majestic passenger liners tied up at piers on the New York side of the river, among them the S.S. *Manhattan*. Black smoke was issuing from her red, white and blue funnels, and tugs had come alongside to usher her out into the stream and escort her downriver. She gave a long, rumbling, blast on her horn and started to back away from the pier.

A cascade of memories swept over me. Happy memories of fair-weather crossings of the North Atlantic Ocean; nocturnal forays into the waterfront districts of Le Havre and St. Pauli; electric nights on the Reeperbahn, drinking beer with young German shipyard workers and Luftwaffe men; and, most of all, dancing and singing in the Zillertal and in cabarets with Meine Liebste Heidi. I couldn't get her image or these lovely lyrics out of my mind:

Du, du liegst mir im Herzen
Du, du liegst mir im Sinn.
Du, du machst mir viel Schmerzen...

My heart ached at the memory of Heidi, standing far below me on the dock that day the previous October, waving goodbye as the *President Roosevelt* moved into the stream. I never imagined it would be my last sight of her. I had intended to return to Hamburg, but it wasn't to be. We exchanged letters for a while, but my itinerant lifestyle made it impossible to maintain a line of communication, and I had not heard from her in months.

I took one last, longing look at the *Manhattan* as she steamed slowly downriver to the open sea. I would have given anything to have been aboard her, to be a member of her crew again, with a warm berth in her fo'c'sle, three hot meals a day, regular pay, and confidence in my future. She was heading east, to scheduled stops at familiar ports. I was heading west, on an unfamiliar conveyance, with unknown ports of call, and no money for a ticket. I had no idea where my next meal was coming from, where I would sleep that night, where I would shave the next morning, or when I would bathe again. I had no idea who I would be sharing a boxcar with, other than my brother. The future was unknowable, and that was both intimidating and exciting.

With a heavy heart, I continued across the bridge with Steve, who seemed lost in his own thoughts. When we reached Fort Lee, on the New Jersey side of the river, we stuck out our thumbs. Four rides, seventy-five miles and eight hours later, we climbed out of the back of a rattly, old pickup truck in Matamoras, Pennsylvania, and walked across the Delaware River bridge to Port Jervis.

Port Jervis

It wasn't hard to find the Erie Railroad yard. As we walked across the bridge, we could hear the "chug-chug-chug" of a steam locomotive approaching the yard from the northwest, punctuated by a long howl from its whistle. We couldn't see the train, but we could see a long, billowing cloud of gray-black smoke rising into the air and advancing steadily left to right over the treeline.

When we reached the New York side of the river, the railyard came into view as we walked through a residential neighborhood. The train was an Erie Railroad passenger train that was coasting into the station at the far end of the rail yard. The yard reminded us of the South Boston rail yard. It was just as dirty, smokey and noisy, but smaller.

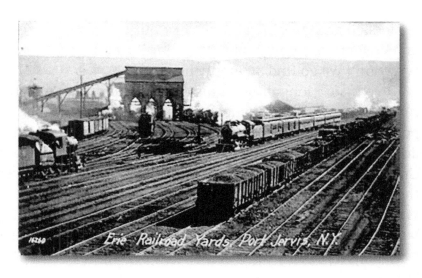

The Port Jervis Rail Yard

Steve and I sat down on a pile of shipping pallets and took a few minutes to survey the scene and plot our next move.

A single track split like an unraveled rope end into seven or eight tracks that ran northwest to southeast for a mile or so, parallel to the river. On the track nearest to us, a long coal train was chugging slowly northward, its straining, tandem steam locomotives belching clouds of dense black smoke from their smokestacks. A variety of boxcars, gondolas and tank cars reposed on most of the other tracks. The tracks on the far side of the yard curved away to the left and entered a large roundhouse. A small switching engine was busy assembling a freight train on one of the inner tracks. The train was about thirty cars long, and was composed of a mixture of boxcars and gondolas, as well as a tanker car or two. Way down the tracks to the east we could just make out a red caboose attached to the tail end of the train.

I looked at Steve. "That looks like our ride, Steve. I don't know where it's going, but it's going to be heading west. Why don't we go find an empty boxcar?"

Steve took a long drag on his cigarette and then exhaled twin streams of blue smoke through his nostrils as he pondered my question. He turned to me and said, "Nah, I don't think that would be such a hot idea, Paul. This isn't Grand Central Station, you know. We can't just mosey over there and select our seats like a couple of paying passengers. We're going to steal a ride on the Erie Railroad, and we gotta be sneaky about it. It's going to be another couple of hours before that train is made up and ready to roll. If we try to board her now, in broad daylight, we'll for sure run into some railroad dicks. What do you say we go into town, get some dinner, and then board the train after sundown? We haven't eaten since breakfast, and I don't see a dining car on this train." He took one last drag on his cigarette before flicking it onto the rail bed, pulled me to my feet, and started walking toward town.

A few minutes later, we were sitting in a booth in Billy's Diner on Main Street, perusing the menu. This figured to be our last meal for a while, so we shot the works and ordered soup, salad, two entrees each, and apple pie a la mode. We handed the menus back to the waitress and gazed out the window to see what was happening in this sleepy burg.

Main Street was almost deserted. Occasionally, a car or a truck would rumble by, or someone would enter or exit the drug store or Woolworth's across the street. A haggard-looking young man paced back and forth in front of the diner, stopping occasionally to stare into the interior. His eyes darted from table to table, as if he was looking for someone. He had an almost feral demeanor, like so many of the men I had been around since leaving home. The brown cap pulled down low over his forehead and a scraggly beard obscured his features. His shirt and trousers, which were at least one size too big for him, were soiled and threadbare, and his shoes were worn and scuffed. He was a walking scarecrow.

While we waited for our food to arrive, the couple at a nearby table finished their meal, paid the tab, and left the restaurant. Moments later, the young man who had been pacing outside the diner walked in and sat down at the table the couple had just vacated. With barely a glance at us or anyone else in the restaurant, he grabbed a fork, shoveled the few remaining food scraps into his mouth, and then picked up the plates and licked them clean. Before the busboy could come to clear the table, he wiped his mouth with a napkin and hurried out the front door.

Steve and I looked at each other in amazement. Was this what fate had in store for us? Would we be licking plates like dogs before we got to Alaska? I wanted to believe I would never debase myself in such a way, no matter how desperate the situation. But I had no way of knowing what travails lay ahead of me on my journey west. Were there limits to my courage and resourcefulness? How much cold, hunger and loneliness could I take? I had already survived many hard tests in my young life, and I was determined to overcome whatever challenges lay before me in the coming months. I thought of my father, dory fishing on the Banks as a boy, struggling to support his family, and of Phil and me digging and clawing for coal and driftwood until our fingers were raw and bleeding on cold winter afternoons, and I knew I could handle whatever the future held in store for me.

The waitress brought our food and we dug in with gusto. When we finished eating, we left a couple of bucks on the table to cover the tab and a tip, grabbed our satchels, and headed back to the rail yard. We stopped at a grocery store along the way and bought some apples, a bunch of bananas, and a box of crackers and stuffed them into our bulging satchels. We returned to our former perch on the pile of shipping pallets just as the sun was sinking below the western horizon and surveyed the scene.

Catching Out

The freight train that had been making up had more than doubled in length while we were gone, and was almost a mile long now. A huge steam locomotive, its bell clanging and clouds of steam streaming from its undercarriage, was slowly backing down the track toward the first car in the train, a rust-colored boxcar with ERIE emblazoned on its side in huge letters. There was an ear-shattering "bang" as the locomotive bumped into the boxcar and the couplers engaged. To my untrained eyes, it looked like the train was complete and ready to leave the yard.

I turned to Steve and said, "We'd better get onboard." I grabbed my satchel and started picking my way across the tracks toward the freight, which I was sure was going to head out of the yard at any minute.

Before I had taken five steps I felt a powerful hand grab my shoulder and jerk me violently backward. I twisted my head around and saw the back of a huge man who was half pulling, half dragging me toward a line of bushes on the far side of the rail yard. I had no idea what his intentions were, but I assumed the worst. I started yelling and swearing as I fought to stay on my feet and release myself from his vise-like grip. Out of the corner of my eye I saw Steve grab his satchel and start running after us. He launched himself at the man, and we all went down in a tumbled, writhing heap. Steve and I both started flailing at the man, who fended off our blows and got back on his feet. He looked at us and shouted, "You dumbass gaycats, don't you know you gotta wait 'til the train's moving before you catch out? We'll have an army of railroad dicks on our heads. C'mon, let's get under cover. Follow me!" The man sprinted to the tree line and quickly disappeared into the undergrowth.

Steve and I were bewildered, but decided we had better take his advice. We scrambled after him, and after clawing through dense underbrush, found ourselves in a small clearing. It was dark in the clearing, and we could barely make out the form of the man who had yanked me off my feet and dragged me away from the train. He was sitting on the ground with his legs crossed, and was fumbling for something in a leather bag that hung from his side. It was too dark to see much, but I could hear muffled voices and the glowing ends of cigarettes in the area on either side of us. We were not alone.

"What's the big idea?" I said, panting to catch my breath. "Why can't we get on the train? And what's a gaycat, anyway?"

The man struck a match to light a cigarette, and in the dim light I could make out the rugged features of a man about Steve's age, or maybe a little older. He had matted, black hair that he had to constantly brush away from his dark eyes, a crooked, somewhat flattened nose, high cheekbones, and a powerful jaw line. The hand that held the cigarette was as big as a pie plate. He was the first American Indian I had ever encountered.

"I've had my eyes on you boys since you came into the yard a couple of hours ago," the man said. "I knew you were gaycats because no hobo with a brain would waltz into a rail yard in broad daylight and loll around like they were waiting for the conductor to usher them to their private compartment. You're lucky the yard bulls didn't see you and turn you over to the harness cops." He took a drag on his cigarette, looked at me, and said, "A gaycat is a greenhorn. Bos like me who've ridden the rails for a while are called dingbats. You won't live long enough to become a dingbat if you don't learn how to stay the Hell away from them friggin' railroad bulls. Some of them are OK, but there's lots of them that are as mean as Hell, and would just as soon throw you off a moving train as look at you, or shoot you in the back. I've seen 'em do it." He took another drag on his cigarette before asking us, "Where you headin', anyway?"

"Alaska," said Steve. "I'm Steve, and this here's my kid brother, Paul. We're heading for the Matanuska Valley. We hear the government is settin' up a farming community up there, and they're lookin' for men to build roads and buildings, and whatnot. We're merchant mariners by trade, but shipping is dead, at least on the East Coast, so we figured, what the Hell, let's give Alaska a try. What do we have to lose?"

"My name's Chester, but they call me Chief," said our new friend. "I'm Lakota Indian, full-blooded. I left the reservation in North Dakota a couple years ago to find work. I've been all over the country, but I haven't found steady employment, nothin' worthwhile, anyways. I've done plenty of harvestin': hay in California and Colorado in early summer; corn and wheat in the Midwest in July and August; hops, berries and fruit in Washington and Oregon in the early fall. The pay is piss poor, but the growers usually put you up in a shelter of some kind, and feed you a couple meals a day."

Chief took a final drag on his cigarette before stubbing it

out. "As far as Alaska goes, I wouldn't put too much stock in any gummint operation up there. If they run it the way they run the Indian reservations, you're gonna be mighty disappointed." Chief gazed silently up at the stars for a few moments before continuing. "Are you guys sure you wanna get on that train? Do you even know where the Hell it's going?"

Steve and I squirmed a little. We really were gaycats. "All I know is it's going west, I hope to Cleveland," I said.

"Yeah, that freight is going to Cleveland," said Chief. "I checked it out with one of the yard men earlier. It'll be pulling out around eleven, about two hours from now. Did you see that flag on the front of the locomotive? The red ball on the white background? That tells you the train is a "hot shot," a fast freight express. If I was goin' to Alaska, I'd head for Chicago and hop on a Union Pacific train to Portland or Seattle, and then catch a ship to Anchorage. I don't know if there's trains goin' to Alaska from Portland or Seattle."

"That's what we were thinking of doing," said Steve. "Or, if shipping picks up, maybe signing onto a ship out of one of those ports."

"Well, there's a lotta miles between here and where you're goin', and if you don't mind taking advice from an ignorant Indian, I think I can teach you a thing or two about the Iron Road before we board that freight later tonight. I've got nothin' better to do, and it don't look like you guys do, either."

"That'd be great, Chief," said Steve. "We're for sure gaycats, as you say, so we'd appreciate any advice you might pass on." We stretched out on the ground, propped our heads on our satchels, looked up at the stars, and listened and learned about the art and science of riding the rails.

"Well, first of all," said Chief, "you gotta know how to catch out, how to board a train without gettin' hurt or caught by the bulls. There's thousands of men ridin' the rails these days. Most of them are good, honest bos, just lookin' for a free ride to somewhere where they can find work. But the railroads don't give nuthin' away for free, and they're worried about theft and sabotage, so they hire railroad bulls, "bo chasers" we call 'em, to terrorize the hobos. Now, there's different kinds of bulls. The bulls that patrol the rail yards we call "yard bulls." "Cinder dicks" are bulls that ride a particular train. Some bos call 'em "shacks." They stay on that one train and patrol it like it was their personal property. The yard bulls usually just chase you out of the yard, or turn you over to the local cops, the "harness bulls." The harness bulls might lock you up in the local jail, or they might take you to a slave farm somewheres, where they make you pick peas or some other bullshit harvestin' work, for pennies a day or nothin'. Or, they might stick you on a chain gang, where you crush rocks or dig trenches for thirty days."

Chief held his hand behind his ear for a moment, as if listening for something. Then he lit another cigarette and continued. "Now, what you gotta understand is, some of these bulls are nasty sons of bitches, I mean real devils. A lotta them are ex-cops who were fired for excessive brutality. They're too mean to hold down a job on a regular police force, but they can get away with anythin' workin' for the railroads. Why, some of them will drag you off a train that's pullin' out of a station and throw you under the wheels, just for the fun of it. They're all armed, too, with clubs, pistols, sawed-off shotguns, and so on. They'll walk from one end of a moving freight to the other, and toss off any hobo they find ridin' the deck or the blinds. It don't matter how fast the train is movin', they'll just say, 'Jump or I'll shoot.'

There's a bull down in Texas, Texas Slim, who brags about killing seventeen hobos. And you'll hear about Denver Bob. Bos I've talked to say they've seen him throw trespassers under the wheels of a train and laugh about it afterward."

"These bulls you're telling us about remind me of the bucko mates my dad had to deal with as a young sailor," said Steve. "Mean bastards who liked to terrorize the crew. They'd beat a man to a pulp just for the exercise. But sometimes they went too far. Dad told us about one bucko he knew, a real prick who pushed the crew to the point of mutiny. Seems he just vanished one night. When the second mate came to relieve him at the end of his watch, he was nowhere to be found. The crew on duty at the time swore they hadn't seen a thing, but one offwatch crewman later told Dad that he had had trouble sleeping that night, and while lying in his bunk in the fo'c'sle he thought he might have heard a brief scuffle on the afterdeck, followed by what sounded like a splash."

All these horror stories were making me a little queasy, so I decided to steer the conversation in another direction. "Chief, what do you mean by riding the deck or the blinds?"

"Ridin' the deck is ridin' on top of the boxcar. It's not the safest place to be on a train, but sometimes a bo's got no choice where he rides. There aren't no open boxcars, or they're already packed with bos. The blinds are the places between the ends of two cars. When you ride the blinds, you gotta stand up and hold on to grab rails, sometimes for hours at a time, in the rain or snow. If you lose your grip, you'll fall under the wheels and be crushed to death. I only ride the blinds when there's no other option. I was riding the blinds on a fast freight with a buddy a couple of years ago. I was on one side, he was on the other. The train rounded a curve. I heard a scream, and when I turned around to see what was going on, my friend was gone. He lost his grip on the hand bar and fell off the train at 85 miles an hour. His family will never know what became of him." Chief looked down at the ground for a few moments, and then looked over at us. "Yeah, avoid the friggin' blinds whenever possible, and don't never ride in a gondola carrying logs or pipes. They don't tie that shit down, and it don't take much to get them to start shiftin', and they can roll right onto your leg and break it, or knock you off the train."

"That's good to know, Chief," said Steve. "How about actually gettin' on a train? Do you just climb aboard, or is there a trick to it?"

Chief shifted his massive bulk, and now was lying on his right side, with one arm under his head. With his free hand, he took out a pouch of chewing tobacco, pulled out a plug, and stuck it under his upper lip before continuing his lecture.

"First of all, Steve, don't ever walk into a rail yard in broad daylight like you boys done this afternoon. Stay outside the yard until dark. When you do enter the yard, stay under cover and scope out the situation. Most of the yard men are okay guys, and you can often approach 'em for information about what train is going where and when. Some of them are pricks who'll turn you in, but more often than not they'll help you. You just have to use your judgment on this, but sometimes you gotta take a chance. These rail yards are huge, with tracks goin' every goddamn which way, and until you've been in the game for a while, it can be friggin' hard to find a train that's goin' where you wanna go. Board the wrong train, and you might find yourself zippin' along at eighty miles an hour in the wrong direction!" Chief chuckled as he said that. I got the impression that he had made that mistake himself at some point in his hoboing career. "And stay away from the local trains. They stop in every little pis-shole of a town, and they'll often pull off onto a siding in the middle of nowhere to let a fast freight pass them, or to drop off an empty boxcar, or some other bullshit. Rattlers, that's another word for fast freights, are the only way to go, 'specially if you boys want to get to Alaska any time soon."

Chief sat up, leaned to one side, and spat out an enormous gob of slimy green chewing tobacco. I heard a "splat" when it struck the ground. He wiped his mouth with the back of his hand, and then continued with his hoboing tutorial. "Now, as far as actually gettin' on the train, you're right, Steve, there's definitely a trick to that. It would be nice if you could just walk up and down the train before it starts movin,' select an empty boxcar, take a minute to check it out, and then climb in and make yourself at home. But the train might not pull out of the yard for another few minutes, or even longer, and then you're an easy target for the cinder bulls. It's much better to catch out on the fly. Listen for two short blasts of the locomotive's whistle. That's the engineer's signal that they're pullin' out. That ol' locomotive may be pulling sixty or a hundred loaded cars, and it takes a while to pick up speed, so you've got a little time. Once the train starts to move, though, you want to start looking for an open boxcar. If you find one, just start running alongside the train, throw your bag inside the car, grab hold of the grab bar, and swing yourself on up into the car."

"Sounds simple," I said.

"It usually is," said Chief. "But timing is everything. If you're fast, you can catch a train that's goin' twenty, thirty miles an hour. They say Jim Thorpe could get on or off trains going sixty miles an hour!" A sly smile came over his face as he said this. "Well, us Indians believe he could, anyway!"

"Just remember, if the train is goin' faster than you're runnin', it'll drag you right off your feet when you grab that bar. Then, your legs are going to be draggin' along and bouncin' off the ground. If you don't swing them up into the car real quick, they'll fall under the wheels, and they'll be calling you Shorty. There's lotsa legless ex-hobos. You'll see them out on the streets, beggin'."

Steve and I looked at each other. What were we getting ourselves into? This hoboing business was not for the faint of heart.

Chief continued. "Some bos like to find a reefer car with an open hatch. A reefer can be a nice place to ride on a hot day like today, but reefers can be dangerous too. You gotta wedge a piece of brake shoe or somethin' in the hatch to make sure the hatch cover stays open. If you crawl in there and someone comes along and closes the hatch, you could freeze to death, or be crushed by tons of ice if they fill the compartment with ice while you're sleepin'."

Chief shifted his position on the ground, spat out his wad of chewing tobacco, and focused his gaze first on Steve, and then on me. "You guys still wanna ride the rails? It might be a little safer on a ship, don't you think? At least there's no railroad bulls out there on the ocean, and you're guaranteed three meals a day and a place to sleep, right?"

Steve and I exchanged knowing glances and we both laughed. "I don't know about that, Chief," I said. "I saw seamen with their skulls bashed in by strikebreakers on the New York waterfront, and my bunkmate had his throat cut one night in Le Havre on my first voyage to Europe. They fished his body out the Seine the next morning. And yeah, you have a place to sleep, but a ship's fo'c'sle is no gentlemen's club. You can be stuck in a cramped, smelly cabin with perverts, thieves, drug addicts, and lunatics. If you have a problem with a guy, you can't complain to the captain, and you can't ask for a new room. You just have to put up with it until you get off the ship, or settle it with your fists. If you climb into a boxcar and don't like the looks of the guys in the car, you can always get off the train at the next stop, or move to another spot."

Chief considered what I said, nodded his head in understanding, and said, "There's lotsa bad guys riding the rails these days, too. You can bet your ass you're going to be sharin' a boxcar with some bad men before you reach Alaska. But most of the guys you run into are genuine OK."

Chief got to his feet suddenly and peered out through an opening in the bushes. The moon had come up, and we could look over his shoulder and see the freight we hoped to boarding soon. There was a deep-throated rumble and a steady hissing sound emanating from the locomotive, but the yard was otherwise quiet. Chief returned to the clearing after a couple of minutes and sat back down on the ground with his legs crossed. "I think we've got another little while yet before that freight starts hauling outta here, maybe fifteen minutes." He lit another cigarette before going on with his hoboing tutorial, took in a huge lungful of smoke, and then settled back down on the ground with his head nestled on a large canvas sack.

"Let me tell you about the different kindsa people you're going to run into riding the rails. First of all, there's hobos, men who travel to work. Tramps are men who travel but don't work. A bum is a guy who don't travel and don't work. "Scenery bums" are kids, mostly, just ridin' the rails for the fun of it. Then you have your "yeggs," tramps who travel from town to town committin' burglaries and cracking safes. They'll pull off a job and then hightail it outta town on the next freight, so they're rarely caught. What you're mostly going to see are "jackrollers" and "dips." A jackroller's a mugger, a dip is a pick-pocket. When you're on the road, you gotta assume everyone you meet is a thief. You learn to sleep with one eye open, whether you're in a boxcar or in a hobo jungle. I see you got them satchels to carry your stuff in. Never let 'em out of your sight."

The silence was suddenly punctured by two ear-piercing blasts from the locomotive's whistle and the incessant, loud clanging of its bell. Chief sprang to his feet, then reached down and picked his canvas sack off the ground and slung it over his shoulder. "Follow me," he said, and started running across the tracks in the direction of the freight train.

We followed closely on the big Indian's heels, desperate to maintain contact with our guide. We became part of a mob, as dozens of men clutching bindles emerged from various hiding places and raced across the tracks toward the freight train that was now moving slowly westward and gaining speed with each loud BANG of its pistons. A column of dense, black smoke billowed up out of the smokestack, and clouds of steam were hissing out of the vents on top of the locomotive and from its undercarriage.

The enormity of our undertaking suddenly struck me as we approached the line of passing boxcars, gondolas, and tankers. I felt as though I were jumping off a cliff blindfolded, in complete ignorance of the height of the cliff, or whether I was jumping into a bottomless abyss or an ocean of opportunity that would give me a new start in life. I suppressed my fear and let my naturally aggressive temperament assert itself as I rehearsed in my mind the technique I would use to board one of the passing boxcars. Steve and I stood on each side of Chief, and waited for his signal. I was anxious to jump aboard one of the empty boxcars that rolled by, but Chief held his hand up to signal patience. The first few cars were already occupied, so I assumed he was waiting for an empty one.

I started to get a little nervous when the caboose came into view. I was afraid there would be no more empty boxcars, and we'd miss our ride. Then, Chief spotted an apparently empty car and grabbed me by the shoulder. "Okay, Paul, remember what I told you. Grab that iron hold, toss your satchel into the car, and swing yourself up and in." He shouted, "Go!" and gave me a firm push toward the car.

I started running alongside the train and matched its speed for a few strides. Then I grabbed the hold bar with my left hand, tossed my satchel into the black interior of the car, and swung my legs up and inside. I barely had time to grab my satchel and scramble away from the door opening before Steve, and then Chief, tumbled in after me in quick succession.

All my fears and misgivings were swept away in an instant, replaced by feelings of pure joy and exultation at the successful start of our ambitious journey to the far end of the continent. At that moment, lying on the wooden floor of that rumbling boxcar, with my heart pounding and adrenaline surging through every nerve and muscle, I felt unbounded confidence that Steve and I would overcome all obstacles in our path. We would fight, fight, fight and survive!

On the Nickel Plate Road

I grabbed my satchel and started crawling away from the

open door of the boxcar on my hands and knees. I couldn't see an inch in front of my face in the Stygian darkness, and had to rely on my senses of hearing and touch. I heard voices, but the loud "clackety-clack" of the wheels made it hard to identify them. I put my hand out and felt someone's leg. The owner yelled, "Get the f*** away from me, you goddam queer!" and yanked his leg violently away from me. I heard Steve calling out to me, but I had no idea where he was. Then, there was a sudden flash of light in the forward end of the boxcar. Chief had lit a stick match and was beckoning to me. Steve sat next to him, leaning against the wall of the car. I got to my feet and walked quickly over to them and plopped down on the wooden floor. The match flickered out before I could survey the scene in the boxcar, but from the muffled voices and occasional shouts, I gathered that we had a lot of company. How many, or what kind of men they were, I couldn't say. There may have been a murderer or a pervert among them, and I should have been too scared to sleep. But it had been a long day and, despite the hard wooden floor and the violent lurching movements of the boxcar, I lay my head down on my satchel and instantly fell into a deep sleep.

I slept like a dead man until Steve shook me awake and ordered me to get up. "Rise and shine, Sleeping Beauty," he said. "We're in the outskirts of Cleveland, and we'll be rolling into the rail yard soon." Steve looked like he needed a shave and a couple of more hours of sleep. I sat up, rubbed the sleep from my eyes, and looked around. Steve had just peeled a banana and was savoring every bite of his meager breakfast. In the early morning light, I could make out a number of motionless human forms scattered around the floor of the boxcar. Chief and another man were standing in the doorway, talking and laughing. I had a surpassing desire to find a place to brush my teeth and shave, but I knew there was no possibility of carrying out my normal morning ablutions, so instead I reached into my satchel and pulled out a couple of apples. I walked over to the doorway, offered one to Chief, and looked out at the passing landscape.

I hadn't gotten a good look at Chief in the dark rail yard the night before, but now, in the early morning light, his tall, erect bearing and wide shoulders seemed even more imposing. And I couldn't help thinking, as I took in his rugged facial features, that with his jet black hair in braids and a couple of feathers dangling from the back of his scalp, he could easily have been the model for the Indian on the Indian Head nickel.

Night was yielding to day as the sun peeked over the eastern horizon and started to bathe the factories and warehouses we were passing in a soft light. Tall smokestacks, solitary or in rows of a half dozen or more, thrust up into the morning sky, but I didn't see any smoke escaping from any of them, and the factory interiors were dark. I spotted only an occasional car or truck moving on the street that paralleled the railroad track. It looked like the Depression had as firm a stranglehold on the Midwest as it had on the East Coast. We passed a long freight train going in the opposite direction, and our locomotive emitted a long, wailing whistle, announcing our arrival in Cleveland to anyone who was interested. The engineer had let up on the throttle, to judge by the diminished tempo of the engine, and the train was coasting into the rail yard.

I finished my apple and tossed the core out of the door just as Steve tossed out his banana peel. I turned to Chief and asked him what his travel plans were.

"I'm goin' back to the reservation for a while, Paul. I need to check on my folks and the rest of the family. Then, I'll probably head over to Iowa or Minnesota for the corn and grain harvest. We'll see," he said, with a notable lack of enthusiasm. "But I'll stay with you fellas until we get to Chicago, assumin' you want company."

I laughed. "We're sticking with you like ticks on a dog, Chief!" I said. "We know we've got to catch out on the Nickel Plate Road, but we have no friggin' idea how to do that."

"Right," said Chief. "And you know what else you don't know?"

"There's a lot we don't know," said Steve, as he lit his first cigarette of the day and inhaled a lungful of smoke. I lit up too, and sat down on my satchel and waited to hear Chief continue our hobo education.

"Well, the most important thing you don't know right now is how to get off a movin' train," said Chief. "Any fool can get off a train, but gettin' off without smashing your face into a switch stand, or falling flat on your face, now that ain't so easy. Now let's watch these professionals get off this sidedoor Pullman."

Chief stepped aside and a couple of hobos approached the doorway as the freight entered the rail yard and slowed to about twenty miles an hour. The first man could have been the older brother of the young man we encountered in Billy's Diner the night before. He was scrawny, unshaven and toothless. His ragged trousers were held up by a length of twine in lieu of a leather belt, and his toes poked through holes in his battered shoes. The second man was in even worse shape, a gaunt wisp of a man dressed in rags that would shame a scarecrow. He was a piteous sight, with wispy tufts of gray hair protruding from under his cap, eyes sunk into his deeply lined, bony face, spindly arms and legs, and an open fly.

The hobos sat on the floor with their legs dangling outside the boxcar. Then they leaned forward and looked toward the front of the train. When the train had slowed to five or six miles an hour, the first man grabbed his bindle, shifted his buttocks over to the edge of the floor, and then dropped down to the ground and ran as fast as he could in the direction of the train before gradually slowing to a walk. The second man followed suit, and we watched them hurry off across the tracks and disappear behind an idle locomotive.

Chief turned to us and said, "It's really pretty easy. You just gotta make sure there's no switch stand up ahead that you could run into, and make damned sure you can run as fast as the train's movin' when you jump off." Chief tossed his apple core away and continued. "One more thing: don't dawdle after you get off the train, or the cinder bulls will be all over your ass. Get the Hell out of the yard as fast as you can, or you'll be in the local hoosegow or on one of them slave farms. Just follow me, I know where the exits are."

An hour later, Steve, Chief and I were rolling out of the Cleveland Nickel Plate Road rail yard, heading west on a fast freight bound for Chicago. We couldn't find an empty boxcar, so we climbed up onto the roof of a full one and found a place to sit down together among the swarm of hobos roosting on the deck like seagulls on a dock railing.

Steve and I shared our crackers and remaining apples and bananas with Chief, and he passed us his canteen, but there was barely enough water left in it to wet our lips. It wasn't much of a repast, but it would have to tide us over until we got off the train. I knew from experience that I could endure

Riding the Deck

hunger, but I wasn't so sure I could make it all the way to Chicago without slaking my thirst. I wished now that I had stopped to take a drink from the fountain that we passed outside the Nickel Plate rail yard earlier that morning. I swore that I would never again pass a water fountain without taking a drink as long as I lived

It had taken the freight a long time, almost half an hour, to get up to speed, but once it did, it was moving too fast for us to remain sitting. We didn't dare sit or stand, for fear of being blown off the train.

I laid down on the deck, covered my face with my hat, and tried to nap. But I was tormented by the images of frosty mugs of beer and ice-cold bottles of Coca-Cola that passed through my mind. And my fair skin was beginning to burn as the sun approached its zenith in the July sky.

As if my physical misery wasn't enough to make sleep impossible, I was terrified at the prospect of being hurled off the train by the violent lurching of the boxcar. To prevent such a calamity, I took off my belt, ran it under the 1" x 3" board that ran fore-and-aft along the top of the car, and then wrapped it around my waist before refastening the buckle. It was impossible to turn over while constrained this way, but immobility was a small price to pay to ensure that I wasn't thrown from a train speeding along at seventy miles an hour. I pulled the brim of my hat down over my eyes again and made another attempt at sleep.

I gave up all hope of napping after a few minutes and decided to distract myself by focusing on the passing scenery. I loosened my belt buckle and sat up part way, leaned on one arm, and took a look around.

We were out of the city now, and passing through verdant farm country. From horizon to horizon, all I could see was thousands upon thousands of acres of corn stalks rising waist-high on either side of the tracks, the deep green of their long, drooping leaves complimenting the azure blue of the cloudless sky. A farmhouse on a hill reminded me of a lighthouse on an island in a great ocean. I envisioned farmers on tractors harvesting the corn later that summer, much the way fishermen in dories would be hauling in cod and halibut on the Grand Banks.

I had been able to divert my attention from my nagging thirst for a few minutes by concentrating my thoughts on the beautiful countryside we were traveling through. But then the tracks started to run alongside a small river. We ran in company with the stream for a mile or so, and I couldn't take my eyes off the blue water flowing lazily toward Lake Erie. I pictured myself jumping into the river and gulping down mouthfuls of the delicious, clear liquid until my stomach burst.

I looked over at my brother and Chief. They were lying on their sides, heads resting on their satchels, staring longingly at the river. Rivulets of sweat were streaming down Steve's face, and his sweat-soaked shirt clung tightly to his torso. Chief had tied a red bandana around his forehead and had taken off his shirt and rolled up the legs of his pants. Most of the other dozen or so bos on the deck of the boxcar were shirtless as well. There was scarcely a sign of life from any of them, other than the occasional languid movement of a hand wiping a sweaty brow. "How long before we get to Chicago, Chief?" I asked. My parched lips and mouth made it hard for me to talk.

"We'll be there in five or six hours, if we live that long," he replied listlessly. I detected a note of weariness in his voice I had not heard before.

"Any chance of getting a drink of water before then?" Steve asked. He was clearly wilting too. The hot Midwest July sun was sapping the life out of us.

"Not 'til Fort Wayne, my friend," Chief replied. "That's a division point, where they change engines and crew. That generally takes 'bout forty-five minutes, so we'll have time to get off the train and look for water. I'm sure there'll be a tap at the water tower." Chief looked up at and squinted at the sun, which was almost directly overhead now. "We should be arrivin' there in 'bout a half hour."

He sat up and took a quick look at the other bos stretched out on our boxcar, and on the cars ahead of and behind ours. A frown had settled on his broad brow when he turned his gaze back toward us. "Problem is, there'll be swarms of thirsty bos all jumpin' off the train lookin' for water, and the yard dicks will be waitin' for us, count on it. There's some mean bulls in the Fort Wayne yard, so we gotta be cagey. It's asparagus-and potato-harvestin' time in northern Indiana, and they'll be lookin' to round up as much free labor as they can to rent out to the local farmers. After you spend a few days hunched over pickin' asparagus and potatoes out of the ground, you'll be wishin' you never left New York." Chief grimaced and reached around and rubbed his lower back.

He was quiet for a couple of minutes, apparently pondering a strategy. Then he said, "Here's my plan, fellas. Them friggin' yard bulls probably have trucks waitin' to haul us out to some slave farm somewhere. If we get off the train and start lookin' around for water, they'll nab us, sure as shit. Hell, there'll be a line of hobos a block long at the water faucet! Now, we could climb inside this here boxcar and hide after some of the bos get off, but the bulls would find us, which would be bad. Or they wouldn't find us, which might be even worse. We'd probably die of thirst before the train pulled into Chicago." He paused for a moment to allow that grim thought to sink in.

"Sounds like we're screwed, Chief," I said. I looked over at Steve. His downcast eyes and drooping shoulders betrayed his sagging spirits. But I was more angry than discouraged. "Dammit, Steve," I said, "we're sailors, not farmers. I'll be damned if I'll let a bunch of railroad bulls shanghai me and haul me off to a potato farm!" I looked over at Chief and said, "There's gotta be a way outta this trap!"

"There is," said Chief. "Here's what we'll do. Soon's the train slows down, we'll hop off and start runnin' for the exits. Don't stop to look around, or the bulls will grab you. Most of the bos are goin' to be headin' for the water tower. We'll go in the opposite direction and find the quickest way out of the yard. We'll find water in a park or a gas station, and maybe get somethin' to eat, too. Then, we'll hide outside the yard and get back on the freight when it starts to pull out."

While we had been strategizing, the engineer had eased off the throttle and the train started to slow. The locomotive emitted a series of long, bellowing whistles that were punctuated by the steady clanging of its bell. We had left open farm country and were entering an urban area. Scattered farms gave way to residential neighborhoods with tree-lined streets interspersed with scattered warehouses and small commercial buildings. After a few minutes, the train entered a large rail yard and was shunted off the main track and onto one of a dozen or so parallel tracks, most of which were occupied by freight trains. Small switching engines were moving up and down the track, attaching boxcars, gondolas or tankers to the trains, or detaching them and ferrying them to another track. I could make out a water tower at the far, western end of the yard. It was a large, red wooden cylinder on stilts with a long black snout extended onto the front end of a steam locomotive. It was a discouragingly long distance from where we were, near the end of a mile-long freight train.

Hobos started climbing down from the cars and heading for the water tower. Just as Chief had predicted, most of them didn't get far before they were set upon by an army of club- and shotgun-wielding cops in blue uniforms who began herding them in groups across the tracks toward a large truck.

We grabbed our satchels, joined the line of hobos shuffling toward the back end of the boxcar, climbed down a series of iron rungs, and jumped off the train. As soon as our feet touched the ground, we lit out toward the rear of the train and then ran across to the north side of the yard and out through an opening in a chain link fence. Once safely outside, we stopped for a minute to catch our breath, and then walked westward until we came to a bend in a river, which we later learned was the Maumee. We walked over to the bank and took a good look at the water, which was slow-moving and murky. Near mad with thirst, I waded into the stream, lowered my face to the water, and was about to suck in a huge mouthful of the muddy water when Chief grabbed me by the shirt and pulled me back onto the bank. "Paul, are you loco? You'll get the screamin' shits if you drink that water!"

Reluctantly, I bowed to Chief's superior judgment in such matters, and we continued walking westward in our quest for food and water, first along the dual tracks that led out of the yard, and then on a street that paralleled the tracks. We passed block after block of warehouses, factories and junkyards before coming to a two-bay auto-repair shop. The large doors of the bays had been swung wide open, giving us a view into the interior of the shop. A black Ford pickup occupied the bay on the left, and a green Buick roadster was parked on the right. We took a couple of steps into the shop and saw the lower half of a man whose head and arms were immersed in the depths of the engine compartment of the roadster. On the wall behind him was a white porcelain sink. We stood there for a few moments, our gazes passing back and forth between the man and the sink.

After what seemed like an eternity, the mechanic pulled his head out from under the hood of the automobile and looked at us with a startled expression. I had no doubt that he was prepared to use the large wrench in his right hand to defend himself if we made a threatening move. We quickly reassured him that we meant him no harm, but would be much obliged if he would permit us to slake our thirst at his sink. He gave us a quick once-over and, taking note of our sorry state, acquiesced to our request. We took turns sucking in huge mouthfuls of cold, delicious water from the spigot. After Chief filled his canteen, we thanked the mechanic and headed back down the street in search of something to eat.

We found a small grocery store in the next block, and bought some fruit and candy bars. We would have looked for a diner where we could sit down and enjoy a decent meal, but we didn't have time for that. Our Chicago-bound train would be pulling out of the yard any minute, so we started walking back to the rail yard, wolfing down candy bars as we went.

Long before we reached the opening in the fence, we heard two loud whistle blasts, followed by the loud clanging of a bell and the deep, accelerating chug-chug-chug of a locomotive getting underway. We had no doubt it was our freight pulling out of the yard. We ran as fast as we could, but by the time we reached the train, it was moving too fast to board. Jim Thorpe may have been equal to the challenge, but not mere mortals. We stood watching forlornly as the red caboose shrank and then disappeared from view as it rounded a bend in the tracks. Steve and I cussed and kicked at the ground, and then turned to our leader.

"What do we do now, Chief?" Steve asked him.

"We'll catch the next freight," he replied. "Let's go find a brakeman." I was amazed at Chief's imperturbability. Missing the train didn't seem to bother him. In fact, nothing seemed to bother him. I admired and tried to emulate his stoicism. I was to learn over the coming months that it was a trait he shared with most hobos.

The Fort Wayne Hobo Jungle

We walked down the tracks for a while until we encountered a heavy-set, middle-aged man in a striped engineer's hat, denim overalls and heavy work gloves working on a switch track. He was not outwardly hostile, so we stopped and engaged him in conversation. Far from hostile, he was downright friendly and helpful. He told us that a hot freight was scheduled to depart the yard at midnight, bound for Chicago. It was being formed up now on Track 7. He even told us about a hobo jungle where we could clean up and rest while waiting for the train. "Just walk right out the west end of the yard, and down the road a piece until you see a bend in the river," he said, pointing to the far western end of the yard. "A hundred yards or so past the bend, you'll see a path leading into the woods. Follow the path and you'll end up in the jungle. You can't miss it."

We thanked the man and continued on our way. Fifteen minutes later, we found the path the brakeman had described, and soon came to a clearing in the woods near the river bank. About a dozen men were scattered around the clearing engaged in activities of one kind or another. Several men sat on wooden boxes, smoking and conversing quietly, while others lay stretched out on the ground, apparently asleep. Down by the river, a naked man was pulling wet clothing out of a drum, wringing it out, and then hanging the articles on tree branches to dry. A little further down the stream, a man sat on the bank with a bamboo fishing pole in one hand and a bottle of beer in the other.

In the center of the clearing, an older, bearded man in a slouch hat stood over a large kettle suspended over a campfire, stirring its contents with a long wooden stick.

A typical "Hobo Jungle"

Next to him, a man was hunched over a board and using a knife to butcher an animal the size of a puppy. I couldn't be sure of the identity of the animal, but it wasn't a dog. It had a long snout, a mouthful of pointy teeth, short, stubby ears, beady eyes, big claws, a white face, a gray body, and a long hairless tail. Every once in a while the butcher put down his knife, scooped up hunks of meat, and dropped them into the kettle.

As we stood watching the cook and his assistant, a younger man walked out of the woods carrying a bundle of sticks. He dropped the bundle on the ground next to the fire and started breaking the longer sticks over his knee and tossing them onto a pile near the fire.

The man stirring the kettle looked up at us, smiled, and said, "Welcome to the Maumee River Hobo Hotel! I'm Jim, and this here's Clem and Hank." We returned his greeting and nodded at Clem, the butcher, and Hank, the wood gatherer. I walked over to the kettle and took a peek inside.

I recognized carrots, potatoes, green beans, and a few chunks of meat. It was a little watery, but a delicious aroma wafted up and filled my nostrils, triggering intense hunger pangs. Almost a full day had elapsed since my last real meal.

Chief peered into the kettle, and then turned to Jim and said, "Looks like you got the beginnin's of a fine Mulligan stew there, Jim. How about if Paul and Steve and I go into town and see if we can find some things to thicken it up a bit?"

"Why, that would be great, Chief. There's a couple of grocers in town who'll give you some produce, maybe even a little meat, if you give 'em a couple hours work. Just put your gear under that tarp over yonder. I'll keep an eye on it for you."

We stowed our satchels under the tarp, and then walked a couple of miles into town and found a grocery. We went to the back door and spoke to the manager, who agreed to give us a sack of fresh vegetables in exchange for a couple of hours of work. We spent the rest of the afternoon stocking shelves, emptying and stacking crates, and sweeping floors. When the two hours had elapsed, the manager was so pleased with the quality of our work that he added two pounds of mutton and a dozen apples to the sack of produce he had promised us. He told us the apples were from a tree Johnny Appleseed had planted near Fort Wayne. I didn't know whether to believe him, but they were delicious, and they gave us an energy boost for the two mile walk back to the hobo jungle.

Just before we turned down the path leading to the hobo jungle, we saw two scrawny men in tattered clothes plucking dandelions and stuffing them in a sack. Then we saw another man in the woods yanking plants out of the ground and stuffing them in his pockets. The plants had long, green leaves and white bulbs. They reminded me of the scallions my mother would put in a soup or a salad.

Chief must have caught the puzzled look on my face. "Them's wild leeks that bo's harvestin', Paul. They'll add a little flavor to our Mulligan stew. So will the dandelions them other fellas are gatherin'. Dandelions, wild leeks, pig weed, sour dock, they're all around us and they're good to eat. You just have to learn what they look like. You can put 'em in a salad or add 'em to a soup."

"It's the law of the hobo jungle," he went on. "Every bo contributes whatever he can to the stew. Even if a man can't bum food from a grocer, he can always grab a bunch of wild plants. Or he can trap rabbits or squirrels or some other critters. They all make good eatin'." Chief's reference to "other critters" put me in mind of the mystery animal that I saw being butchered and added to the stew kettle earlier. I tried not to let my imagination run wild.

Chief went on with his tutorial. "If you want to feel welcome in the jungle, chip in with the work. Help clean up after supper, and make sure there's plenty of wood on the firewood pile. If you brew up coffee in the morning, make sure you leave some grounds in the pot for the next bo. If you find a sheet of plywood or corrugated iron laying by the side of the road, haul it back to the jungle. Someone can use it to build a shelter. And when you leave the jungle, make sure it's tidy so the fellas that come after you don't have to clean up your mess."

Chief stopped and turned to us and said, "The most important thing to keep in mind when you walk into a hobo jungle is, figure out who the jungle buzzards are, and ask their permission before you settle in, help yourself to stew, or sit down by the fire. You gotta give them time to size you up and decide if you're OK. If there's enough stew, they'll let you have some. If there isn't, they'll tell you. If they get a bad feeling about you, they'll ask you to move on."

"What the f*** is a jungle buzzard?" Steve asked.

"A jungle buzzard's a hobo who stays in the jungle for more than a few days. They're older guys, generally, who wanna take a break from the trains for a spell. But some of them hang out in the jungle and prey on the younger bos, gaycats like you and Paul. They'll get you to do all the work, hustlin' food, collectin' firewood. Some of 'em will try to get in your pants. You gotta watch out for that type. Jim's a buzzard, but I haven't been around him long enough to size him up. He seems alright, but it don't matter to us, 'cause we're catching that express freight in a few hours."

The hobo jungle was bustling with activity when we walked into the clearing with our booty. A few more bos had joined the encampment, and we had no trouble finding willing hands to help prepare the vegetables and mutton for the kettle. When we had completed our culinary chores, Steve and I headed down to the river. We stripped off our soiled clothes, gave them a good scrubbing, and then went for a swim. The river water was murky, but it was far cleaner than the water at Stetson's Coal Pier in South Boston, where we used to swim on hot summer days. At least I didn't see any dead rats floating in it, and it was cool and refreshing. When we got out of the water, we changed into clean clothes and hung our laundry out to dry on a tree branch near the cooking fire.

I noticed that our clothes had plenty of company in the tree branches. There was a suit jacket on a hanger hooked on a branch next to Steve's underwear, as well as assorted other articles of clothing, pots and pans, a canvas bag containing eating utensils, towels, a razor, and even a small mirror!

There was no clock in the jungle, but hungry hobos don't need a timepiece to tell them it's chow time. The seductive aroma emanating from the kettle had suffused the clearing, and it was impossible to resist its magnetic allure. Steve, Chief and I joined the line of bos that had formed at the kettle, where Jim and Clem were ladling steaming cupfuls of Mulligan stew into the tin cans the men held out to them. When we reached the front of the line, Jim dug his ladle deep down into the depths of the kettle to make sure we got our fair share of the meat we had scored at the grocery store that afternoon. I appreciated the gesture, though I knew it was unlikely that mutton was the only meat Jim's ladle had dredged up. But my hunger overpowered my anxiety, and I sat down on a log with Steve and Chief and dug in.

Quiet prevailed in the clearing for a few minutes while everyone slurped down the Mulligan stew. I had to admit it was delicious, despite my qualms about the provenance of some of the ingredients.

The silence was broken by a small, gray-haired man sitting by himself on an upturned wooden soapbox. "Goddam, Jim, you went and outdid yourself this time," the elfen figure blurted out in a deep, Southern drawl. He put down his spoon and wiped his mouth with the back of his hand before continuing to sing the praises of Jim's stew. "That's about the best Mulligan stew I've tasted this side of the Mississippi. What's your secret, if you don't mind my askin'?"

"No secret, Ted," Jim responded. "Just the usual formula, a little of this, a little of that, I throw whatever edibles people bring me into the pot and let it cook for a few hours. Paul and his brother, Steve, and Chief, them's the ones you should thank for gettin' the mutton. That and the wild leeks, that's what makes it so good."

"Yeah, I can taste them wild leeks, sure 'nuff. And dandelions, too. But I could swear there's something different about this Mulligan stew, Jim. Can't quite put my finger on it, but it's got somethin' extra, maybe a new spice or some herb I haven't tasted before."

"I think it's the meat," said the hobo sitting across from Jim, a gaunt man wearing wire-rimmed spectacles. He was poking the contents of his tin can with his spoon, and examining it closely with an inquisitive eye. "It's different, a little more tender than mutton, at least some of it is." He looked in our direction and asked, "Are you sure it was mutton the butcher gave you guys, and not veal? This is tastier than mutton, more like rabbit or squirrel. Ummm-ummm!" He scraped the bottom of his tin can and licked the spoon clean.

I looked over at Clem, but he avoided my eyes. Then I looked at Chief, who had a knowing look on his face, but didn't comment on the stew. Then, Ted piped up again. "Jim, I seen you settin' up traps in the woods hereabouts. What kinds of critters do you catch in your traps?"

All eyes trained on Jim, who hesitated for a moment before answering. "Well, all kinds of critters. You know, rabbits, squirrels, an occasional bird."

Ted pondered Jim's response for a few moments before asking him, "Do you ever catch any exotic critters, you know, muskrats, weasels, snakes, or suchlike?"

"Well, sure," Jim responded, looking down at the ground. "I catch all kindsa things." He clearly did not care to be too specific in his response to Ted's query. But the question remained hanging in the air. I'm sure every man Jack of us sitting there, savoring the pleasant aftertaste of the superb stew, was mentally reviewing the range of crawling, creeping, flying, and slithering fauna that could possibly have wandered into Jim's trap, and from there into the soup kettle. The one image that occupied my mind was of the creature that I had observed Clem butchering when we first arrived in the jungle. No longer able to contain my growing curiosity, fear and revulsion, I blurted out: "By the way, Clem, what was that animal you were butchering this afternoon?"

All eyes now turned to Clem. Absolute silence prevailed in the jungle for what seemed like minutes, although it only took him a few seconds to say, "That was a possum, Paul. You saw it. What the Hell did you think it was, a pussy cat?"

An audible sigh passed through the collective lips of the group. The tension that had been building over the past few minutes had crested and broken, and now everyone was enjoying a good laugh, partly at my expense. I was embarrassed. Apparently, possum was standard fare in hobo jungles, either fried, roasted or cooked in a stew. I had never seen a possum before, and I had feared that the animal I saw Clem cutting into stew stock was a rat. I had certainly seen plenty of rats of that size when Phil and I scavenged bottles in the South Boston dump. I was relieved, but I did not join the hobos who lined up at the kettle for second helpings of the Mulligan-possum stew.

Ted sat down next to me while he scarfed down the last few spoonfuls of his stew. "I gotta tell you, Paul, I was gettin' worried there for awhile. I've heard tell of hobos puttin' everything under the sun into Mulligan stew, stuff you wouldn't believe, sich as snakes, toads, moles, and so on. And I'm OK with all that, but I was stayin' in a jungle in Kansas back in '35 or '36 where the jungle buzzard who was in charge of the stew was caught puttin' an armadillo in the kettle. A goddam armadillo, for Christ's sake! Now, I can sink my teeth into jus' about any critter that sports fur, and even an occasional snake, but I draw the line on armadillos." He gave an involuntary shudder and got up and walked down to the river bank and rinsed out his tin can and spoon.

It didn't take long to clean up after supper. There were tin cans, spoons, the kettle and a few cooking utensils to wash, but no tables to wipe down, floor to sweep, or leftovers to put away. As darkness settled over the encampment, we tossed a few hefty sticks onto the campfire and gathered around to smoke and tell tall tales of the road. At least I thought the bos were spinning tales, trying to outdo one another with fables of derring-do, or scare the bejesus out of gaycats like Steve and me. At the time I found the stories hard to credit. My experiences riding the rails over the next few months were to teach me otherwise, however.

Jim, who had been riding the rails for fifteen years, talked about a near-death experience he had had "riding the rods." Up until the 1920s, boxcars had long, steel rods running lengthwise on their undersurface to support heavy loads. Bos would place boards across the rods to ride on, or would lie on a single rod and hang on for dear life, riding just inches above the tracks. It was the most dangerous place to ride on a train, but a desperate hobo would ride the rods if there was no alternative. One night, Jim caught a hot freight out of Chicago, riding a single rod. After the train got up to speed, a terrific vibration started up, and it didn't take him long to come to the realization that the train had a "flat wheel." One of the wheels on his side of the boxcar had a flat spot that was causing the pounding vibration that started in his hands and spread throughout his body.

Jack London "Riding the Rods"

"It was like using a f***in' jackhammer, except worse, because you couldn't let go, even for a second, or you'd lose your grip and be ground into hamburger by the wheels. And the faster that ol' train went, the worse it vibrated. I thought it was goin' to shake my teeth loose and turn my brain and my innards into jelly. I had to hang onto that f***in' rod all the way to St.Louis! Jesus H. Christ! That was the last time I ever rode the rods. I'd rather deck a boxcar in a blizzard than go through that kind of Hell again!"

I was thankful that boxcars were no longer equipped with rods. But a tall, gangly hobo named Russ gave us something else to think about. Steve and I had heard plenty of stories about railroad bulls terrorizing hobos, throwing them off trains, shanghaiing them and renting them to slave farms, or sticking them on chain gangs, but Russ told us about another breed of bulls that went beyond terrorizing hobos.

Back in 1935, Russ had caught a Chicago-bound hot freight

out of Kansas City one cold, drizzly November afternoon. The train was swarming with bos, and Russ was in a boxcar with a dozen other men. He had been riding the rails for years, and something didn't feel right. He hadn't seen a single bull, either in the yard or on the train. He smelled a rat.

Russ stopped to light a cigarette and took a deep drag on it before continuing with his story. "I figgered I'd caught a lucky break, me and all them other bos. Maybe the bulls were on strike! Ha! Anyway, I found an empty spot on the floor of that boxcar and curled up in a Hoover blanket (that's a newspaper, for you gaycats), and went to sleep. It was a short nap, because fifteen or twenty miles outside of Kansas City, the train started to slow down, and then it came to a stop. Just stopped, out there miles from nowhere. 'What in Sam Hell is goin' on?' I says to the bo next to me. The man just shrugged his shoulders. No one knew what to make of it.

"Next thing I know, there's a heap of shoutin' and cussin', and a couple of cinder dicks open the door to our boxcar and order us out. Bulls armed with shotguns and clubs were all over that train, roustin' bos off the decks and blinds, and flushin' 'em outta the boxcars. Some of the bos resisted, and the bulls treated them pretty rough, kickin' and clubbin' them somethin' awful. Well, pretty soon, they had all the bos, mebbe 200 of us, off the train and lined up along the tracks. Then, the bulls went down the line, and ordered every bo to empty his pockets. They took half of each man's money. If a bo said he didn't have no money, the bull would pat him down, and then rummage through his bindle. If they found any money, they'd keep the whole amount, and tell the bo that was his punishment for lyin'. When they was all done robbin' us, the bull in charge of the operation said now that we had all paid the railroad for our ride, they were goin' to let us back on the train. That ride cost me a buck, but I talked to a coupla brothers who said they were headin' home to Minnesota after working the hops and fruit harvest in Washington and Oregon. They had near $200 between the two of them, enough money to keep their family back home in groceries through the winter. Those boys paid 50 bucks apiece for their boxcar ride to Chi-Town!" Russ took a final drag on his cigarette before flicking it angrily into the fire.

Railroad Bulls

"I've been robbed by bulls before," said Clem, the possum butcher. He had been sipping whisky out of a hip flask while listening to the conversation. "Hell, one time, in Nebraska, the local I was ridin' pulled off onto a siding, waitin' for an express to pass in t'other direction. All of a sudden, the boxcar door comes flyin' open and two bulls order us out at gunpoint. They had us strip off our clothes, then they went through everything lookin' for money. They turned our hats inside-out, even checked our underwear and belts, and inside our shoes. They took everythin' they found, the pricks. They went right down the line, strippin' and robbin' every bo on that train."

Clem took a long swig out of his flask and returned it to his trouser pocket before going on. "I gotta be fair, though, I have crossed paths with one or two good bulls. Years ago, when I was just fifteen years old, I was tryin' to catch out in the Burlington Northern yard in Topeka. This yard bull caught me just as I was climbin' into a boxcar. He ordered me outta the car, and escorted me outta the yard. I figured he was going to haul me off to the pokey, but instead he took out his wallet, gave me a dollar, and told me where I

Railroad Bulls

could find a diner to get a meal. Then, he told me the freight I had tried to catch out on wasn't scheduled to leave for another hour. He told me to hide in the bushes just outside the yard, and hop on the train after it started to pull out. Yeah, a lot of bulls are mean bastards, but some are alright."

The conversation around the campfire went on this vein for a while longer, with the veteran hobos swapping tales of adventure and misfortune, recounting gruesome accidents; weird traveling companions; panhandling; and describing flophouses, mission houses, and jails they had stayed in. I was getting a little depressed hearing about the horrors of the road, and I guess Steve was too, because he pulled out his Marine Band harmonica and started playing some tunes to lighten the mood, starting with "I've Been Workin' on the Railroad." He played softly at first, but with more passion as the bos gathered around the fire and started to sing along. He played "Irish Washerwoman" and "Drunken Sailor," and ended with "Shenandoah." My brother was a virtuoso with the harmonica, and his playing lifted everyone's spirits.

By the time the last, melancholy notes of "Shenandoah" floated out of Steve's harmonica, the fire had burned low, the sun had long since set, and the moon was rising in the east. Chief looked up at the night sky, and clapped me on the shoulder. "Paul, our train will be leaving soon. Grab your satchel and we'll head back to the yard."

We thanked Jim and the other bos for their hospitality and took our leave. An hour later, we were on a side-car Pullman, barreling down the Nickel Plate Road on a hot freight, bound for the Windy City.

Chicago

The freight train pulled into Chicago in the pre-dawn hours. The moon had dropped below the western horizon, and the massive rail yard, which dwarfed the other yards we had been in, was cast in shadows, illuminated only dimly by lights mounted on tall poles at 100-yard intervals. Chief had been in this yard before, which was lucky for Steve and me. Without a guide, we'd have been like rats in a maze. We followed closely behind Chief as he started walking north toward a street overpass.

We hadn't gone more than a few car lengths when a man in a police uniform suddenly stepped out of the shadows, shined a flashlight in our eyes, pointed a revolver at us, and demanded, "What are you? Jew? German? Irish?"

"Irish!" Steve and I shouted out in unison. My heart started pounding, and I had to fight the instinct to run. The man gave us a long, hard look, grunted, and then turned the gun in Chief's direction.

"How about you?" he shouted. "You sure as Hell don't look Irish!"

We heard a "click" as the man cocked the gun, and my mouth went dry as I watched him push the barrel into Chief's massive chest. I thought I was witnessing our friend's last moments on this earth. But Chief maintained his usual calm demeanor and, with a note of pride in his voice, said to the man, "I'm Lakota Sioux. American Indian!"

The bull stared at Chief for a few moments, and then uncocked and lowered the gun. I have no doubt that, had he not liked our answers, he would have shot us, cleaned out our pockets and satchels, and thrown our bodies into the nearby Chicago River. Our deaths would barely be noted by the local authorities. Just three more John Does for potter's field, and neither Chief's family nor ours would ever learn what became of their sons. Life was cheap in Depression-era America.

The cop asked us what we were doing in the yard. We explained that we had just gotten off a freight train, and were trying to find our way out of the yard. He pointed with his club toward the overpass we had been walking toward. "That's Roosevelt Road up there," he said. "To the right there's a path leadin' up to the street. Walk east a few blocks and you'll be in Grant Park. You can catch a few hours sleep there, or in the hobo jungle down behind the Field Museum south of the park. Good luck to you!" The man holstered his revolver and walked off into the night.

Chief turned to us and laughed, "Welcome to Chicago!"

We found a place to sleep in a wooded section of Grant Park, but after a few hours we were rousted out of the park by a couple of Chicago's Finest. We walked north on Lake Shore Drive for a few blocks, and watched the sun rise up out of Lake Michigan and slowly bathe the city's concrete canyons in warm sunshine.

We ate breakfast at a greasy spoon diner in the Loop. There was no possum stew on the menu, but there was traditional breakfast fare, and we ordered heaping platefuls of scrambled eggs, bacon, sausage, hot cakes, and toast, and pot after pot of black coffee. Thus fortified, we sallied forth to explore the Windy City.

We wandered around the Loop for a while. The streets were crammed with cars, trucks, double-decker buses and trolleys, while electric trains rambled noisily overhead on the elevated platform, what Chicagoans called the "El." The sidewalks were packed with somber-faced men and women, the men in fedoras and dark suits and the women in long skirts or dresses and high heels, rushing to their Loop offices to start another work day.

I reflected on the difference between myself and these office workers. I didn't have a job; I was living hand to mouth; I was sleeping in boxcars, hobo jungles, and public parks; and I had no near family except my brother. But I nourished the hope that my prospects would improve once I reached the promised land, the Matanuska Valley in Alaska. The people scurrying down the sidewalk were well dressed and appeared to be eating regularly, but they didn't look particularly happy. They seemed to be resigned to their fate. I hoped I never found myself in their shoes, locked into a secure but miserable existence as a wage slave in a dreary office in a crowded city. For them, every day was the same old grind. For me, every day was a new adventure. I wouldn't have traded places with any of them.

We walked up Michigan Avenue and crossed over the Chicago River and past the Wrigley Building on the left and Tribune Tower on the right. We continued up North Michigan Avenue for a few blocks, stopping frequently to stare at the merchandise on display in the shop windows. Fancy women's boutiques, haberdasheries, jewelers, furriers, toy stores, department stores and gourmet restaurants and cafes lined both sides of the street. This was the famous Gold Coast, one of the most affluent neighborhoods in America. It far surpassed Boston's Back Bay or Beacon Hill in sumptuous elegance.

We were shocked by the displays of opulence in these shops. It was as though we had left our world and entered another reality. It was inconceivable to us that there were people in America in 1938 who not only had enough to eat, but were able to indulge themselves with fancy clothes, mink stoles, Rolex watches, and other baubles. These were the people who lived in the brownstone mansions and posh apartment buildings that occupied most of the side streets. The entrances to these regal residences were attended by liveried doormen, and chauffeured Lincoln roadsters and Cadillac coupes were parked at the curbside, ready to whisk their owners off to social engagements or business meetings.

When we reached the palatial Drake Hotel, we turned around and headed back down Michigan Avenue, not stopping to gaze into any more storefronts or gape at the fancy residences. We felt conspicuously shabby in our tattered shirts, patched pants, and scuffed boots. The well-dressed and well-coiffed men and women we passed on the sidewalk seemed to avert their gaze and quicken their pace as they passed us, or moved to the far edge of the sidewalk, as if we were carriers of some fearful contagion. A nightstick-swiveling beat cop gave us the fish eye, and we feared he might arrest us for trespassing, or for being poor. We had gone down the rabbit hole and entered a world as alien and inhospitable to us as Wonderland was to Alice. We needed to return to our grimy and harsh, but familiar, hobo world.

We walked back to Grant Park and the three of us sat down on a bench near Buckingham Fountain, lit up cigarettes, and took in the scene. It was a beautiful summer day, with only scattered wisps of clouds in the azure sky, and a gentle southeasterly breeze sweeping in off Lake Michigan. Tourists with cameras hanging from their necks wandered around the park, snapping photographs of the fountain or the Chicago skyline, and office workers on their lunch breaks relaxed on benches or stretched out on the manicured lawns surrounding the fountain. Sailboats and motor yachts rode to their moorings in Monroe Harbor just to the east of the park.

Steve and I ruminated for a while about the possibility of hiring on as crew on one of the larger yachts. We couldn't conceive that a wealthy yachtsman wouldn't leap at the chance to add a couple of young men with our seafaring ex-perience to his crew. Our dad had been a professional captain for rich yacht owners, and he was well compensated for his work and seemed to enjoy it. Bill and Steve often accompanied him when he took his clients out for a sail, and marveled at being paid for having fun.

It was a pipe dream, of course. Chief brought us back to the harsh reality of our present situation by reminding us that we were just visitors in this beautiful city, and we couldn't spend the rest of the summer lounging around Grant Park. Our stomachs were growling after our long jaunt that morning,

Grant Park

but after splurging on a huge breakfast, we didn't think we could afford much in the way of lunch. And we hadn't given a thought to where we'd lay our heads down that night.

Chief said he knew a place where we could get a free meal. "It's a mission place, over on the main stem. All ya gotta do is sing a few hymns, and tell 'em you've put your life in Jesus's hands, and they'll give ya a meal."

"What's the "main stem"? I asked. I felt as though I needed a dictionary to keep up with all the hobo lingo I was picking up.

"The main stem's the downtown area of a town or city," Chief explained. "It's where a bo goes to find work, or pan-handle, or 'throw down', as we say in the trade. In Chicago, West Madison Street, west of the Loop, is the main stem." I wondered what a couple of gaycats like Steve and I would do without our Sioux Indian guide.

"We'd be lost without you, Chief!" said Steve. We had no idea at the time how prophetic his words would prove to be.

"You guys are smart, you'd figure it out," said Chief. "Look, let's plan our next move. I need to get back to the rez, and you guys need to get to Alaska before the snow flies. We can hop an Illinois Central freight to Sioux Falls. From there, we can catch out on a Northern Pacific freight to North Dakota, and you fellas can continue on to the coast from there. I'm ready to move on tonight, if you guys are."

"Sounds good, Chief," said Steve. We ground out our cigarettes, grabbed our satchels, and started walking north through the park. When we reached Madison Street, we turned west and continued on until we crossed the Chicago River and entered Skid Row.

We had gone down another rabbit hole, but the world we had entered this time could not have been more different from the Gold Coast. North Michigan Avenue was a world of comfort, style, security, and hopefulness. West Madison Street was a hellish world of depravity, despair, and shattered dreams. It was mean, ugly, sordid and depressing. It was shocking to all the senses: garish signs hawking 15-cent hot dogs "with all the trimmings" and 29-cent pints of wine; pawn shops; strip joints; flophouses; the moans of men vomiting up rotgut whiskey in alleyways; the stench of vomit and urine emanating from the drunks passed out in doorways and in the gutters; mounds of garbage lining the sidewalks; scarecrow figures rummaging through trash cans searching for discarded food scraps; hookers lolling in the doorways of dive hotels, unable to disguise their apathy and shame with lipstick and rouge.

Chief led us a couple of more blocks down West Madison Street until we came to a storefront with a large neon cross hanging over the entranceway proclaiming "JESUS SAVES." Another sign identified the establishment as the BREAD OF LIFE MISSION.

While we stood in line waiting to enter the establishment, Chief offered us some advice. "Put on your most pious face, guys. The meeker and holier you look, the less they'll feel the need to save your wretched asses from eternal Hellfire. Act all arrogant and defiant, and they'll be on you like stink on a hog with the 'come to Jesus' shit. And when the singin' starts, belt out the words like you really mean them. Do that, and they'll give you a little extra when you go through the serving line."

We were greeted at the entrance by Brother James. He was a rather portly, middle-aged man with swept-back gray hair, penetrating blue eyes, and a stentorian voice. "Men, have you heard the Good Word? Enter, pray and sing with the other lost sheep, and then share the bread of life with us." He handed each of us a hymnal and ushered us into a large room containing several rows of folding chairs. Most of the chairs were occupied by men who appeared to be in desperate need of both food and prayer, the former more urgently than the latter. A small lectern was positioned at the front of the room facing the assembled penitents, and comforting bible verses adorned the walls. A matronly woman, presumably Brother James's wife, was seated at an upright piano and thumbing through the pages of the hymnal on the music rack. We sat down in the last row of seats, tried to look pious, and waited for the service to begin. A heavenly aroma wafting into the chamber made the waiting almost unbearable.

Brother James ushered a few more salvation seekers into the room, and as soon as the last seat was filled, he advanced to the lectern, opened his hymnal, and then turned to the pianist and said, "Sister Jane, let us sing."

The little congregation, half-heartedly at first, started to croak out the words to "A Mighty Fortress is Our God." Brother James's powerful baritone easily overpowered the combined voices of the assembled multitude, and he looked over at Sister Jane and gave her a signal to turn up the intensity of her playing a notch or two. She launched into the second verse of the hymn with heightened Christian fervor, and the rest of us instinctively started to sing with more passion. An approving smile spread across Brother James's broad brow as we belted out a sincere, if not exactly euphonious, rendition of "Rock of Ages."

As the last words of the hymn floated from our lips, Brother James put down his hymnal and launched into a fire-and-brimstone sermon, a real scorcher that left many of us in an agonized state of spiritual distress, convinced that, unless we mended our wicked ways, we would spend eternity roasting in the biblical lake of fire. But, after showing us the awful fate awaiting the unrepentant among us, Brother James led us in the hope-restoring singing of "Amazing Grace."

Through many danger, toils and snares
We have already come
'Twas grace that brought us safe thus far
And grace will lead us home

I had come to the Bread of Life Mission seeking only nutritional sustenance. I had no expectation of or desire for moral instruction or spiritual enlightenment. But the words of that beautiful old hymn touched my soul as I thought of the "dangers, toils and snares" I had already come through in my brief lifetime, and of the unknown moral and physical challenges that lay ahead of me in the coming weeks, months and years. Was it luck or grace that guided me to enroll in the CCC just as I had run out of options at home in South Boston? Was it luck or grace that kept me from being swept off the stern of the *Halo* that night off Cape Hatteras? Was it luck or grace that saved me from freezing to death in a snowstorm, saved by a state trooper who just happened to shine his flashlight into the cab of the truck I had taken refuge in? Was it luck or grace that led to our fortuitous encounter with Chief that night in the Port Jervis rail yard? And was it luck, or grace, that stayed the trigger finger of the yard bull last night? I didn't know the answers to these questions, but from that point on, I knew that grace, a divine and mysterious force, was a guiding and protective presence in my life.

As promised, after tending to our spiritual needs, Brother James addressed our corporeal needs by leading us to a dining area, where Sister Jane ladled out steaming cupfuls of a hearty stew, and we helped ourselves to sandwiches and coffee before sitting down to eat at a massive oaken table. This was the preacher's chance to double down on his message of salvation and redemption, and he went at it with true religious fervor. He went around the table asking each man if he had taken Jesus Christ into his life, and if he knew that the Savior would always be with him, whatever path he traveled in life. I couldn't resist asking Brother James, a bit sarcastically, if Jesus would be with Steve, Chief, and me in the boxcar later that night as we rumbled across the prairie. I was stunned and touched by his reply.

"Why certainly, Paul. Jesus is always with you. Remember

Ruth 1:16: '...for whither thou goest, I will go; and where thou lodgest, I will lodge.'"

We finished our meal and, on Sister Jane's insistence, stuffed our satchels with sandwiches before thanking our hosts and taking our leave of the Bread of Life Mission. I was to have a range of different experiences, not all good, in several mission houses before I reached the West Coast, but Brother James's kindness and inspiring words left a lasting impression on at least one teenage wanderer.

Twilight was descending on the City of the Broad Shoulders as we made our way east on West Madison Street toward the Illinois Central rail yard. The plan was for Steve and me to wait on Roosevelt Road while Chief stole into the yard and scoped out which freight trains were heading west to Sioux Falls that night. Then, we'd all hide in the shadows and catch out when the train started to roll out of the yard. After our close call the night before, we just wanted to get out of Chicago with our lives.

We had just crossed Clinton Street when we approached, of all things, a bookstore. It was flanked on one side by a liquor store offering wine at 15 cents a glass, and on the other by a pawn shop. I was a hopeless bibliophile, and could no more pass a bookstore without stopping than an alcoholic could pass a bar without going in for a drink. Despite its shabby exterior and gloomy interior, I was tempted to go in and browse. My misgivings melted away when I saw the sign over the front window: "SCARCE-RARE-UNUSUAL." I told Steve I would only be a minute, and stepped over the two drunks passed out in the entranceway and entered the store.

As it turned out, my brief foray into that skid row bookstore had fateful consequences. Chief had apparently continued walking down West Madison Street, not realizing that we had stopped to dawdle, and now he was nowhere in sight. We walked fast, thinking we would catch up with him in a block or two. We didn't, but we didn't panic. We figured he would probably wait for us at the Roosevelt Road overpass. But when we reached the path leading from Roosevelt Road down to the yard, there was no Chief. We peered down into the yard to see if we could spot him, but by this time night had fallen, and most of the yard was cast in shadows.

We decided to sit tight, confident that our friend would show up eventually. But after waiting a couple of hours, and listening to one train after another pull out of the yard, we started to fret. We decided to risk a run-in with the yard bulls and sneak into the yard to look for Chief. We wandered around for a few minutes, staying hidden in the shadows as much as possible, and kept a sharp eye out for our comrade.

Suddenly, we saw a large man trundle down the path and run alongside a long freight train that was slowly picking up speed.

"That's him!" said Steve. I wasn't so sure, but I followed my brother in pursuit of the figure. We shouted out to him as we ran, but he didn't slow down, and he didn't respond to our calls. He looked like Chief; a big guy with broad shoulders, carrying a satchel like Chief's. He probably couldn't hear our shouts over the sound of the train. It had to be Chief!

We had nearly caught up to him when he grabbed the door frame of an open boxcar and hauled himself into the black interior. Steve and I followed him into the car in quick succession, and lay on our backs panting for a minute or two. As soon as I caught my breath, I looked around the car. I could see a glowing cigarette tip in the inky blackness, but nothing more. "Where've you been, Chief? Trying to ditch us?" I asked, in a kidding manner.

"Who the f*** is Chief?" responded the man in a gruff voice.

An icy chill ran down my spine as I realized what had happened. We had just climbed into a boxcar headed we knew not where, and had lost Chief, our loyal friend and guide, probably forever. I was afraid to ask the obvious question: where was this train headed?

Steve introduced us to our new boxcar mate, and asked him where he was going. The man said his name was Sam, and he was heading home after being on the road for several months. "Where's home, Sam?" I asked, hoping that home was somewhere along the route from Chicago to Seattle.

The scene was surreal. It was though we were in a seance and talking to a ghost. The glowing red tip of Sam's cigarette, bobbing up and down and then flaring up as he took a long drag, was the only visible evidence that we were communicating with a living human being and not some disembodied spirit.

Sam hesitated for a few long seconds before responding to my query. Finally, he spat out the words "Nawlins."

"New Orleans?!" Steve gasped, and I had an impulse to jump off the train. But we were going far too fast to entertain such a notion. Now we were in the soup, and we had to think fast to get back on the right track, so to speak.

"One more question, Sam," I said. "Are we on an express freight, or a local?" I prayed it was a local. If so, we could get off the train before traveling too far south. With luck, we could hop a freight back to Chicago and catch out on a westbound train before the night was out.

"This here train's a hot freight," said Sam. "Next stop's Cairo, down at the very southern tip of Illinois." He pronounced Illinois with an "ess" sound at the end.

I had never heard of Cairo, Illinois. It sounded as foreign and as exotic to me as Cairo, Egypt, and as improbable a destination. Sam assured us it wasn't that far, maybe five or six hours. We'd be pulling into the Cairo yard around daybreak. Steve and I decided we would get off there and catch the next train going back north or west.

Sam tossed his cigarette butt out the door and then crawled to one end of the boxcar. He was snoring like a chainsaw within minutes. My brother and I crawled to the other end of the car, and Steve was soon engaged in a spirited snoring contest with Sam. I slept fitfully for a few hours, tormented by guilt. If I hadn't stopped to browse in that friggin' bookstore, we'd be headed to the Dakotas with our Lakota Sioux Indian friend and mentor. Instead, we were sharing a boxcar with a stranger, 4,000 miles from our final destination, and hurtling in the wrong direction at eighty miles an hour.

Heading West

We didn't linger in Cairo. We hopped the next freight heading north without bothering to find out where it was going, or whether it was an express or a local train. It turned out to be a local, and it stopped at a half dozen small yards and sidings before pulling into Quincy, Illinois, three hours northwest of St. Louis, Missouri. It took us all day to get to the small Mississippi River town, and by the time we did, we were hungry and thirsty, so we got off.

We walked to the main stem and washed dishes in Rosie's Diner in exchange for a meal. Then we found our way to the Quincy hobo jungle, where we slept under the stars for a few hours before rising in the predawn darkness to catch a westbound freight. We couldn't find an empty boxcar, so we rode the blinds 200 miles across the state of Missouri to Kansas City, Kansas.

Riding the blinds was about as much fun as riding a bucking bronco standing up. It was like standing lookout duty high up in a ship's crow's nest during a gale, but much more dangerous. Decking a boxcar was enjoyable in comparison. Steve and I rode back-to-back, each of us standing on the bottom rung of an iron ladder attached to the end of a boxcar, and hung on with both hands to another rung at shoulder height. We couldn't sit down, and we could only communicate by yelling at the top of our lungs over the roar of the wind and the loud clacking of the wheels. After an hour or so, the bottoms of our feet were aching. We could briefly relieve the pressure by shifting our weight from one foot to the other, or from the balls of our feet to the heels, but the pain was constant. Worse than the physical pain was the fear that we would lose our grip and fall under the wheels of the train. I was tremendously relieved when, after hanging on for dear life for three hours, we approached the outskirts of Kansas City. When the freight pulled into the Kansas City rail yard and onto a parallel track, Steve and I released our death grip on the iron rungs and leaped to the ground before the train slowed to a complete stop. We hustled out of the yard before the yard dicks spotted us, and went to the main stem to scrounge up something to eat.

Into the Dust Bowl

A couple of hours later, we were heading west again, on an express freight bound for Denver, Colorado. We had climbed aboard an empty boxcar with eight other hobos, six men and two girls who were trying to pass as boys. The girls had tucked their hair under their hats, and had smeared dirt over their faces to disguise their feminine features. They wore sweaters to flatten their busts, despite the August heat, and rarely spoke, using nods and other gestures to communicate. They kept to themselves in one corner of the boxcar, and the men left them alone.

Steve and I sorely missed Chief's companionship and leadership, but we were growing steadily more confident in our hoboing skills. We figured we had made it about one third of the way to Seattle so far, and felt that nothing could stop us now.

It was a glorious mid-summer day, and hot, so we left the sliding doors on both sides of the boxcar open to let in as much sunlight and fresh air as possible. I had always pictured Kansas as one of the flattest places on earth, and I was surprised at how hilly it actually was. Not Vermont hilly, but not as flat as a billiard ball, either.

We sat on the floor of the boxcar as the train sped along, our feet hanging out of the door, soaking up the sun's rays and breathing in lungfuls of fresh Kansas air. Every so often we would spot a biplane crop-dusting the fields. It looked like the pilot was having great fun, swooping down almost to ground level to release a cloud of chemicals, then soaring up into the air, turning tightly, and swooping down again to dust the next section of field. He must have felt as though he were on a roller coaster as he followed the hilly contour of the land.

Steve took out his harmonica and started playing some of his favorite tunes, with me singing along, starting with "I've Been Working on the Railroad" and "She'll Be Coming Around the Mountain." Steve was a virtuoso on the harmonica, and when I looked around the boxcar, I saw a smile on every bo's face. Some were singing, and most of the bos were tapping their toes in time with the music. When Steve launched into "Irish Washerwoman," I got up and danced a jig.

Steve concluded the impromptu harmonica concert with

a soulful rendition of "Red River Valley." By the time he had started on the second verse, the whole group was singing along. I saw more than one man wiping away a tear..

The words and the music took me back to Camp Mansfield, lying around the barracks on cold winter nights, lonely and pining for home. One of the men would start strumming a guitar, and we would sing "Red River Valley," "Shenandoah," and other mournful ballads until the bugler played taps. The communal singing soothed our aching hearts, and drew us closer together as young men far from our homes and loved ones, struggling to find a way out of the economic miasma that had clouded our futures. My spirits soared when I thought of all I had accomplished since then: I had taken the first steps toward a career in the Merchant Marine, and had sent money home to my parents every month since I left home. But my spirits flagged when I reflected on my current circumstances. Here I was, eithteen years old, a ninth-grade dropout, alone in the world except for my brother, dressed in rags, scrounging and scavenging for food, sleeping in boxcars and hobo jungles, and with only the faint prospect of improving my circumstances if I could reach far-off Alaska. At moments like this, I plumbed the depths of depression, but pride wouldn't allow me to wallow in self pity. I was a fighter and a survivor!

Almost imperceptibly, the Kansas landscape was changing as we rolled steadily westward across the state. We had passed mile after mile of lush, verdant fields of soybeans and corn in the eastern part of the state, but as the train rolled further west, there seemed to be more fallow than planted fields, and the plants were stunted, withered and broken. Corn that should have been waist high was half that height. In some of the fields, only the scattered tops of plants were visible above the surface, and the black, rich earth we had seen earlier looked more like sterile sand than life-nourishing soil.

It wasn't only the fields that had a deserted, lifeless appearance. We passed one derelict farm after another, the half-open doors and windows of houses and barns evidencing the sudden departure of their erstwhile occupants. Pastures and corrals were empty, and there was nary a human, a farm animal, or even a dog or cat to be seen. I had heard stories of huge dust storms raging across the prairie in recent years, sucking up millions of tons of topsoil and sand into gigantic clouds, and then depositing the debris helter-skelter over the countryside. The result was the Dust Bowl, and we were riding through the heart of it. It was as though a tsunami of dust, soil, and dirt had surged through the region, piling high up against the sides of houses and outbuildings and remained frozen there. Whatever crops had been in the ground had been obliterated. Tractors, trucks and wagons were abandoned in the fields, buried up to their axles in dirt. Outhouses and windmills lay on their sides, knocked off their foundations. The tumbleweed blowing across the arid landscape was the only sign of life in this bleak landscape. I tried to imagine what became of the poor farm folk who were driven from their homes and livelihood by the cataclysm. I was to meet more than a few of them in the coming weeks, in flop houses, hobo jungles and church missions from Kansas to Oregon.

The train roared across the border into Colorado early that afternoon, and Steve and I decided we'd get off the train at the first stop. We had been riding in the same boxcar all the way across Missouri and Kansas, a distance of over 700 miles, and had not had a decent meal in twenty-four hours. The train had made a few coal and water stops along the way, so we had been able to keep our water flasks full, but we had become obsessed with thoughts of food. I would have greedily devoured any dish put in front of me. My mouth watered at the memory of the delicious possum stew we had enjoyed in the Fort Wayne hobo jungle, and I would not have turned down a hot bowl of armadillo stew if it had been offered to me.

The freight pulled into a rail yard in a small town a couple of hours before sunset, and Steve and I were on the ground and running for the exit before it had come to a stop. We had no idea where we could find food, but we followed a group of bos who told us we were in La Junta, Colorado, and that they were heading for the hobo jungle on the Arkansas River. We followed them as far as the turnoff to the riverside encampment, and then proceeded into town to buy ingredients to add to a mulligan stew. We had nearly depleted our capital, but we had enough money to buy a bag of potatoes and carrots, as well as some fruit to hold us over until the stew was ready.

As we anticipated, when we arrived at the hobo jungle there was a fire going and a kettle positioned over the fire. Hobos were scattered around the area, napping, playing cards, or hanging laundry on tree branches. No one was tending the kettle, and it appeared to contain little more than water and a few herbs. An older man with a pipe anchored in his mouth was kneeling over a large turtle which he had just placed upside down on a tree stump near the kettle. He looked at us, grunted "Hello," and then used a pocket knife to sever the head of the flailing amphibian. The man then set about butchering the turtle, wielding his well-honed knife with surgical precision to carve the animal's surprisingly ample flesh into one-inch square cubes which he deposited in the kettle. Steve and I added our contribution to the stew, and followed the path down to the river to clean up.

We returned to the jungle to find the camp in an uproar. A man, a young bo from Tennessee named Grayson, was sitting on a log holding a bloody rag to his face. When he moved it momentarily to reposition the makeshift bandage, we could see a long gash running from his left cheek to his chin and incipient shiners in both eyes. A few men were standing over him, cursing him. No one offered him first aid.

Most of the bos were gathered around the two girl hobos on the other side of the camp. The girls were sitting on wooden crates, and the older-appearing of the two had her arms wrapped around the younger one, who was sobbing uncontrollably. The younger girl's shirt was in tatters, and her arms and face were covered in scrapes and bruises.

The girls, seventeen-year-old Helen and her fifteen-year-old sister May, had fled their home in the Upper Peninsula of Michigan a few weeks earlier to escape their abusive stepfather. They were headed to California, where relatives had offered to take them in. They had encountered the usual difficulties hobos face on the road, but thus far had been able to avoid the unwanted attention of unscrupulous men by dressing as boys and keeping low profiles. Their strategy had worked until that evening when Grayson had surreptitiously followed May into the woods, where she had gone to relieve herself. Helen heard May's screams, ran into the woods, and found Grayson on top of May, ripping at her pants and shirt. Helen pulled a stiletto out of her sock and lunged at Grayson, slashing his face with the razor-sharp blade. The shouting and screaming soon attracted the attention of the other hobos. Several of the men subdued Grayson, while others helped May to her feet and assisted her back to the jungle.

The men were so angry at Grayson that I was sure they were going to beat him to death. But cooler heads prevailed and he was hauled before a summary kangaroo court. It was an open-and-shut case. Grayson was quickly convicted of attempted rape, and the court then spent several minutes debating what his punishment should be. Most of the bos wanted to take him to the La Junta police station, but one man suggested tarring and feathering him and depositing him in a boxcar on the next outbound freight train.

The court decided to let Helen and May select the punishment. The sisters deliberated privately for a few minutes, and then told the court what they wanted to see happen. They knew that if the bos turned Grayson over to the police, May would never get justice. Grayson would say that May had enticed him into the woods, only to lose her romantic fervor when she realized that Grayson was interested in more than just hugs and kisses. It would be May's word against Grayson's, with Helen as the only witness. Bringing charges against Grayson would require the girls to appear in court and be humiliated by the defendant's lawyer, who would cast them both as immoral tramps. What other kind of girls would travel across the country in boxcars with hobos?

The sisters asked the court to take Grayson to the rail yard and put him on the first train heading east. The court agreed to honor the girls' request, and several bos were selected to carry out the sentence. Grayson gathered up his belongings, and a contingent of hobos escorted him to the rail yard, where he was thrown into a cattle car headed to the Chicago stockyards.

Grayson eluded formal justice that evening, but I am sure that May and Helen took comfort in the fact that his conscience, if he had one, would be pricked every time he looked in a mirror, or saw a passerby involuntarily recoil at the sight of the hideous scar that marred his otherwise handsome visage.

After Grayson's sentence was carried out and calm had returned to the hobo jungle, we enjoyed some delicious turtle soup and then told stories around the campfire for a while.

One story in particular caught my attention. It was about a man who caught out in a boxcar in Minnesota with a couple of teenage boys who were running away from home. It was a warm day, and he sat in one doorway with his legs dangling out while the two friends sat in the other doorway with their legs hanging out. Peering ahead, he could see that the train was approaching a bridge. Suddenly, he was thrown violently through the air and slammed into the back end of the boxcar. The soles had been torn off his shoes, and his feet were bruised and bleeding. The two boys who had been sitting in the other doorway were gone. Apparently, their feet had caught the sides of the narrow railroad bridge and they had been thrown from the train and, no doubt, killed.

I shuddered as I listened to this sad story. Steve and I had ridden for hours that day with our legs dangling from the doorway of the boxcar. Luckily for us, the train hadn't crossed any narrow railroad bridges.

Steve usually played a wide range of music on his harmonica, but that night he played mostly sad tunes. I was beginning to worry about my brother. He was sentimental by nature, and prone to melancholy. I feared he was beginning to lose heart.

The next morning, Steve and I decided to take a break from our travels to earn some money. Neither of us had slept much since leaving New York, and our diet, while exotic at times, had been skimpy. We had to take our belts in a notch or two, and our clothes were hanging loosely on our lean frames. Our cash reserves had dwindled to pocket change and the $5 Mrs. Higgins had given each of us. If we had any hope of reaching the Matanuska Valley, we had to put food in our bellies and cash in our wallets.

We walked into La Junta and sat down at the counter in Fred's Diner. Everything on the menu looked good, but we had barely enough money to buy breakfast for one of us, so we asked for one order of ham and eggs, home fries, toast and coffee, and an extra plate, so we could share the meal.

To our astonishment, ten minutes later the waitress deposited a heaping breakfast platter and a steaming mug of coffee in front of each of us. We started to protest that there had been a misunderstanding, but she looked over at the kitchen doorway where a balding, middle-aged man in a cook's smock was leaning against the doorframe and smiling at us. "It's OK, Fred says it's on the house."

We waved to Fred and thanked him before digging into the eggs, ham and home fries. We couldn't believe our luck, and we ate quickly before we woke up from what had to be a dream.

As we were finishing our meal, Fred came over to chat. He said he knew we were hobos the minute we walked through the door. He had spent time riding the rails when he was younger, and he recognized the "lean and hungry look" of the itinerant worker. He had known hunger, and there was no way he was going to let us walk out of his diner with half-empty bellies.

Fred told us that La Junta and the entire southeastern corner of Colorado and neighboring parts of Oklahoma,

New Mexico, Kansas, and Texas had been devastated by drought and dust storms over the last few years. He described apocalyptic dust clouds that roared across the plains, blotted out the sun, and covered the land with a thick coat of dust and sand. They called them "black blizzards." The dust was so thick at times that people had to wear goggles and masks when they went outside. Sand driven by gale-force winds would wear the paint off cars and trucks. Livestock and people suffocated, and hundreds died from "dust pneumonia." Crops were destroyed, farms and barns were buried under mountains of sand and dirt, and entire herds of cattle had to be destroyed for lack of forage. Hundreds of families, who had been dispossessed when banks foreclosed on their farms, loaded all their earthly possessions on their cars and migrated west, mostly to California. There had been a rash of suicides, and most of the people who remained in the area were disheartened and depressed. The only thing that kept La Junta from becoming a ghost town was the business generated by the railroad.

While Fred was giving us the lowdown on La Junta, we noticed a mountain of dishes, pots and pans piled up in the kitchen sink. We offered to make the mountain disappear, and Fred accepted our offer. When we were done, Fred offered us jobs as dishwashers. He offered to pay us 25 cents an hour and give us a free breakfast and dinner in exchange for coming in for a couple of hours every morning and evening to wash dishes and clean up the kitchen. We agreed to take him up on the offer, but only for a week. We shook hands on the deal, and Steve and I left the diner to take a look around La Junta.

We walked around the small town for a while, and then followed State Route 109 a couple of miles out into the countryside and wandered through several abandoned farms. It was a windy day, and heavy, dark clouds scudded overhead. The soil looked incapable of sustaining life. There were no trees, and only a few sparsely-leaved bushes.

The farmhouses could more accurately be described as shacks than proper houses. The shingles on the roofs had been bleached to a pale shade of gray by the sun, as had the clapboard siding. Most of the window panes were either broken or missing, and front doors were ajar or lying on the ground, blown off their hinges by the gale-force winds that periodically ravaged the area. Porch foundations had settled unevenly, causing the plank floors to open widely. The roofs of many of the houses had collapsed.

We ventured into one of the derelict farmhouses. Sand covered the floors and piled up against the interior walls. Sheets of newsprint had been stuffed into the sills, tops and sides of windows to keep sand from blowing in through the cracks. Newsprint had likewise been pasted over the un-sheathed inner surfaces of exterior walls to block sand from seeping through the seams in the exterior sheathing.

In the kitchen, a thick coat of sand covered the plank flooring, and had even insinuated itself under the linoleum. A cast-iron cooking stove stood in the center of the room, with a sheet-metal chimney passing up through the ceiling. Cabinet and cupboard doors hung loosely from their hinges, or were missing. The cupboard drawers had all been pulled out and lay in pieces on the floor. A soapstone sink and tub with a hand pump stood against one wall. The house had no running water, but there was an outhouse at the rear of the structure.

It was a sad scene, made more poignant by the personal items left behind by the family that had left for greener pas-

A typical Dust Bowl scene

tures: articles of clothing, threadbare and beyond repair; worn-out shoes; broken dishes, glassware, and cooking utensils; rag dolls; a strapless baseball glove; marbles; and articles that had probably been passed down through several generations, items of no material value, but perhaps of incalculable sentimental value to some now-departed child or adult, who had left it behind in their desperate flight from what had become an earthly Hell.

The barn and a few small outbuildings were all in a state of near collapse, with sagging roofs, and distorted frames. They would probably come tumbling down in the next windstorm. We found a rusted hay rake buried to its axles in sand near the barn. It was hard to imagine the implement ever again being used to harvest wheat, just as it was hard to imagine the farmer who once worked the farm ever recovering from the calamity that had overwhelmed him and his family. But, though I didn't know the man, I knew I wouldn't bet against him. Some men, and women, cannot be beaten.

Steve and I spent the next week fattening up on Fred's cooking and putting a few bucks in our pockets washing dishes and doing odd jobs around town. We slept in the hobo jungle, where we met some interesting characters and heard some interesting stories sitting around the fire at night. I discounted the more improbable of these stories, but some had the ring of truth.

One bo, a husky farm boy from Lancaster, Pennsylvania, told us how he and a friend nearly froze to death one night when they were trapped inside a reefer. They had propped the hatch open when they entered the car, but someone, probably a railroad bull, had slammed the hatch shut during the night. They tried to climb up to the hatch to open it, but the walls of the car were coated in ice, and were too slippery for them to gain a hand- or foothold. When the train pulled onto a siding later that night, they screamed for all they were worth until a brakeman came along and opened the hatch. The boy said he and his buddy shivered for hours after their rescue, and never climbed into a reefer again.

On our last night in the La Junta jungle, the conversation turned to odd jobs men had done during their travels. One man said he had gone to Washington to pick apples the previous September, but arrived before the apples were ready to be harvested. He ran into a brakeman who supplemented his trainman's wages by trapping coyotes, for which the state paid an attractive bounty. The brakeman offered the bo 25 cents for every rattlesnake he brought him, which he would then use as coyote bait.

Steve and I found the rattlesnake hunter's story amusing, but we were not amused when another bo described his experience in the Matanuska Valley that spring. Like us, he had heard that there was a demand for men with road-building or construction skills. But when he arrived at the experimental community, he discovered that morale among the settlers was low, and many of the original colonists had given up and returned home. They had found the climate too harsh, the growing season too short, the soil too rocky, and freight prices too high to make farming pay. There was little construction activity, and no job openings, so he gave up and went back on the road. This was deflating news. Steve and I exchanged glances. Were we pursuing a pipe dream? We had a lot to think about.

We had planned to catch out on a Denver-bound express freight early the next morning, but when a brakeman in the railyard told us that the next one wasn't scheduled to pull out of the yard until that afternoon, we decided to hitchhike instead. We walked to the edge of town on US 50 and stuck out our thumbs. There wasn't much traffic on the highway, and after a dozen or so cars and trucks passed us without even slowing down, we figured we had better start walking. We didn't anticipate walking the entire 180 miles to Denver, but it was easier to walk than to stand idly in the hot sun.

Most of the vehicles that passed us were Model A Ford trucks or Model T sedans loaded down with families and all their worldly possessions, following the sun west to the California or Oregon Promised Land in hopes of securing a new lease on life. Steve and I marveled at the amount of furniture, housewares, baggage and human beings these vehicles could carry. We marveled that the engines had the power to propel these overloaded vehicles forward, and that their axles didn't crack under the tremendous weight they were asked to bear.

One truck tested the limits of Henry Ford's engineering genius. Dad was at the wheel while Mom rode shotgun with a toddler on her lap. Numerous ragamuffin children sat or stood atop a hillock of housewares, carpets, steamer trunks, bedding, bed springs, mattresses, sofas, couches, kitchen chairs, washboards, laundry baskets, and bicycles. A spare tire was lashed to the door frame, and jerry cans and suitcases were secured to the running boards. A mongrel dog sat wagging his tail atop the peak of the haystack, while a chicken coop harboring a brood of hens was precariously secured to the tailgate. A small American flag was attached to the right head lamp. Mom, Dad and all the children gave us a friendly wave as they chugged by. I have no doubt they would have offered us a ride if they could have found room for us on that traveling haystack!

Steve and I came to regret our decision to hitchhike to Denver. By mid-afternoon, around the time that express freight train was pulling out of the La Junta rail yard, we had traveled only sixteen miles down US 50, at least half of that distance on foot. It took us two and a half days to reach Colorado Springs, where we snuck into the rail yard and boarded a northbound freight. Half of the vehicles that passed us on the highway were Dust Bowl refugees who didn't have room for us, and most of the remaining drivers were wary of giving a lift to a couple of scruffy-looking young men of unknown character. We calculated that we walked about 86 of the 110 miles from La Junta, sleeping in deserted farm buildings at night, filling our water bottles from the Arkansas River, and nibbling on pears and apples we bought in La Junta.

Steve boosted our flagging spirits during the long stretches

"California or Bust!"

between rides by playing some of our favorite tunes on his harmonica. We laughed at the lyrics of "Home on the Range," especially "Where seldom is heard a discouraging word." There was plenty to be discouraged about, but we tried to lose ourselves in the music, and for the most part we were successful.

We met some interesting people on that hitchhiking venture. One of our first rides was in a long-haul truck. The driver seemed like a normal human being, a skinny guy about Steve's age with a western drawl and a large plug of chewing tobacco tucked under his lip. He maintained a calm demeanor until another truck attempted to pass us. Then, he became a man possessed. He pulled himself up straight in his seat, stared menacingly into the rear view mirror, turned red in the face, and started cussing.

"That sumbitch ain't going to pass me. You bet your sweet

asses he ain't." Then he stood on the accelerator and shifted the screaming engine into progressively higher gears until we had left the would-be overtaker in the dust. As soon as the challenger disappeared from sight, the driver slipped back into his previous relaxed persona and offered us each a plug of chewing tobacco. This scene repeated itself every time a truck tried to pass us. He seemed not to mind being passed by a car, but he could not abide being passed by another truck. At first it was exciting, like riding in an Indianapolis race car. But, after the truck almost flipped over while rounding a bend in the road at high speed, Steve and I decided we'd had enough excitement for one day. When we stopped for gas in a small town, we got off the truck.

Three more short rides and hours of walking brought us to Pueblo, where we spent the night in a gospel mission. We hit the road early the next morning, and resumed our thumbing/walking journey to Denver. Early that evening, we were picked up by two middle-aged guys who were running away from their wives. They were heading to Denver, where they intended to go on a bender to celebrate their emancipation from loveless marriages.

They had already started the bender. They passed a bottle of whisky back and forth, and offered us a bottle of our own, which we declined. They were downright giddy, probably due in equal parts to slipping the bonds of matrimony and the strong spirits they were imbibing. The sedan meandered from one side of the road to the other as we slowly progressed northward on US 87. If it weren't for our fatigue and our blistered feet, Steve and I probably would have asked to be let out. But we decided to stick it out with the runaway husbands until we got to a sizable town.

As we were approaching Colorado Springs, the car's headlights suddenly went out, and the engine stopped. We had run out of gas. The car coasted to a stop in the middle of the highway. Steve and I got out and pushed the Chevy well off the road, said a quick goodbye to the men, who were sound asleep, and started walking,

We found the Colorado Springs rail yard just in time to catch a northbound freight. We climbed into a boxcar and debated what our next move should be. Steve was ready to give up on the Matanuska Valley, but I wasn't ready to throw in the towel yet. We agreed to get off the train in Denver and see what we could find out about what was happening in Alaska. Maybe things had turned around over the past few months and construction workers were in demand again.

We spent that night in a Salvation Army homeless shelter near the rail yard in Denver. The Army addressed most, if not all, of our needs. First, the man at the front desk directed us to the shower room, where we were issued clean, white night shirts to wear while they fumigated and laundered our clothing. Then, we were given a bottle of kerosene and instructed to apply it to our entire body, scalp and crotch included, to kill head lice ("walking dandruff"), body lice ("seam squirrels"), and crabs ("crotch crickets"). Finally, we were given towels and Castile soap and told to rinse off the kerosene in the shower. At five o'clock we were herded into the chapel, where we agreed to become soldiers for Christ, listened to a coma-inducing sermon, and sang "Onward, Christian Soldiers" and other spirituals.

At the conclusion of the church service, we filed into the dining room and were given a steaming bowl of beef stew, rolls, and coffee, plus apple pie for dessert. We sat down at a table and swapped tales with other homeless men, most of whom were hobos like ourselves. We asked if they knew anything about the Matanuska Valley Colony. Few of the bos had ever heard of it, but a couple of men from Washington state chuckled when we brought it up while finishing our dessert.

"It's a friggin' fiasco," said one of the men. "Goddam gummint screwed it up. Brought in all these families from Minnesota and Wisconsin who couldn't make a go of farming in the Midwest, on some of the best farmland anywhere. Hell, I heard many of them weren't even farmers, just people on relief that the local relief administrators just wanted to get out of their hair."

"Yeah, they've made a hash of it," said the other man. "They rushed those families out to Alaska before they had set up any support system, schools, hospitals, and so on. There was a measles outbreak there the first year, and only one doctor in the whole damn valley to take care of hundreds of patients. And most of the land is too rocky to till anyway. Most of the colonists gave up and went home after a few months. Can't blame 'em. I had a friend of mine, a carpenter, who packed his tool bag and went up there looking for work. He stayed for a couple of months, but came back last January. The work was sporadic, the government was slow to pay, and it was the most boringest place he'd ever been. No bars or nothin' where a man could unwind after workin' hard all day." He swallowed his last forkful of apple pie, looked at us and asked "Are you fella's thinkin' of goin' up there?"

Steve and I looked at each other. "We were," I said. "But we may have to change our plans."

"Lights out" was at nine o'clock. Workers spread sawdust on the dining room floor and handed out newsprint for us to wrap ourselves in. Linen and pillows would have been nice, but Hoover blankets were better than nothing.

The next morning, we retrieved our laundered and fumigated clothes and went to the dining room for a breakfast of oatmeal, donuts and coffee. Then, Steve and I went to a nearby park and talked things over. We agreed to give up on Alaska. It had been pie in the sky all along. But what to do next? Continue on to the West Coast, or go back to New York? Steve said he had had enough of hoboing, and just wanted to return to New York and ship out. I was equally determined to go on to Portland or Seattle. They were both busy ports, and I was confident we could find a ship there. Besides, I had been looking forward to traveling through the Rocky Mountain states and seeing a part of America I had only seen in westerns. I had to admit, though, that my main motivation for pushing on was a reluctance to admit defeat. I knew I'd hate myself if I gave up now.

Steve wasn't buying my argument. Maybe he was just more sensible than me, or simply didn't have my sense of adventure. Whatever the case, we reluctantly agreed to part ways. That afternoon, he headed over to the Rock Island Line yard to catch an eastbound freight, and I returned to the Union Pacific yard and caught out on a westbound freight.

Sailor on Horseback

It took Steve and me five weeks to ride the rails 2,000 miles from New York to Denver. It took me three months to travel 1,200 miles from Denver to Portland. But I spent only a fraction of that time in boxcars, and for many weeks I was miles from the nearest railroad. I retain many happy memories of the days and weeks I spent slowly working my way across the western United States, but I had some terrifying experiences as well, and they haunted my dreams for years.

My solo journey got off to a slow start, as I had unwittingly boarded a local train. I had hoped to ride nothing but express freights all the way to Portland, but I hadn't yet learned to distinguish local trains from express trains.

We stopped at a couple of sidings to allow fast freights to pass, and didn't arrive at Fort Collins until daybreak. I decided to get off the train, eat breakfast, and sleep in the local hobo jungle for a few hours before catching out again that evening.

That night I was back on the road, sharing a boxcar with a couple of older men who told me they were "harvest bos." They were headed to Washington state to harvest hops and fruit. They had done every manner of work, but they preferred harvesting. I told them I didn't think that I was cut out for agricultural work, being a merchant seaman by trade. I thought they were kidding when they suggested that I should give sheep herding a try.

"Best job I ever had," said one of the men. "You get to ride a horse around all day way up in the Rockies. You gotta like dogs, of course, but the dogs do most of the work, keeping wolves and coyotes away from the sheep. You won't get rich herdin' sheep, but they give you a place to stay and feed you pretty good. You should give it a shot."

I was intrigued by the idea, but I had never been on a horse. "No problem. They'll teach you to ride," said the other bo. "Before you know it, you'll be trottin' around the mountains like you was Hopalong Cassidy. This time of year, late summer and early fall, them sheep ranchers are lookin' for men to take their flocks down out of the high mountain meadows. We'll be stopping in Medicine Bow soon. You get off there and you'll find a job sheepherding in no time."

I took the men's advice and got off the train in Medicine Bow, Wyoming, a small town on the Continental Divide. It was pitch black and the town was buttoned up for the night, so I walked into the police department and asked if I could sleep in one of their cells for a few hours. The sheriff showed me into a cell and gave me some blankets and a pillow. In the morning, a deputy served me breakfast and asked me if I would be interested in herding sheep for $2 a day. I jumped at the offer, and before noon I was hired as a camp tender and sheep herder by Ghost Creek Ranch, and took my first riding lesson. My primary job was to bring supplies to the sheep herders who were moving the flock down to corrals near town as it got colder and grass cover thinned out at higher elevations. We hauled the supplies on pack horses or in horse-drawn wagons, and slept under the stars.

As my riding skills improved, I spent more time herding sheep, working with the dogs to keep the flock intact and protect them from predators. The biggest threat was coyotes and wolves, but black bears would grab sheep who wandered into the woods on a hot day to "shade out." The dogs did most of the work, but they seemed to enjoy it, and the sheep seemed to appreciate the dogs. I often saw an ewe licking a dog's face. On the other hand, as protective as the dogs were, they had no compunctions about eating a dead lamb.

By late September we had moved the flock down to the main ranch and the men were preparing them for market. Sheep herding had been a welcome respite from hoboing, but I was anxious to reach the coast before winter set in, so I hung up my spurs and headed back out on the road.

Defending My Virtue

The most fearsome predators I encountered on the high mountain plateau were the bears and wolves who were always looking to pluck off a wayward sheep. There were predators of a different kind riding the rails, skulking in the dark corners of boxcars and on the edges of hobo jungles, constantly on the lookout for vulnerable young hobos to take advantage of.

I rode out of Medicine Bow one night on a Union Pacific freight bound for Ogden, Utah. I had climbed into what appeared to be an empty boxcar, and settled down in a corner and quickly fell asleep. I couldn't have been asleep for more than a half hour when I was awakened by the sound of heavy breathing just inches from my face and rough hands tugging at my belt buckle. I couldn't see my assailant in the Stygian darkness, but I instinctively struck out with both fists and landed enough blows to cause the man to retreat momentarily. He lay there for a few minutes catching his breath. I quietly got on my hands and knees and crawled toward the far end of the boxcar, laid on my side, and waited. Eventually, his breathing became inaudible, and I closed my eyes and drifted back to sleep.

My respite was brief. I was yanked back into full wakefulness by the sound of the man shuffling across the floor of the boxcar, cooing, "C'mon, Honey. Let's have some fun, you and me." I knew it was only a matter of time before he found me, and I prepared to launch myself at the man and beat him senseless as soon as he came within range of my fists. The instant I felt his hand on my leg, I released a savage barrage of kicks and punches at my invisible target. Few of them struck home, but I felt my fists smash into bone and cartilage at least a couple of times, and it was evident from the man's howling that at least one of my kicks struck a sensitive part of his anatomy. Cursing and moaning, he withdrew to the far end of the boxcar to lick his wounds. I wiped blood off my hands, whether his or mine I couldn't tell, and laid back down in my end of the boxcar. I stayed awake for as long as I could, but after the man's groaning turned into snoring, I let down my guard and fell back to sleep.

I slept very little that night. The man was determined to have his way with me, and I was equally determined to defend my honor. I felt as though he and I were contestants in a fifteen-round championship fight. He would attempt to ravish me, I would fight him off, and he would retreat to his corner to recover from the pummeling I gave him. Then, the bell would ring for the next round and we'd go at it again. It was exhausting, and it's good that I wasn't carrying a knife in my sock, as was my habit when visiting the Reeperbahn or LeHavre. I would have used it on the man, or thrown him out the door of the speeding train if I could have.

At daybreak, the train slowed and came to a stop in the Ogden rail yard. Before I climbed out of the boxcar, I went over and took a look at my tormentor, who was lying on his back and snoring loudly. He was a big man of about thirty, with BORN TO RAISE HELL tattooed across one arm. His eyes were swollen shut, his nose was crooked, and a rivulet of blood ran down from one corner of his mouth onto his chin. I looked at my hands. They were swollen and bruised, and so sore I could barely move my fingers. To this day, my knuckles bear the scars of that epic battle. And from that day on, I always wore two pairs of pants when I climbed into a boxcar at night. One with the zipper in the front, and the other with the zipper in the back.

Gandy Dancing

Getting into a boxcar that was harboring a pervert had been a stroke of bad luck, but Lady Fortune showed me her sunny side later that day. After polishing off a stack of hotcakes in a greasy spoon diner near the rail yard, I walked to a nearby park and found a place to sleep behind a clump of bushes. When I woke up a few hours later, I walked back to the railyard to see if I could catch out on a westbound freight. A friendly brakeman gave me an appraising once-over and asked me if I wanted to be a gandy dancer. I must have given him a funny look, because he quickly explained that gandy dancers were men who repaired the railroad track. He told me that the UP was hiring men to beef up their section crews. There was a lot of work that had to be completed before the snow flew, and they needed men who could swing an eight-pound spike maul or wield a twenty-five-pound lining bar ten hours a day. I thanked the man for the tip and went over to the UP personnel office. When I told the hiring agent about my CCC experience, he hired me on the spot. I would receive the princely wage of 25 cents an hour, less 90 cents a day for meals and lodging, and was assigned to a crew that was working on a section of track along the Snake River, a few miles west of Pocatello, Idaho.

Late that afternoon, I hitched a ride on a UP work train that was bringing a load of supplies to the section I had been assigned to. There were twenty of us in the section crew, all of us young, fit and happy to have a job. We lived in an old Pullman car that had been pulled onto a siding, lifted off the tracks, and placed on blocks. The Pullman served as our dormitory and dining hall, as well as storage shed for tools and supplies.

Every morning, we would propel ourselves on hand carts to a section of track that needed repairs. We became proficient at replacing worn rails or rotten ties, raising or lowering the track, pulling weeds out of the rail bed, adding crushed rock ballast to the rail bed, and "lining" the track.

Every curved section of track needed to be "lined" period-ically. When a train rounded a curved section of track, it ex-erted a centrifugal force on the rails that caused a tiny outward shift of the track. Over time, these small shifts would deform the track enough to cause a derailment if the track wasn't realigned. The foreman would sight down the track, and whenever he saw a deflection in the rails, he would line half of the crew along the inner side of one rail and the other half on the outer side of the neighboring rail. We'd dig the point of our gandy, or lining bar, into the gravel under the rail and, in rhythm with a chant called out by one of the men, heave our bar against the rail with all our might. With each heave, the track would move a fraction of an inch. By this means, a team of twenty men, heaving in unison and taking advantage of the magic of leverage, was able to shift a 4,000-pound section of track back into position. It reminded me of the way that square rigger crews, working to the rhythm of a sea chantey, would heave on capstan bars to raise spars or anchors weighing thousands of pounds. Section crews were called gandy dancers because of the way they rhythmically heaved on their lining bars.

Lining track was hard work, but lifting the ties and rails off the work train and into position was even harder, and more dangerous. We used rail tongs to carry the 1,700-pound, twenty-eight-foot long rails into position, and then used spike mauls to drive spikes through fissure plates and into the ties. Finally, we spread crushed rock around the ties with ballast forks and tamped it down with tamping bars. This was, by far, the most physically demanding work I had ever done.

We worked ten hours a day, five days a week, and blew most of our meager earnings in Pocatello bars every Saturday

Gandy dancers working in unison to align track

night. On Sunday afternoons, a few of us would pack a picnic lunch and ride a hand cart to a section of track that bordered the Snake River where we would swim, fish for cutthroat trout, or sleep off our hangovers.

After a few weeks of gandy dancing on the Union Pacific, I had developed thick calluses on my hands and added a few pounds of muscle to my lean frame. But I hadn't added any heft to my wallet, nor was I able to hone my navigation or ship-handling skills working on the railroad, so I decided to move on to Portland, where I hoped to find a ship and continue my climb up the hawse pipe to become a Merchant Marine officer.

The Near-Death Jump

I caught a westbound freight train out of Pocatello late one night. I had stuffed a couple of sandwiches and a bottle of water in my satchel, and had hoped to ride the train all the way to Portland. Fate, in the form of a surly brakeman, intervened, however. A few miles west of Boise, the train pulled onto a siding to let a passenger train pass us. The brakeman, who had gotten off the train to throw the switch, noticed the open door of the boxcar and shined his flashlight into the interior. I tried to make myself invisible, but he spotted me, and ordered me out of the car. I climbed out, and then pleaded with him to let me get back into the boxcar. But he was a mean cuss. He just scowled at me and called me a lousy bum. He stood next to me as the train started moving again, and then climbed aboard the caboose.

I watched in anger and disbelief as the light from the caboose grew fainter and fainter before finally blinking out. It was a moonless, starless night, and I couldn't see my hand in front of my face. I started walking back toward Boise, stepping from one tie to the next. It made for an awkward, slow gait, but I had no other way to navigate in the inky darkness. I thought about curling up next to the track and sleeping until dawn, but it was mid-October, and it was too cold to sleep outdoors without a sleeping bag. So, I kept plodding along.

After an hour or so, I started to hear the sound of running water, and I realized I was approaching a river. When I could hear the water moving under my feet, I knew I was on a bridge. This was confirmed when I put a foot down in the space between ties and felt nothing. I was a little nervous about proceeding blindly across the bridge, but I didn't have much choice. I continued on, slowly, making sure of my footing with each step.

I was making steady progress across the bridge when a tiny pinprick of light appeared in the west. It grew steadily larger and brighter, and I realized with horror that it was the headlight of an approaching locomotive. I had no idea how long the bridge was, or my relative position on the bridge. Could I make it to the far shore before the train arrived, or should I turn around and retrace my steps? It was a moot point. The train was bearing down on me fast, and I had to get off the bridge fast, or be squashed by the speeding locomotive.

I reached out in the darkness, hoping to find a railing or some kind of structure I could hang onto while the train passed. I felt nothing. With the locomotive less than 50 yards away and roaring toward the bridge at high speed, I sat down on the end of a tie, turned my body around so I was facing the track, and lowered myself until I was hanging by both arms from the tie.

While I hung there, with thousands of tons of loaded boxcars and gondolas roaring by, I did a quick mental computation. How long would I have to hang there? Assuming the train was going sixty miles an hour, I calculated it would take one minute for a mile-long section of train to pass my location. If the train was one mile long, I would have to hang on for one minute, and if it were two miles long, I would have to hang on for two minutes. I thought I could hold on for a minute, but not much more than that. As I hung there, with my fingers turning to rubber and searing pain spreading across my arms and shoulders, I wondered how far I would fall if I lost my grip on the tie. I also wondered how deep the water was at that spot, or if there were any rocks in the area. I pictured myself lying in shallow water with two broken legs or a broken back, or dead.

Finally, after what seemed like an eternity, the last few cars rumbled past, and I tried to hoist myself back up onto the bridge. I didn't have enough strength left to pull myself up, so I started to swing my legs side to side, hoping to generate enough momentum to swing my torso onto the track. But I lost my grip on the tie and fell. About six inches. To my utter astonishment, and great relief, I was standing on solid ground. In the early dawn light I saw that I was standing on the grassy riverbank, ten feet from the water's edge. I sat on the bank for a few minutes, silently giving thanks to God for sparing me, and started back down the track toward Boise after my heart stopped pounding in my chest.

Portland

Three days later, I jumped down from a boxcar for what I hoped would be the last time. I was in the Union Pacific Albina Yard on the Willamette River, in Portland, Oregon. I was stiff, sore and hungry after riding hobo-class 3,000 miles across America on the Erie, Nickel Plate, Illinois Central, and Union Pacific railroads. I was also broke. The few dollars I had earned sheep herding, gandy dancing, and picking sugar beets on the UP were gone, spent on food and some new clothing I had bought at my last layover in Messner, Oregon. Three months riding the rails had turned my meager wardrobe into a collection of rags. My boots were in a sorry state as well, but I would have to continue buttressing them with cardboard sole inserts until I had the money to replace them. I still had the $5 that Mary Higgins had given me, but I was saving that for a dire emergency.

I checked into a Salvation Army shelter, and spent the next few days at the union hall, hoping to find an OS berth on a ship. Any ship. I didn't care where the ship was going, what cargo it carried, or who the skipper was. I just wanted steady work, regular meals, and a place to sleep where I didn't have to worry about railroad bulls and perverts. But the few berths that opened up were snapped up by older sea-men with more seniority than me.

I was desperate. I was down to my last dollar, and trying to survive on the bowl of oatmeal and the cup of coffee served at the shelter every morning, supplemented by an occasional hot meal earned washing dishes at a diner or restaurant.

One afternoon, I wandered over to the Portland waterfront with the idea of boarding one of the vessels, presenting my seaman's papers, and asking for a meal. I was hoping, naively as it turned out, that the crew would extend that courtesy to a fellow mariner who was down on his luck.

At random, I approached the gangway of the S.S. *William Luckenbach*, showed my credentials to the quartermaster, and requested permission to come aboard to visit the galley. The man took a cursory look at my documents, then returned them to me and told me to go away. I was angry and humil-iated, but there was nothing I could do about it. After all, I was a panhandler, a stranger who meant nothing to him.

Demoralized by this experience, I realized that my hoboing days were not over. If I couldn't get a ship in Portland, I'd try somewhere else.

San Francisco

I returned to the UP yard and, under the cover of darkness, boarded a southbound freight. It was a rough trip. On the first leg of the journey, I rode in a gondola loaded with iron pipes. One of the other bos had his leg broken when the car lurched suddenly, causing the pile of pipes he was standing on to shift. We heard what sounded like a gunshot, and it took a few moments for us to realize that the "gunshot" was the sound of his shinbone breaking. We did what we could to comfort the poor guy, but we couldn't do much for him until the train pulled into the Redding, California, rail yard. Most of the bos riding the gondola disappeared when the train came to a stop, but a few of us remained behind and started lifting the heavy pipes off the man. Before long, the yard bulls were swarming over the gondola, supervising our efforts to remove the man from the gondola, but not lifting a finger to help.

We splinted the man's broken leg and lifted him down to the ground and placed him in the back of a truck. He was whisked off to the hospital, and we Good Samaritans were whisked off to the local police station. We were charged with trespassing and spent the night in jail. The next morning, we appeared before a judge who gave us a stern lecture, and then dismissed the charges.

That night, I caught out on a San Francisco-bound freight train. I spent the next few days, and the last of my money, in a flophouse near the Embarcadero. When my money ran out, I spent a few nights in jail as a guest of the city. I reported to the union hiring hall every morning, and looked for work in the afternoons. I was almost at the end of my tether when, on November 23, the day before Thanksgiving, I landed an OS berth on, of all vessels, the S.S. *William Luckenbach!*

I boarded the *William Luckenbach* "schooner rigged," dressed in rags and wearing cardboard shoes. Crew members gave me their hand-me-downs, and I made my own oilskins out of sugar-bag cloth, which I waterproofed with a mixture of fish oil, lamp black, varnish, and Japanese dryer. The sailor who had turned me away from the ship in Portland was shocked when he saw me on the *Luckenbach*, now a member of the crew and no longer a beggar. He was embarrassed, so I didn't let other members of the crew know that we had a history. He was young, but several years older than me. He had a physical advantage over me, and let me know this in his own, subtle, but strong-arm way.

I was overjoyed to have found a ship. Months of riding the rails across America had tested my mettle. My faith in my country and the capitalist system wavered at times, but I never doubted my ability to survive any challenge. I was in a state of near starvation, and it would be many weeks before I regained my physical strength, but I knew I would emerge physically and spiritually stronger from my experiences.

During the course of my wanderings in the streets of San Francisco, before I landed a berth on the *William Luckenbach*, I had come across a unique San Francisco institution, Bernstein's Fish Grotto. It was a popular seafood restaurant with a nautical theme. Diners entered the restaurant through an opening in the bow of a mock ship. The interior was divided into several dining rooms decorated to resemble cabins. The day before, I had stood outside the restaurant, drooling as I looked over the menu. A person could enjoy a complete dinner, soup to nuts, for $2.00. I swore that I would treat myself to a sumptuous meal there if I ever had two bucks to rub together.

Now that I had a job and a place to sleep, and knew where my next meal was coming from, I briefly considered eating Thanksgiving dinner at Bernstein's the next day. But then I thought of all the homeless men I would pass on my way from the dock to Bernstein's Fish Grotto, and realized I couldn't do it with a clear conscience. The *Luckenbach's* cook had announced that he would be serving a full turkey dinner the next day, so I wouldn't even have to leave the ship to celebrate Thanksgiving in the traditional style, or pay for it.

I thought about the $5 that Mary Higgins had given me

The SS *William Luckenbach*

for emergencies. There had been many times over the past few months when I had been tempted to spend the money on a meal and a bed, but something had held me back. I'm not sure what it was. Maybe I just didn't want to admit to myself that I had reached rock bottom. My pride wouldn't let me draw on that last resource until I had exhausted all other options. I had come very close to that point. But I had always found a way to move on from disaster, often through the intercession of strangers, like Chief, Brother James, Fred in La Junta, the sheriff in Medicine Bow, or the judge in Redding. I climbed into my berth in the fo'c'sle that night with a plan in mind, and slept better than I had in months.

The next afternoon, I walked over to Union Square and sat on a bench. It was a sunny November afternoon, but the cold wind that blew in from the Pacific Ocean seemed to penetrate right through my canvas jacket. I sat there for a while, observing the down-and-out men who loitered in the park. Some were panhandling, while others were curled up in Hoover blankets, perhaps sleeping off hangovers.

A couple of young men of about my age caught my eye. They were sitting on a bench and perusing a newspaper. They were clean shaven and quiet, and I guessed from their neat but threadbare clothing that they were checking the Help Wanted section of the paper. I approached them, and a brief conversation confirmed my initial assessment. They were brothers from Bellingham, Washington, who had been riding the rails and hitchhiking up and down the West Coast for months looking for work. They had had short stints harvesting crops, working in lumber camps, and crewing on fishing boats, but had been unable to find steady work. They had not eaten yet that day, and had no idea whether they would. I told them I could help them with that, and asked them to follow me.

A few minutes later, we were standing outside Bernstein's Fish Grotto. The boys looked at me quizzically, but I just opened the door and ushered them inside. I had a word with the maitre d', who promptly led us to a table. After the brothers were seated, I handed the older boy Mary Higgins' five-dollar bill, wished them both a happy Thanksgiving, and left.

I returned to the *William Luckenbach* and enjoyed Thanksgiving dinner with my new shipmates. That evening, I took a few minutes to compose a letter to Mary Higgins. I recounted the highlights of our trip, leaving out most of the lowlights, and confessed that Steve and I had chosen to ride hobo-class rather than Pullman class in order to conserve our meager resources. I was sure she would understand, and I was sure she would approve of the way I had used the $5 she had given me. I wrote a longer letter to my parents, put both letters in the mail, and reported for duty on the midnight watch.

Early the next morning, we cast off our docking lines, steamed past Alcatraz Island, and rode the outgoing tide past the Golden Gate, bound for New York by way of the Panama Canal.

EIGHT

BACK TO SEA

I MADE DOZENS OF VOYAGES on the S.S. *William Luckenbach* over the next six months. She wasn't the prettiest vessel afloat, or the fastest, but she was my home, my livelihood, and my school as I continued to master the art and science of seamanship and navigation. She was launched as S.S. *Pommern* in Bremen, Germany, in 1913, for the North German Lloyd Line, and carried livestock to Australia until the start of World War I. She was seized by the U.S. Navy in 1917, renamed the U.S.S. *Rappahannock*, and put to work ferrying horses and cattle to the American Expeditionary Forces in Europe. The Navy put her in mothballs in 1924, and she remained in the reserve fleet until the Luckenbach Steamship Company bought her in 1933 and renamed her the *William Luckenbach*. She was now making regular runs carrying general cargo between East Coast and West Coast ports by way of the Panama Canal.

The *William Luckenbach* was a large cargo vessel for her time. She was 497 feet long, had a beam of fifty-nine feet, and displaced 17,300 tons. She was an excellent school ship for me because she visited a lot of ports. We would steam from Boston to New York to Philadelphia, transit the Panama Canal, and then make brief stops in San Pedro, San Francisco, Portland, Bellingham, and Seattle or Tacoma. All that moving in and out of crowded ports provided me with an intensive course in ship and cargo handling. When I was off duty, I would study my *American Practical Navigator*, and practice celestial navigation whenever I could borrow a sextant from one of the officers. A couple of the older ABs in the crew took me under their wing. Old Pete, a Latvian sailor, taught me the finer points of marlinespike seamanship. After a few weeks under his tutelage I had mastered dozens of different knots, hitches, splices, lashings and whippings, as well as the proper maintenance and storage of rope. Frenchy Villeaux, a Cajun from the bayous of Louisiana, schooled me in the intricacies of cargo handling, an essential skill for a sailor on an intercoastal freighter. Frenchy must have seen something in my character that he liked, because one night in the fo'c'sle, as I was dozing off, I heard him say to another sailor, "Paul's a poor boy, but he's an honest one."

In my father's day, the crew of a wooden ship was kept constantly at work tuning and repairing the rigging and spars of the vessel, or holystoning the decks on their hands and knees. The *William Luckenbach* had little rigging for the crew to fuss with, and we used powerful electric scrubbers to keep the teak decks clean. But we had to wage a constant battle against rust. We were busy loading and unloading cargo when we were in port, but once we entered tropical waters the bosun would put us to work with chipping hammers and wire brushes. After we cleared the rust from a section of the superstructure, we would apply a primer coat of red lead paint, and then a topcoat of black, white or gray enamel. *William Luckenbach* had acres of steel plate, and

Paul Gill, dressed for shore leave

miles of iron rails, exposed to the elements, so the chipping and painting never ended.

If chipping and painting was my least favorite shipboard chore, taking a trick at the wheel was my favorite. I used to enjoy approaching land at night, watching the shore lights get bigger and more numerous as we approached the harbor entrance. I learned early on that the words of a harbor pilot are advice, technically, and that they become commands when the captain repeats them. The pilot calmly calls out, and the captain confirms, "Half Ahead," "Slow Ahead," "Dead Slow Ahead," "Steady as She Goes," "Slow Astern." I loved the way the captain, pilot, and quartermaster worked with crisp efficiency to maneuver the 17,000 ton ship to the dock, the quartermaster responding to helm orders, the watch officer relaying engine commands to the engine room by means of the engine room telegraph.

My stint on the S.S. *William Luckenbach* came to an abrupt end in San Francisco on June 1, 1939. The NMU (National Maritime Union) in Portland went out on strike against the companies operating oil terminals in that port, and this action froze shipping all up and down the West Coast. I was lucky to find part time work as a dock walloper (longshoreman) on the Embarcadero and as a rigger in the Todd Shipyard at Hunter's Point. If I had to be shorebound for a spell, I couldn't have chosen a better port to be marooned in than San Francisco, one of the world's great sailor towns. For the first time in a long while, I had a few coins in my pocket and the chance to enjoy a normal social life.

U.S.A.T. *Republic*

I received my Able Seaman license on May 22, 1939, and signed on the U.S. Army Transport *Republic* as AB on July 17, 1939. The *Republic* was launched as the S.S. *Servian* in the Harland & Wolff yard in Belfast in 1907, the yard that built RMS *Titanic*. She served as a transatlantic passenger liner for several years, and then as a troopship during World War I. After a stint in the transatlantic passenger service for the United States Lines in the 1920s, she was purchased by the U.S. Army and refitted as a troopship. Starting in 1932, she transported troops and supplies from the Brooklyn Army Terminal to Fort Mason in San Francisco by way of the Panama Canal, and then on to Pearl Harbor, Hawaii.

The *Republic* was a big ship. She was 599 feet long, had a

Paul Gill's Able Seaman license

beam of sixty-eight feet, and displaced 33,000 tons. Her cruising speed was only 14.5 knots, so the 5,000-mile voyage from Brooklyn to Panama to San Francisco took two weeks, and the 2,400-mile passage from San Francisco to Honolulu took another week. But she carried thousands of tons of supplies and over 2,500 troops to Pearl Harbor on every trip. I often wondered why all this manpower and materiel was being shipped to the Pacific. I found out, eventually.

I had two stints on *Republic*, the first from July 17, 1939, to June 4, 1940, the second from November 17, 1940, to March 24, 1941. During the course of many long passages, I got to know the officers and crew of the ship well. They were a competent and harmonious group, essential ingredients to the making of a happy ship. Captain Olson was a reserved man with many years of command experience and a no-nonsense demeanor. Tom Cleaves was the Chief Mate, and Gus Karlson was the bosun. Dr. Bruce was the ship's doctor. The Deck and Engine Departments were manned mostly by Americans, with a smattering of Kanakas (native Hawaiians), and the Steward's Department was staffed largely by Filipinos.

Army officers and their families were quartered in state-rooms, and enlisted men slept in triple-decker bunks on the lower decks. Dances, parties and special entertainment were put on for the officers and their families every night, while the troops watched movies on the afterdeck. Before watching the movie, the troops were required to participate in public prayers, led by a chaplain, and a religious song fest.

The Kanakas in our crew were great sailors. They were as much at home high in the *Republic's* rigging as they would have been in the crown of a coconut tree harvesting coconuts. I felt that they were a challenge to my own nautical high-wire ability, and I let them know that I was a match for them aloft in the ship's rigging, on the yards, spars, booms, and masts high above the deck, or working over the ship's side

U.S.A.T. *Republic* transiting the Panama Canal

while underway. The Kanakas loved the friendly rivalry, and so did I.

We had regular lifeboat drills on the *Republic*. I was always the stroke oar; I sat in the sternmost seat in the boat and set the pace. The other oarsmen would synchronize their strokes with mine. There were always a few men who could not help "catching crabs" with their oars. When they didn't feather their oars, the blade would catch the top of a wave, create a lot of spray, and reduce the speed of the boat.

One of the benefits of having Kanaka shipmates was that I could count on being invited to hula dances and luaus when the *Republic* was docked in Pearl Harbor. I spent many hours at Waikiki Beach surfing and riding the waves in outrigger canoes. I acquired a certain degree of proficiency in these sports, and picked up enough Hawaiian to engage in simple conversation with the lovely Hawaiian girls I met in Honolulu.

I loved Pearl Harbor, and felt as though I had a home on the *Republic*, but after five round trips from New York to San Francisco to Honolulu, I needed a change of scenery. I signed off the ship in New York on June 4, 1940, one month shy of my 20th birthday.

On the Beach

The employment situation was only marginally improved from two years earlier when I left New York to seek my fortune in Alaska. I did find part-time work at the Fletcher Shipyard and the Tietjen & Lang drydock in Hoboken. At night, I frequented some of my favorite haunts, reunited with old friends, and made some new friends as well.

On July 13, 1940, I signed on the collier S.S. *Michael Tracy* as crew relief for one round trip voyage to Newport News, Virginia. When I returned to New York at the completion of this assignment, I spent a week with my brother, Bill, doing steeplejack work on New York City high rise buildings.

S.S. *Uruguay*

I checked the shipping news section of the New York Times every morning to see what ships were arriving and departing, and went down to the NMU hiring hall if a big passenger liner was in port. I wanted to find a berth on a liner because they went to interesting ports. My due diligence paid dividends on July 25 when I landed an AB berth on the passenger liner S.S. *Uruguay*. The *Uruguay* was launched in Newport News, Virginia, as the S.S. *California* in 1927. She was 574 feet long, had a beam of eighty feet, displaced 20,183 tons, and had a cruising speed of 18 knots. The Moore McCormack Line took over as her operator in 1938, and started regular New York-Barbados-Rio de Janeiro-Santos-Montevideo- Buenos Aires-Trinidad-New York passenger service.

The S.S. *Uruguay* sailed with the outgoing tide on the morning of July 26, 1940. Five days out from New York, we made a brief stop in Bridgetown, Barbados, and then set a course for Rio de Janeiro. When I reported for duty on the forenoon watch three days later, I and seven other crew members were told to report to the foredeck for lookout duty. We were puzzled by this odd command, but we duly complied.

When we arrived on the foredeck, we were greeted by a few of the older members of the crew, who told us that we were Slimy Pollywogs and that we were being subpoenaed to appear before King Neptune and his court to answer charges of impersonating sailors and trespassing in Neptune's kingdom. We were issued oilskins, boxing gloves for mittens, and a pair of binoculars, and were told to man the rails and

SS *Uraguay*

keep a sharp lookout for Davy Jones, King Neptune's Royal Emissary. He would be arriving soon to officiate at a trial to determine whether we were landlubbers or true sailormen worthy of induction into the Mysteries of the Deep. If we survived the ordeal they planned for us, we would become Trusty Shellbacks.

It was miserable wearing oilskins in the sweltering equatorial heat, and impossible to handle binoculars while wearing boxing gloves, but we went along with the Crossing the Line ritual and pretended to scan the ocean for King Neptune and his court. After a few minutes, our shellback crewmates, sailors who had crossed the equator before, started appearing on deck costumed as surgeons, barbers, judges, mermaids, and bears. A hubbub arose on the starboard bow when King Neptune, followed by Her Highness Amphitrite, Davy Jones, and the Royal Baby, climbed over the rail and proceeded to the foredeck. There, they greeted the captain, and asked if there were any pollywogs on board. After being informed that there were seven pollywogs among the crew, King Neptune took his seat on a makeshift throne and stamped his trident scepter on the deck to signal that he was ready for the inquisition of the Slimy Pollywogs to begin. We pollywogs were stripped to our underwear and brought before the King and his Royal Court.

Before the interrogation began, we were given a "truth serum" consisting of hot sauce and aftershave lotion, followed by a raw egg. Neptune then asked us a number of ridiculous questions, such as "What does Davy Jones keep in his locker?" and "Who cuts the grass in Fiddlers' Green?"

After the interrogation, we were put through a trial by ordeal. First, the barbers lathered our faces with a paint/pitch concoction, and then shaved us with a piece of rusty metal strapping. Next, we were pelted with mushy fruit and ordered to crawl on our hands and knees through chutes filled with rotting garbage. Then, we were brought before the Royal Baby (the hairiest, fattest member of the crew) and compelled to kiss his belly, which had been smeared with lard and coated with hair clippings. Finally, after we kissed a sea hag's foot and King Neptune's ring, we were thrown into a large tub of sea water and dunked repeatedly by bears.

Davy Jones, after conferring with King Neptune, announced to the ship's company that the seven pollywogs, having survived our trial by ordeal, were now Trusty Shellbacks and Loyal Sons of King Neptune. We had leave to sail the southerly waters of King Neptune's Briny Kingdom, and a duty to put Slimy Pollywogs to the test on any future voyage to southern hemisphere ports.

Davy Jones, as King Neptune's Royal Scribe issued each

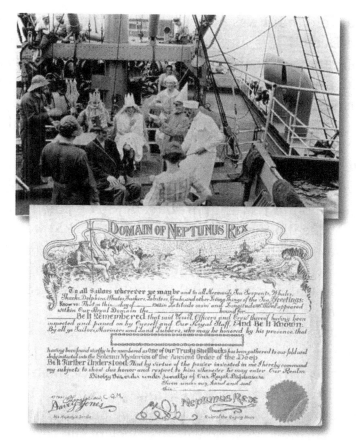

The Shellback Ceremony celebrating a seaman's first crossing of the equator. *Top*: King Neptune holding court. *Bottom*: Sample of a Trusty Shellback certificate.

newly-minted Trusty Shellback a certificate attesting to his initiation into the Solemn Mysteries of the Deep on August 8, 1940, at longitude 34.57 degrees west, latitude 00.00 degrees. The document was signed by Davy Jones, Royal Scribe, and Neptunus Rex, Ruler of the Raging Main, dipped in a bucket of sea water, and presented to each proud new shellback.

I was told that I was now a member of the Ancient Order of the Deep. I was already a member of the Order of the Ditch (Panama Canal) and, before my seafaring career concluded, I would also become a member of the Order of the Spanish Main (South American coast), the Order of the Blue Nose (Arctic Circle), and the Order of the Rock (Gibraltar).

Rio de Janeiro

Having purged its crew of Slimy Pollywogs, the *Uruguay* proceeded on to its next port of call, Rio de Janeiro, Brazil. Many of the old tars on board told me that Rio was an exceptionally beautiful city and a great sailortown. Some said they preferred Rio to Honolulu. If Rio could be mentioned in the same breath as Honolulu, I couldn't wait to see *Cidade Maravilhosa*, the Marvelous City.

Although fraternization with the passengers was strictly verboten, I had become friendly with a First Class passenger during the voyage, a Brazilian woman of German ancestry named Ilse. Ilse was a very attractive woman a few years older than me, who first caught my eye one afternoon when I was repairing a hoist on the afterdeck of the *Uruguay*. She was playing shuffleboard with another passenger, and we had a brief, flirtatious exchange.

After that initial conversation, we kept bumping into one another, and not entirely randomly. Ilse's English was not as good as my German, so we spoke *auf Deutsch*. This arrangement gave me a chance to work on my German, and thwarted eavesdroppers.

Ilse was returning to Rio after visiting relatives in New York. She worked in her father's chemical firm, and had her own apartment in Cosme Velho, a residential neighborhood on Corcovado Mountain, near the statue of Christ the Redeemer. She offered to show me around Rio. I accepted her offer, of course.

The old tars had not exaggerated Rio's beauty. As we approached the Brazilian coast, the sun was starting to peek over the eastern horizon, and only the tops of the many mountains surrounding the city were visible. Then, as we steamed closer, and the sun began its diurnal journey across the sky, we could make out Christ the Redeemer standing benevolent watch over the sleeping city, and Sugarloaf Mountain thrusting skyward out of the sea, like some giant finger pointing heavenward, marking the entrance to Guanabara Bay.

As a member of the forward mooring party, I had an unrestricted view of the stunning panorama that was opening before us. And it became more beautiful and interesting as we neared the shore and lights started to come on in buildings throughout the city. We pulled alongside the dock at Pier Maua, secured the mooring lines, and commenced discharging cargo and passengers. The off-watch members of the crew flooded the streets of Rio, while the rest of us spent the afternoon taking on cargo for Montevideo and Buenos Aires, counting down the hours and minutes until we, too, could sample the offerings of this exotic seaport.

As agreed, I met Ilse on the quay when I knocked off my shift, and she took me on an abbreviated tour of her native city in her red Mercedes Cabriolet. I had to pinch myself. Less than two years ago, I had been a hobo, riding boxcars across America in search of work. Now, I was being driven around Rio de Janeiro, Brazil, in a luxury automobile by a beautiful young woman. Clearly, Ilse and I came from different strata of society, but that didn't seem to matter to her.

I had to be back on the ship by 0800 hours the next

morning to stand my watch, so Ilse gave me a very quick tour
of Rio. We ate dinner at a restaurant near the Copacabana
and afterwards strolled along the praia until the sun disappeared behind Tijuca Peak. The tour concluded with a verti-
go-inducing drive up the winding Estrada do Corcovado to
the gigantic art deco statue of Christ the Redeemer. The
panoramic view of nighttime Rio de Janeiro from atop Corcovado was stunning, but the 100-foot high statue itself was
mesmerizing. I expected to feel diminished by the massive
structure, but it had the opposite effect on me. The all-
powerful but compassionate, all-forgiving essence of Jesus
Christ was brilliantly expressed by the wispy smile, the long,
almost femine hands, and the beckoning outstretched arms.
This was the Christ whose guiding and protective presence I
had felt at some of the most perilous points in my life
journey. What a blessing for the people of Rio to have such a
paternal figure looking over them from on high!

From Cordovado, Ilse drove us to her apartment. In the
morning she drove me back to Pier Maua and we sat in her
Mercedes talking for a few minutes before I went back on
board the ship.

Ilse told me she wanted to see me again when the *Uruguay*
returned to Rio, but I was noncommittal. I had learned from
my painful experience with Heidi that it was futile for a
sailor to make a commitment to any one woman. I believed
in free love, and wanted to avoid romantic entanglements.
We kissed goodbye, and I went on board, changed into work
clothes, and reported for duty on the forenoon watch. An
hour later, the *Uruguay* was rounding Sugarloaf Mountain
and steering for Santos, our next port of call.

Santos, Montevideo, and Buenos Aires all had their charms,
but they paled in comparison to Rio de Janeiro. I would

have liked to explore each of these port cities, but we were never in port long enough to venture much beyond the waterfront bars and nightclubs. When the Uruguay returned to Rio a couple of weeks later, I set off to explore Rio on my own and met a lovely young Brazilian girl named Marcia on the Copacabana. Marcia was a dark-eyed beauty about my age who worked as a secretary for a Rio shipping firm. Her company did a lot of business with American shipping companies, and she spoke passable English.

Marcia and I spent the afternoon touring Rio by tram and on foot before I returned to the ship to stand the overnight watch. Before we parted, Marcia told me she wanted to see me again when the *Uruguay* returned to Rio in a few weeks. I told her I would love to see her again too, but I couldn't make any promises. I wasn't even sure I would still be on the *Uruguay* when she returned to Rio. Marcia just smiled and said she would see me at the quay in a few weeks. "Whatever will be, will be," I said. I was a fatalist, and at the tender age of twenty, I had already seen enough of life to know that only a fool would map out the future course of his life in ink. I was as vulnerable to the "slings and arrows of outrageous fortune" as the next man, and knew that whatever plans I made for the future were just scribbles in the sand.

When the *Uruguay* returned to Rio a few weeks later, I was again assigned to the forward mooring party. As usual, there was a large, enthusiastic throng at the pierside to welcome the arriving passengers. As the tugboats nudged into our slip, I heard a chorus of *Ois* and *Olas* rising up from the crowd. I knew enough Portuguese to recognize the words for "hello." I was used to hearing a torrent of joyful greetings flying back and forth between passengers and quayside greeters whenever Uruguay tied up at a pier. What I was not used to hearing was, "Hallo, Paul! *Guten morgen!*" It didn't take me long to pick Ilse out of the crowd, waving excitedly. And I waved back just as excitedly.

Ilse faded out of view as the ship glided into her slip. I was preparing to throw a monkey fist secured to a heaving line to a dockworker when I heard a familiar voice cry out from below, "Hello, Paulo! Welcome back to Rio!" I froze. I hoped that somewhere in the throng of passengers crowding the rail there was a man named Paulo who was the target of that enthusiastic greeting. But I quickly spotted the beaming Marcia in the crowd, jumping up and down and waving excitedly. I waved back to her and flashed her a big smile. But I wasn't smiling on the inside. My life had just gotten very complicated. Two beautiful young ladies were standing on opposite ends of the pier, each ignorant of the other's existence, waiting for me to run down the gangway, gather her up in my arms and smother her with kisses. I was on the horns of a dilemma. What to do? I had to think fast and come up with a plan to deal with the ticklish situation I found myself in. I pondered the situation while I helped secure the mooring lines, and the logical solution came to me in a sudden flash of insight.

I leaned over the bow of the ship and shouted to Marcia to meet me at the gangway at 6:00 p.m. Then I ran down to the stern of the vessel, located Ilse in the crowd, and shouted out the same message. She said, "*Bis später!*" (See you later) and left.

Nervous, and not knowing what to expect, I walked down the gangway at precisely 6:00 p.m. As instructed, the two *senhoritas* were waiting for me on the pier. At first, they cast curious glances at one another. And then, as it dawned on them that they were both there to see me, their smiles turned into scowls. I quickly ushered them over to a bench and asked them to sit down before open hostilities could break out.

We had a long talk. Each girl admitted that I had not led them on, and that she had come to greet me at the pier that morning of her own volition. I told them that I liked them both very much, and would be happy to have a date with either one of them that night, or with both of them. I would be leaving Rio for the last time the next morning and didn't expect to ever see either of them again. I told them I was at their disposal and would honor their decision. The girls scrutinized one another for a few moments, and the scowls slowly transformed into smiles as they each looped an arm in one of mine and we walked to Ilse's parked Mercedes.

Republic Redux and S.S. *J.S. Luckenbach*

I signed off the S.S. *Uruguay* in New York on October 14, 1940, and spent the next month working as a rigger in the Fletcher shipyard in Hoboken. With the arrival of cool weather in November, my thoughts again turned to tropical climes, and I signed on for another stint as AB on the USAT R*epublic*. I spent the winter voyaging through mostly tropical waters, ferrying troops and supplies from Brooklyn to San Francisco to Honolulu. I signed off the *Republic* in San Francisco on March 24, goofed off for a week, and then signed onto the S.S. *J.S. Luckenbach* as AB on April 2, 1941.

The S.S. *South Bend* was built in Philadelphia in 1919 for the Luckenbach Steamship Company. She was taken over by the U.S. Navy and was converted to a troopship. From May to August of 1919, she brought 5,000 troops home from France. She was then returned to her owner, renamed S.S. *J.L. Luckenbach*, and put into service as an intercoastal steamer, hauling general cargo between East and West Coast ports by way of the Panama Canal.

Later that spring, I learned that the U.S. Maritime Service at Fort Trumbull, in New London, Connecticut, had opened its Officer Candidate School to any American merchant mariner who had accrued more than fourteen months of sea duty. Successful candidates would be commissioned as ensigns in the Merchant Marine and would be eligible to sit for the Coast Guard Third Mate licensing exam. I saw this as a golden opportunity to shoot up the hawse pipe to the bridge, and immediately sent in my application. When the *J.L. Luckenbach* docked at the Brooklyn Army Terminal on May 28, a letter of acceptance was waiting for me. I immediately signed off the ship and started to prepare to go back to the classroom for the first time since I dropped out of school at age fourteen. During my four and a half year career as a merchant seaman, I had risen from galley boy to Able Seaman. I had sailed on nine different vessels to seaports in the far corners of the world, from Hamburg to Buenos Aires to Honolulu, and had steered these ships over the waters of the North and South Atlantic Oceans, the Pacific Ocean, and the North and Caribbean Seas. At the age of twenty-one, I had become a seasoned sailor and I felt well-prepared for the next step forward in my career as a professional mariner.

NINE

FORT TRUMBULL AND
MARY EVANS

A FTER I SIGNED OFF THE *J.L. Luckenbach*, I spent a few days at home in South Boston visiting my parents. Dad was delighted to see two of his sons advance to the bridge so quickly. He had had to put in many hard years "before the mast" before he moved to the quarterdeck. Bill had just earned his Second Mate ticket, and I would be eligible to take the Third Mate licensing exam in December if I successfully completed the Officer Training School course. Both Mom and Dad were thrilled that I would be "on the beach" for an extended period of time, and just a short train ride from Boston.

I returned to New York and fattened my bank account a little working in the Fletcher and the Tietjen & Lang shipyards in Hoboken. With mybrother Bill's help, I got some jobs doing exterior repairs on the St. Regis Hotel on Fifth Avenue and other Manhattan high-rise buildings. It was scaffolding work, and the high winds aloft made it almost impossible to keep the scaffolding anchored to the buildings. But, dangerous as the work was, the pay was four times that of a shipyard worker.

On July 9, 1941, I reported to Fort Trumbull, a formidable stone structure built on the west bank of the Thames River in New London, Connecticut, between 1839 and 1852.

I got my dormitory assignment and class schedule and settled in. I was looking forward to returning to the classroom for the first time in six years. I should have been apprehensive, but I wasn't. I had an unquenchable thirst for knowledge, and I did not need to be in a formal educational setting to maintain my intellectual focus. I had spent countless off-watch hours in ships' foc's'les or high up in the crow's nest teaching myself algebra, geometry, and trigonometry. I was blessed with a natural aptitude for mathematics, and was able to perform complicated computations in my head. I had started to teach myself celestial navigation, and I was excited at the prospect of learning how to determine a ship's position anywhere on the globe. Little did I know how vital this skill would prove to be in the coming months!

Officer candidates were enrolled in either the Deck Department course or the Engine Department course. The syllabus for the Deck Department was comprehensive, with classes in navigation, mathematics, seamanship, boat handling, cargo handling, marine history and traditions, and first aid.

Almost all of the instructors were licensed Merchant Mariner officers, and they drew heavily on their "real world" experience, as well as movies and models, to demonstrate their points.

The Fort Trumbull Officer Training School was run like a military organization. Reveille was at 0600 hours, which gave us forty minutes to perform our morning ablutions and tidy up our rooms. Breakfast was served at 0640, and

amazon Gift Receipt

Send a Thank You Note

You can learn more about your gift or start a return here too.

Scan using the Amazon app or visit

https://a.co/d/cZSVnF3

ARMAGEDDON IN THE ARCTIC OCEAN: Up the Hawse Pipe Galley Boy to Third Mate on a Legendary Liberty Ship in th Bigge...

Order ID: 114-41124098-1509807   Ordered on February 23, 202...

classes ran from 0800 until 1615, with a forty-five-minute break for lunch. The evenings were devoted to study and preparation for the next day's classes. Every Saturday morning there was a formal inspection and review of the regiment, and we were given liberty from noon Saturday until 2000 Sunday.

If I was caught up on my academic work, I went home on the weekends. I enjoyed catching up with Janet, and my brothers, when they were home between ships. The food service at Fort Trumbull was good, but it was great to savor Mom's wonderful home cooking after scrounging or eating galley food for so many years. I didn't mention the possum stew and other delectables I often dined on in the hobo jungles. My proper English mother would have been scandalized.

I hadn't seen Steve since we parted ways in Denver. We sat for hours in the family kitchen drinking beer and regaling Mom and Dad with stories of our railroading adventures. Of course, we omitted some of the more unseemly incidents, such as my night-long battle with the sexual pervert in the boxcar in Wyoming, and the attempted rape of the young girl in the hobo jungle in La Junta, California. But both Mom and Dad were intrigued by Chief, and said they wished they could have met him.

Steve had had some unpleasant encounters with railroad bulls on his journey back East, but he made it back to New York in relatively good shape and a little wiser for his hoboing experiences. He had shipped out on a number of different ships over the past three years, making passages to Europe, primarily.

Times were hard when I left my hometown in 1936 to follow the sea. Lingering unpleasant memories made me reluctant to return at first, but conditions had changed since the outbreak of war in Europe in 1939. There had been a surge in war production and shipbuilding in the area, and employment opportunities were better than they had been in years. Good times were back for the people of Boston, and for this "Son of the Bean and the Cod" as well. Decked out in a U.S. Maritime Service Chief Petty Officer's brass-buttoned uniform, with red hash marks on the sleeves denoting my years at sea, I liked to think I cut a dashing figure.

On one of my weekend visits to Boston that fall, Phil introduced me to Maura (Mary) Evans, an Irish lass who had come to America with her large family as a girl of eight. Standing there, in the portal between the dining room and living room of her Dorchester home, I was struck dumb by the beauty of this girl, intoxicated by her captivating Irish smile as she greeted me with a warm welcome to her home. I was at a complete loss for words as I gazed admiringly at her stylish mode of fall dress, her elegant mink coat, matching fur headpiece, smartly complementary tan leather shoes, handbag and gloves.

She was a breathtaking beauty, and before I realized what was happening I had fallen deeply in love with her. It was an instantaneous *fait accompli*, a deep love that I did not know I was capable of experiencing. I could not resist it, and it completely overwhelmed me.

I did not want this to happen because I was not prepared to have a meaningful relationship with any woman. My future involved the sea, war or not, and there was no room in my life for love and marriage. But I had no sooner laid eyes on this beautiful girl than I felt a powerful urge to hold her close and confess my love for her.

Sailors had a reputation for having a girl in every port. I had had my dalliances, but once I met Maura, she monopolized

Paul Gill and Mary Evans

my thoughts and I had no room in my heart or my life for any other girl. Our relationship rapidly blossomed into a spellbinding romance and, just weeks after that magical first meeting, I proposed to her at a Boston Bruins hockey game in Boston Garden. We were engaged to be married, but we decided to put off setting a wedding date for the time being.

The Japanese attacked Pearl Harbor on December 7, 1941, and I graduated from the Fort Trumbull Officer Training School and was commissioned an ensign in the U.S. Maritime Service three days later. The Coast Guard issued my Third Mate's ticket later that month. I was now licensed to navigate American vessels of any tonnage on any ocean.

The United States Lines offered me a berth as Third Mate on the S.S. *Nathanael Greene*, a Liberty Ship under construction in Wilmington, North Carolina. I accepted the position, and agreed to join the ship after she completed her sea trials, loaded her cargo, and signed on her crew at the end of March. The *Greene* was scheduled to depart New York on April 1, her ultimate destination Archangel in north Russia.

The S.S. *Nathanael Greene* was named after Revolutionary War Major General Nathanael Greene, a native of Rhode Island, who was considered General George Washington's most talented and most successful officer. The third of the 2,710 Liberty Ships to be built, she was 441 feet long, had a beam of 57 feet and a draft of 28 feet, and she displaced 7,366 tons. Her triple-expansion steam engine generated 2,500 horsepower, and her top speed was 11 knots.

While waiting for the *Greene* to be fitted out and complete her sea trials, I worked as a rigger in the Quincy, Massachusetts, Fore River Shipyard. I worked on the construction and fitting out of the U.S. Navy destroyers U.S.S. *Barton* and U.S.S. *Barclay*, the cruiser U.S.S. *San Juan*, and the battleship U.S.S. *Massachusetts*.

As the time approached for my departure, Maura and I experienced heart-wrenching sadness. Although we never spoke of it, we both realized that there was a good chance that we would never see each other again once I left for Russia. Every day, newspapers were full of stories of German U-boats sinking American merchant ships within sight of land off the East

The launching of S.S. *Nathanael Greene*, Wilmington, North Carolina, January 17, 1942

and Gulf Coasts. At that early stage in the war, more American merchant seamen had lost their lives to enemy action than had all branches of the military combined.

I was filled with remorse, ashamed that I had let our love affair blossom as it had, only to then sail away as though our love had never existed. I felt so cruel and selfish, but I had to go. As a ship rigger, I could easily obtain a draft deferment. But I was a professional mariner, not a shipyard worker, and my proper and natural role in life was to be on the bridge of a ship, whether or not there was a war going on.

In the meanwhile, relations with Maura's family deteriorated. Our betrothal, far from cementing bonds, alienated me from them. Naturally, they loved her and wanted to protect her. They did not want her to marry a sailor who had a girl in every port, or who would someday leave her on a sudden impulse to return to the sea, never to be seen again. They could not see that a woman could marry a professional seafarer and enjoy a happy married life.

Maura's mother refused to talk with her future son-in-law, and this complicated life for everyone. But this did not change our feelings for one another one bit. I was about to depart on a hazardous voyage under extremely dangerous war conditions, and we didn't know when or if we would ever see each other again. I felt very sad that Maura was suffering for my sake. It would not have helped to point out to Mrs. Evans that seafarers in my family had followed the sea for generations and had never encountered the kind of marital problems that she had conjured up. Nevertheless, I sensed that something would happen during the coming voyage that would remove the dark cloud which had cast a shadow over our relationship.

On March 31, 1942, I bid a tearful farewell to Maura at South Station in Boston, and boarded the train that would take me to New York City, the S.S. *Nathanael Greene*, and an unknowable future.

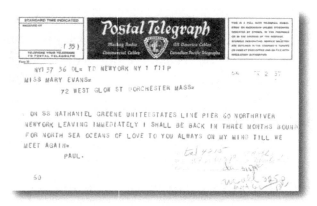

Telegram Paul sent to Mary

TEN

S.S. *NATHANAEL GREENE* SAILS TO THE WAR ZONE

The *Greene* Departs New York

DOCKED AT THE UNITED STATES Lines Pier 60 on the North River in New York Harbor, the S.S. *Nathanael Greene* was prepared to depart on its maiden voyage to north Russia to deliver ammunition and weapons to our Soviet ally.

I reported aboard ship at 0600 hours on April 1, 1942, and signed the ship's articles as Third Mate. I was assigned to the 4-to-8 watch; I would be on duty from 4:00 a.m. to 8:00 a.m. and from 4:00 p.m. to 8:00 p.m. when we were at sea. I reported to the bridge and introduced myself to Captain George Vickers, Chief Mate John Jones, and the other deck officers.

This was my first berth as a ship's officer, Third Mate, responsible to the ship's master for sailing operations and navigation on the morning and evening 4-to-8 watches. After six years of life in the fo'c'sle sailing as a seaman before the mast on American merchant ships, it was ego inflating to now be, at the age of twenty-one, an officer and a gentleman in the American Merchant Marine.

SS *Nathanael Greene*

We were scheduled to depart from port at 7 o'clock in the morning on my watch on the bridge. The pilot boarded at 6:30 a.m. and joined Captain Vickers in the wheelhouse on the bridge, warming up with a cup of coffee. The morning air was cold and damp, which was not unusual for New York Harbor at this time of year.

The quartermaster stood by at the wheel, and I was at the engine room telegraph, both of us waiting for orders from the captain. The Third Assistant Engineer and the engine room Black Gang on watch were at their stations, awaiting orders from the bridge. The Chief Mate was overseeing deck activities, issuing orders to the bosun at the gangway and to the mates at the bow and stern to order the deckhands to let go and haul in the fore and aft spring lines from the dock bollards. The deckhands then hauled the gangway aboard and were stationed at the bitts fore and aft with the mates, ready to let go and haul in the ship's bow, stern and breast mooring lines from the dock bollards.

The tug boats that had been ordered to move the ship away from the pier and out into the channel whistled as they came alongside, and the captain and pilot swung into action with orders. The course and speed were set by the pilot, who gave compass headings and wheel maneuvers to the quartermaster at the wheel, and engine room instructions to the mate at the engine room telegraph.

In turn, the captain shouted orders to the mates stationed at the bow and stern to take tug boat tow lines and to cast off and haul in the dock mooring lines. All orders were quickly carried out and the tug lines were let go when the vessel entered the channel and made way under her own power.

The *Greene* started downstream on the outgoing tide. When we reached the battery at the southern tip of Manhattan, we turned up into the East River and steamed along the east shore of Manhattan, past Roosevelt Island, and through Hell Gate, all the while fighting the powerful 5-knot current. When we came abreast of Rikers Island, the Jacob's ladder was thrown over the ship's side, and the pilot waved good luck to the master and crew before he descended to the waiting launch. Compass heading orders were issued to the quartermaster, who brought the ship's head on a course for Long Island Sound and a northeasterly passage along the New England coast, through the Cape Cod Canal, and then on to Halifax, Nova Scotia. There, the *Greene* would join a convoy for the crossing of the North Atlantic to Glasgow, Scotland.

Regular sea watches of four hours on and eight hours off were set for the deck and engine room merchant crews, and similar gun-station watches were set for the Naval Armed Guard crew members.

I was relieved from duty at the end of my morning watch by Mr. Smith, the 8-to-12 watch officer. I paused at the ship's rail on the Boat Deck outside my cabin to relax for a few moments, and to review the day's events before proceeding to the Officers' Mess for breakfast.

The silhouette of the Manhattan skyline was slowly dropping below the horizon as the ship steamed northeasterly through the waters of Long Island Sound. The surface of the water was calm, displaying not so much as a ripple in the calm air. The odd serenity of the scene invited reflection.

I thought back to the many exciting evenings I had spent drinking beer and dancing with young *Deutschen* in cabarets and *biergarten* on the Reeperbahn, or the afternoons I had spent strolling along the promenades of the Alster Pavilion with Heidi. How had things come to this pass that I would soon be locked in mortal combat in the frigid waters of the Arctic Ocean with the easy-going, intelligent and fun-loving young Germans I had once counted as friends? How was it possible that young *deutsche Matrosen* (German seamen) were at this very moment cruising these waters in U-boats, searching for American merchant ships such as the *Greene* to send to the bottom of the sea with a well-aimed torpedo?

As I leaned against the ship's rail, my attention was drawn to the life rafts suspended aloft against the mast shrouds, and the lifeboats swung out on their davits high over the sea below, ready for quick release and launching. I fought to suppress the images flashing through my mind of a stricken *Nathanael Greene*, smoke billowing from her superstructure, in a sinking condition, her officers and crew scrambling into these lifeboats. I knew these were not fantastical images, and that such a scene had a fair likelihood of becoming reality, whether on the broad North Atlantic, in the frozen wastes of the Arctic Ocean, or in the warm waters of the Mediterranean Sea, only God knew.

Then, my thoughts turned to my four merchant seamen brothers, all of them out there somewhere on the high seas hauling cargoes to Great Britain, the lone European power still fighting Nazi Germany. It comforted me to know that I was not the only one in the family braving U-boat-infested waters to bring material aid and moral comfort to our British allies, but I knew I wouldn't stop worrying about them until the war was over and peace returned once again to the oceans of the world.

Then, I thought of my personal situation. I was no stranger to a ship's wheelhouse. The better part of my seafaring years had been spent as quartermaster on many a ship's bridge, working with masters and mates in fair weather and foul. I was confident that I would prove to be a top-notch Merchant Marine officer. My only deficiencies had been a lack of comprehensive training in piloting and navigation for coastal and deep-water sailing and an insufficient understanding of the fundamentals of astronomy, oceanography, and meteorology. All of these deficiencies had been remedied by the training I received at Fort Trumbull. Now that I had completed the classroom work and acquired a Third Mate's license, all I needed was more real-world experience in ship handling, piloting, and navigation. I knew that it was only a matter of time before I would advance to a master's position on my own ship. I had learned the ropes of basic seamanship and ship-handling operations as a deckhand, and now I needed to acquire comparable expertise as a ship's navigator on the bridge.

Finally, my thoughts turned to Maura, and of our future together. I promised myself that, whatever challenges lay before me, I would survive and return to my one true love and make her my wife.

Halifax

At 7:30 p.m. on April 3, we arrived at the pilot station outside off Halifax, Nova Scotia. We picked up our pilot, steamed past a burning oil tanker at the harbor entrance, proceeded to Bedford Basin, and dropped anchor among fifty-two other merchant ships.

We remained in Halifax until April 11, 1942. I spent those eight days getting acquainted with the merchant crew and the sailors of the Naval Armed Guard, familiarizing myself with the *Greene's* construction, character and equipment, and learning what other men knew about the coming voyage and ports of call.

Captain George A. Vickers, "the skipper," was a master who ruled with an iron hand, with discipline for all and respect for none. He was a man of about forty-five years of age, twenty-five of which were spent following the sea. He was a fo'c'sle man who had worked his way "up the hawse pipe" to command of the bridge. He was of medium build and stature, with wavy gray hair that gave him a distinguished appearance. He was handsome and a real captain. He was also a hardass, like my father, who gave stern orders to officers and crew alike, with little regard for their rank. This caused some resentment among those with wavering hearts, but the skill and courage he displayed during battle won the respect and admiration of all hands, merchant and naval.

Radio operator John McNally, "Sparks," was a handsome young Irishman from Swanton, Vermont. John was always aglow with his vibrant personality, ready to laugh at the slightest provocation. He was well liked by the entire ship's company.

This was John's first trip to sea, yet he carried himself with the saltiness of a born sailor. With his handsome face and winning personality, he captured the hearts of young ladies wherever he went.

Chief Mate John Jones was a Welshman, but I did not know the origins of the Second Mate, Peter Smith, or any of the men in the Engine Department.

In addition to the forty-one members of the merchant crew, we had an eighteen-man Naval Armed Guard contingent on board the *Nathanael Greene*, under the command of Lt. (JG) Roy Billings. This was a young crew, and the first sea voyage for most of them. Nor did any of them have combat experience. By comparison, the merchant crewmen were world traveled and street wise, wary of newcomers to the sea, and toughened by years of sea duty.

From the beginning of the voyage, there was mutual and growing respect between the merchant and navy seamen. Both the merchant crew and the navy crew had a role to play in the safe operation of the vessel and protecting it from enemy action. It wasn't long before the two groups thought of themselves as the "ship's crew" rather than as separate merchant and navy crews. We were all patriotic Americans, and that was all that mattered. We sailed on a merchant man-of-war, a fighting ship.

The *Nathanael Greene* Sails for Scotland

Early in the morning of April 11, 1942, we weighed anchor

and headed seaward in two-column formation, our destination Loch Long, Scotland. The convoy (SC79) shifted from two columns to a broad-front formation after clearing Halifax harbor, and steamed in a zig-zag pattern until we approached the Scottish coast, when we reverted to a two-column formation.

Sixty-one merchant ships were escorted by seven Canadian corvettes until we reached British waters, where we picked up Royal Navy destroyers.

We ran through snow squalls for much of the voyage, and the ship rolled and pitched in heavy seas. The Armed Guard manned the gun stations around the clock, and were seasick for much of the passage. When the bad weather abated after we entered British waters, the escorts flew barrage balloons to thwart enemy air attacks.

We arrived at Loch Long at 11:25 a.m. on April 25 and dropped the hook. We remained at anchor for a month awaiting sailing orders. Sea watches were discontinued except for the anchor watches maintained by the members of both the deck and engine departments. Time passed ever so slowly, and it seemed that the forestay anchor ball would never be hauled down.

Members of both the merchant and gun crews made frequent visits to Glasgow and Edinburgh to see the sights and to enjoy some nightlife. The war had left its mark on both of these cities. There was a chronic shortage of food and consumer goods, and long work days, nightly blackouts and fear of bombing attacks sapped the morale of the Scots.

To while away the hours in the Loch, we tested our marksmanship with our .30-caliber Springfield rifles. These archaic weapons would be of no use whatsoever against enemy ships or aircraft. Fortunately, they were replaced by the M-1 rifle, a much more powerful weapon.

This rifle practice made me think back to my time in Hamburg, where almost every nightclub had a shooting gallery where the customers could demonstrate their marksmanship and win prizes for their sweethearts. These shooting galleries were very popular with the young German men, especially among the soldiers, sailors and airmen. It was a thrill to compete with them, especially with the Luftwaffe men I befriended. They were good, but I held my own, which was impressive inasmuch as the only shooting experience I had was with BB rifles as a young boy. Never did I imagine that I would someday, not too many years hence, be engaged in a real-life, face-to-face, shooting competition with such young men, this time shooting to kill.

When I demonstrated the marksmanship skills that I had developed, the armed guard and merchant crew were most impressed. I baffled them with my ability to shoot cans out of the air with the Springfield rifle. I was proud of myself, because I had no previous experience with this rifle. Maybe my keen marksmanship could be ascribed to the hours I spent with my twin brother at the dump, sifting through the trash for redeemable whiskey bottles, and tossing an occasional bottle at a rat foraging for food, or at a seagull squawking overhead. This was our early artillery practice, and it paid dividends in later years.

Loch Long to Sunderland, England

On May 25, 1942, Captain Vickers attended a convoy conference on another vessel, and when he returned he gave the command to prepare the *Greene* to put to sea. We sailed along the Scottish coast in a small convoy to Loch Ewe, where we anchored on May 27. The captain attended another conference, where he received orders to set sail the next day for the Firth of Forth, on the east coast of Scotland, in the North Sea. We sailed in company with the S.S. *Charles McCormack* and the S.S. *Point San Pedro*, and arrived at the Firth on May 30th at 11:00 a.m. and dropped anchor. Captain Vickers and John McNally attended yet another convoy conference. We weighed anchor the next morning and departed for Sunderland, England, about one-hundred miles down the coast, on the North Sea.

We docked in Sunderland on June 3, and several Oerlikon 20mm anti-aircraft guns were installed on the *Nathanael Greene*. We started training on these wonderful weapons as soon as they were bolted to the deck. The Oerlikon was a highly effective close-range anti-aircraft gun, capable of firing up to 300 rounds per minute. We trained every day for six days, until we had proven to our instructors that we could handle the weapons.

Enemy Air Raids

We had been sailing between Scottish and English ports since we arrived in the United Kingdom in April. Some of these ports had been severely damaged by enemy air raids and reduced to a mass of ruins. I experienced my first air raid while we were in Sunderland. Around 1:30 a.m. on June 5th, I was awakened by the general alarm to report to my gun station. I assumed it was only a drill.

Suddenly, a terrific explosion sounded close by. I flew to my station! By this time, the sky was all lit up with exploding AA (anti-aircraft) shells and manganese flares dropped by enemy aircraft to illuminate their targets on the ground below. What a powerful barrage the English were putting up with their AA guns! It sounded like one continuous roar of thunder. The enemy bombers were apparently targeting the docks and ships. The bombs made a blood-curdling whistle as they fell earthward.

We had received orders not to open fire lest we give our ship's position away. We could hear the shrapnel falling on the ships' decks all around us, and when a whistling bomb sounded close by, we would drop to the deck to seek cover. It was extremely frightening. We had no idea how many planes were attacking us, but the ceaseless roar of their engines as they soared overhead and the length of the attack indicated that the Nazis were attempting to inflict serious damage on the port of Sunderland. RAF (Royal Air Force) Spitfire and Hurricane fighter aircraft drove the Luftwaffe bombers off and back to France, and the "ALL CLEAR" siren was finally sounded at around 4:00 a.m.

Later that morning, the traitorous Lord Haw-Haw (his real name was William Joyce), broadcast in English on German radio that the previous night's air raid had demolished Sunderland's docking facilities. The British authorities did not reveal the actual extent of the damages, as was their standard policy. I was soon to learn that the Germans were excellent propagandists, but the British were better fighters.

Sunderland to Middlesbrough

On June 14, 1942, the *Greene* steamed a few miles down the English coast and a mile up the River Tees to the port of Middlesbrough. We were idle until June 21, when we started transferring Canadian Matilda and Valentine tanks from S.S. *Reigh Count* to the *Greene*. That night, engine-room cadet Bob Gordon and I went to the Grand Hotel and tied one on. On the night of June 25-26, a massive air armada flew overhead and out over the North Sea. We learned the next day that this was a 1,000-bomber RAF raid on Bremen, a revenge attack to atone for the British defeat at Tobruk in North Africa.

The *Greene* Returns to Loch Ewe

On June 27, we departed Middlesbrough, steamed north for two days, and anchored off Methil in the Firth of Forth on June 29. Captain Vickers attended a convoy conference in Methil, and was appointed commodore of a small convoy that left for Loch Ewe the next morning. We arrived in Loch Ewe on July 1, 1942, and dropped the hook.

Reykjavik, Iceland

On July 2, we departed Loch Ewe and, after a passage of three days, dropped the hook in Hvalfjord, a long fjord near Reykjavik. It was an uneventful passage other than for our accidentally attempting to shoot down a British Hudson bomber that was flying reconnaissance over the convoy.

On July 8, the battleship U.S.S. *Washington*, the cruisers U.S.S. *Tuscaloosa* and U.S.S. *Wichita*, and the Royal Navy battlecruiser H.M.S. *Renown* all came to anchor in Hvalfjord. During the three weeks we were in Hvalfjord awaiting sailing instructions, we saw several severely-damaged merchant ships straggle into the anchorage. One vessel had lost her bow and was towed stern-first by a destroyer. From what little we could gather from conversations with the crews of these ships, conditions on the Russian run sounded too unbelievable to be true. Rumor had it that as soon as a convoy cleared the minefields north of Iceland, high-flying German Condor reconnaissance planes started shadowing the convoy, updating U-boats in the vicinity and Luftwaffe units based in Norway on the convoy's position, speed and bearing. Submarine and air attacks would gradually increase in frequency and intensity, culminating in all-out attacks when the convoy reached the waters between Bear Island and Spitsbergen (now called Svalbard) in an effort to destroy the merchant ships and their escorts.

I learned after the war that these ships were all part of the ill-fated convoy PQ17. Acting on intelligence indicating that heavy German surface units, including the battleship *Tirpitz,* had sortied and were about to pounce on the convoy, First Sea Lord Dudley Pound feared that the Royal Navy escorts would be unable to protect the convoy, and ordered it to scatter. U-boats and Luftwaffe torpedo aircraft and bombers savaged the convoy. Twenty-three merchant ships were sunk, and only eleven made it to Russian ports. As it turned out, *Tirpitz* never left its anchorage in Trondheimfjord.

Desperate for ways to pass the time while riding at anchor waiting for sailing orders, we organized a boat race on July 9. The Deck gang defeated the Engine Room gang, naturally. Occasionally, the crew would organize softball games ashore as well.

On July 16, a large convoy of merchant ships arrived in the anchorage from the United States. The next day, I visited the hospital ship U.S.S. *Herman Melville* to pick up medical supplies for the *Greene.* That afternoon, seven more Navy gunners joined our Armed Guard, raising their numbers to twenty-six from the original nineteen. One of these sailors looked like he was fourteen years old!

On July 22, I visited the S.S. *Mary Luckenbach* to see her Second Mate and her bosun, both of whom I had sailed with on her sister ship, the S.S. *J.L. Luckenbach.*

On July 25, merchant ships slowly started slipping out of the anchorage. Twenty-seven ships remained at anchor in the fjord.

On July 27, Captain Vickers and John McNally went ashore

to collect sand to use in case the ship was struck by incendiary bombs. They came back empty-handed.

The crew was in the grip of channel fever. We wanted to get on with the trip, come what may. Nerves were taut to begin with, but things got worse when the *Greene* went aground on the night of July 29, on Second Mate Smith's watch. Captain Vickers was in a rage, and the night was shattered with his blasting attack on Smith's seamanship. Sleep was impossible for the rest of the night.

Back to Loch Long

On August 3, 1942, we weighed anchor and steamed in convoy formation on a southeasterly course, bound for Loch Long. The convoy zig-zagged and maintained a speed of 7 knots. The scuttlebutt was that we were headed for Russia by way of the Persian Gulf. This was wishful thinking, as it turned out. We ran into heavy fog as we passed the Hebrides, and the convoy went into two-column formation. We arrived in Loch Long on August 8 and anchored. Liberty launches made two trips daily between the ship and Gourock. From Gourock we walked to Greenock, and from Greenock we took a bus to Glasgow, about a half-hour trip. In Glasgow, we generally stayed at Mrs. Maxwell's Bed and Breakfast, near the Hotel Beresford, a favorite watering hole for visiting American seamen and servicemen.

Several large American army transports pulled into Loch Long while we were anchored there, including one ship, the U.S.S. *Wakefield*, that I immediately recognized as the former S.S.*Manhattan,* the passenger liner I had made two voyages to Europe on in 1937. The *Manhattan* had been requisitioned by the U.S.Navy, renamed the U.S.S. *Wakefield*, and converted to a troopship.

Gourock on Loch Long, Scotland

On August 20, Captain Vickers attended a commodore's conference with the masters of the other thirty-two merchant ships anchored in Loch Long. At 3:00 p.m. the next afternoon, we weighed anchor and sailed for Loch Ewe. The morale of the *Greene's* crew was poor at this point, as we seemed to be just moving from one desolate anchorage to another and not accomplishing anything.

We arrived at Loch Ewe at 9:00 a.m. on August 23, 1942. The next day, S.S. *Empire Morn* and the Liberty Ship S.S. *Patrick Henry* joined the forming convoy, and the S.S. *Benjamin Rush* arrived on August 28.

On August 26, officers of the British rescue ship *Copeland* came aboard the *Nathanael Greene* to tell us what to expect from the Germans on our voyage to Archangel.

It was clear to every member of the *Nathanael Greene's*

crew that, four months after arriving in the United Kingdom loaded to the gunwales with war materiel, and after swinging at anchor in one remote anchorage after another, day after endless day, the balloon was going up.

ELEVEN

ARMAGEDDON IN THE
ARCTIC OCEAN

Wednesday, September 2, 1942

A T LAST THE DAY HAS arrived to sail for Archangel, U.S.S.R., our destined port of discharge. Five months ago yesterday we sailed from New York, thinking that, at the longest, the trip would take about three and a half months. But we were in for disappointment. I had hoped and planned for a short voyage. But now, tired of speculating and hoping against hope, I am inclined to be fatalistic, so let come what may. The decision has at last been made. We were now en route to Archangel, Russia, by way of the North Atlantic Ocean, the Arctic Ocean, the Barents Sea, the White Sea, and the Dvina River.

The Loch was bustling with activity as the convoy's merchant ships and naval escort vessels readied for the voyage. Last-minute tasks included loading fuel, taking on water, replenishing ship's stores and supplies, checking armament and ammunition readiness, final dispatches of ship's mail and crew correspondence and, lastly, attendance by all captains and senior officers at the commodore's conference for receipt of their final sailing orders.

Captain Vickers returned from the commodore's conference early that afternoon and we weighed anchor soon after. We maneuvered into convoy column position and proceeded seaward, bound for Archangel, Russia. By nightfall, we had cleared the minefields and were well out to sea. Winds of gale force from the southwest, with heavy squalls and a rough, heavy, confused sea and ground swells shielded the convoy from enemy craft throughout the night.

When I was relieved of my watch at 8:00 p.m., I turned in, clothes and all, ready for any emergency that might occur during the night. Though I was very tired, I found it difficult to sleep. My thoughts rambled through the recent past, and I wondered whether I would ever return home or see Mary again. Before leaving Loch Ewe, I had written and mailed letters to Mary, her mother, Mom and Dad, and my sister, Jean, and her husband, Jim. These letters could have been my last. I did not know what to write; I didn't want to frighten them.

Thursday, September 3, 1942

Vessel rolling and pitching in rough, heavy southwesterly sea and swell. Moderate southwesterly gale with heavy rain squalls prevailing throughout the day. Late in the afternoon, the vessel started shipping water over her decks and hatches. Laboring and straining, rolling 20-25 degrees at times. Visibility lowering. About 9:00 p.m., we shipped a heavy sea forward which shifted the deck cargo. The strength of the wind increased to a strong gale. Cargo was dangerously adrift in #4 hold after a heavy roll of the vessel, so the master decided to "heave to" to wind and sea for the safety

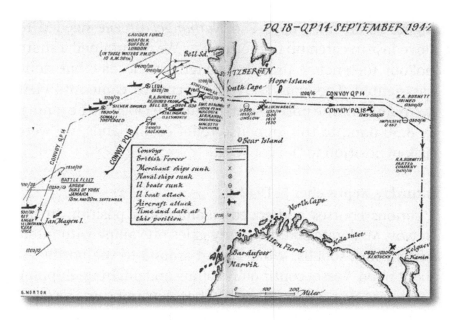

Route of convoy PQ18 and initial U-boat dispositions

of the vessel. Other vessels in the convoy were also having difficulty and hove to as well.

Within a few hours, we had lost sight of all other convoy vessels. The menace of enemy aircraft was then added to the stress of severe weather conditions. We were in a precarious predicament. Our vessel was well armed and prepared for enemy action under convoy conditions, but under the present circumstances we were no match for an enemy submarine or surface vessel attack.

Friday, September 4, 1942

At dawn, wind and sea let up some, so the master ordered the helmsman to bring the ship's head around to the north-west, and orders were given to ring up FULL AHEAD on the engine room telegraph. The *Nathanael Greene* needed to move fast to catch up to the convoy. We maintained a sharp lookout for enemy aircraft throughout the day, but none was sighted. The main body of the convoy came into view two points off the port bow at around 7 o'clock that evening. By 8:30 p.m., to the immense relief of all hands, we were back in position in the convoy.

Saturday, September 5, 1942

Various courses and speeds maintaining position in the convoy. Moderate southwesterly gales prevailing with intermittent rain squalls. Wind hauled around to the northwest about noon. Vessel continually rolling and pitching, shipping heavy seas over the decks and hatches. A warning was received from the commodore that enemy submarines were in the vicinity. Destroyers continuously dropping depth charges.

Sunday, September 6, 1942

Wind and sea conditions remained the same throughout the day. Vessels of the convoy endeavoring, with extreme difficulty, to maintain their proper convoy positions, yet this is generally impossible due to the severe weather conditions.

Monday, September 7, 1942

The weather conditions improved within the lee of Iceland, which was sighted at 7:30 a.m. The convoy remained in sight of land throughout the day.

Tuesday, September 8, 1942

This morning, ten more merchant ships joined the convoy off the west coast of Iceland, bringing the total number of merchantmen in the convoy to forty-three. The escorting warships apparently include twenty destroyers, two AA cruisers, two light cruisers, two submarines, and three rescue vessels. The convoy was now headed northeast after an alteration of course this afternoon off the northwest coast of Iceland. The waters that the convoy was now steaming through were treacherous. They were heavily mined, and many of our own convoy vessels had ended their voyage at this point. Strong northeasterly winds with heavy rain squalls prevailing, with a rough, heavy sea and swell.

Wednesday, September 9, 1942

Convoy steaming through dense fog banks. Frequent heavy snow squalls with blinding sleet from the north as the mercury dropped to 32 degrees Fahrenheit. Vessel rolling and pitching heavily and shipping seas over the foredeck.

Thursday, September 10, 1942

Wind and sea moderated in the early hours of the morning, as the convoy passed through occasional patches of fog. Destroyers commenced dropping depth charges. Convoy continuously maneuvering to evade U-boat attacks. Depth charges are being dropped so relentlessly and the explosions are so powerful that the ship is in a constant state of vibration. This keeps us in a state of heightened anxiety, not knowing whether an explosion is a depth charge going off nearby or we have been struck by a torpedo. A British aircraft carrier, HMS *Avenger*, joined the convoy. The inner group of escort destroyers and cruisers formed a tighter ring around the merchant ships, endeavoring to form an impregnable defensive ring against enemy submarines.

Friday, September 11, 1942

While communicating with the commodore in Morse code at 4:30 this morning, we could hear an aircraft circling over the convoy. Dense fog made it impossible to determine the approach bearing of the aircraft. Suddenly, it dove to a height of about 300 feet over the *Greene*, and then immediately ascended to a higher altitude. It was only visible for two or three seconds, but it had all the markings of a German Dornier long-distance bomber. Two hours later, we received a message from the commodore telling us that we could expect an air raid attack that night or the next day.

The *Nathanael Greene* was experiencing difficulty maintaining our assigned column position because of the poor station-keeping performance of the vessel ahead of us. The commodore approved our request to switch positions with this vessel, the SS *John Penn*, from position #72 to position #73.

The convoy fought heavy seas and swells most of the day in a moderate northeasterly gale and blinding snow squalls. We dreaded the thought of taking to our lifeboats in such conditions.

Saturday, September 12, 1942

Prevailing weather conditions unchanged. The convoy is now north of the Arctic Circle (latitude 66 degrees, 33.00 minutes north) and in the Arctic Ocean. We have passed many half-submerged lifeboats and liferafts, with oars, life jackets and flotsam close by. They were badly damaged by enemy action, and we cringed at the thought of what had happened to their former occupants.

Sunday, September 13, 1942

From this day until our arrival in the U.S.S.R., we were in-

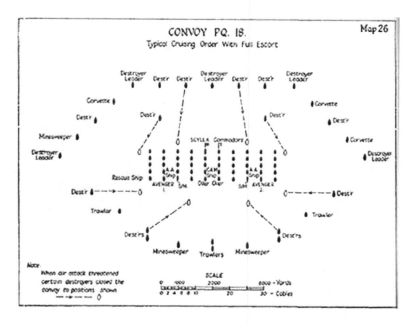

Convoy PQ18 Cruising Order

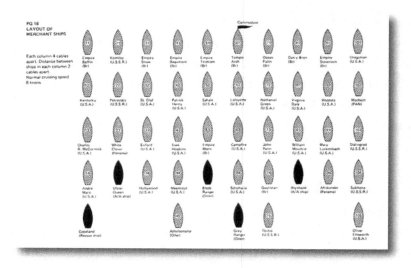

Convoy PQ18 Merchant Ships Formation. SS *Nathanael Greene* was originally #72, but changed places with #73 SS *John Penn* on September 11.

This painting was done by US Navy artist Lt. Commander Griffith Coale, USNR, while serving on a vessel escorting this convoy. It is titled "Convoy Off Iceland--Increasing Gale."

volved in the biggest convoy battle of World War II, according to the British Admiralty. We were attacked night and day from the air and from the sea. Forty-four out of about 120 attacking Luftwaffe aircraft were destroyed. The S.S. *Nathanael Greene* was credited with the destruction of nine enemy aircraft, and was recognized by the commodore as the fightingest merchant vessel in the convoy. The convoy's escorts destroyed at least four U-boats.

U-boat Attack

After being relieved of my 4:00 a.m. to 8:00 a.m. watch and having breakfast, I walked out to the boat deck to see how the vessels astern of us were holding their stations in the convoy. It was about 9:00 a.m., and other members of the crew were walking the decks and casually studying the positions of other vessels in the convoy.

Without warning, the cold still morning air was split by the sound of a thunderous explosion on our starboard quarter. A Russian vessel, the *Stalingrad*, had been torpedoed by a U-boat. What remained of her crew could be seen swimming in the ice-cold, white-capped water. Destroyers raced to the vicinity of the sinking vessel and dropped depth charge after depth charge. Minutes later, another horrendous explosion ripped through the air, again from the starboard quarter. An American vessel, the Liberty Ship S.S. *Oliver Ellsworth*, had been torpedoed by another U-boat. Her crew quickly took to the lifeboats and abandoned ship.

The *Stalingrad* was going down fast by the stern. Suddenly, her bow tilted up to the heavens, as if begging God for salvation, and then quickly disappeared beneath the waves. The *Oliver Ellsworth* was sinking slowly. After her lifeboats cleared the fatally-wounded vessel, destroyers moved in and shelled her, sending her to the bottom so that the enemy couldn't salvage her.

The convoy maintained its course and speed during the enemy action, and the *Stalingrad* and *Oliver Ellsworth* survivors were picked up by the rescue craft that steamed astern of the convoy.

The general alarm had been sounded for submarine attack, and all hands had rushed to their stations with their helmets and life jackets, prepared for action. I was in charge of ammunition readiness for the four-inch surface gun and the machine guns at the stern gun stations. Lieutenant Roy Billings of the Naval Armed Guard had advised me that over 20,000 rounds of ammunition had been clipped and readied at my gun station, and that there was no need to clip any more in the magazine.

A sharp lookout was maintained for U-boats. Sporadic

machine gun fire could be heard from vessels astern of us which were shooting at the water. The destroyers did not let up on their depth-charge attack against the submerged submarines. The air temperature dropped to well below freezing, which added to our misery. The U-boats continued to harass us until about 11:30 a.m., when we were dismissed from our gun stations. We went to the messrooms amidships for lunch, leaving the Naval Armed Guard on the lookout for the enemy.

Heinkel 111s Attack

No sooner had we left our gun stations than the general alarm sounded for enemy aircraft attack. We raced to our stations and searched the horizon for the enemy. We found them. God almighty! They were approaching from the south, the convoy's starboard side. They were coming right out of the sun, and we were almost blinded when we looked in their direction. It looked like a swarm of giant black locusts was coming to attack us!

There was a warning shout from amidships. A submarine was sighted close by on our starboard bow! Our three-inch AA gun at the bow station opened fire at it, followed by machine gun fire from all of our gun stations. The gunfire quickly forced the U-boat to dive.

The enemy planes were flying just a few feet over the surface of the water on our starboard bow, towards the head of the convoy. I started to count them: 1, 2...13, 14..."Damn it! Look at them!" I yelled. There were too many to count. My God! The way they maneuvered, too! Hedgehopping over the seas and zig-zagging. Our anti-aircraft defense and gun-laying training at the Royal Navy base in Sunderland was most comprehensive, but did not prepare us for this mode of attack!

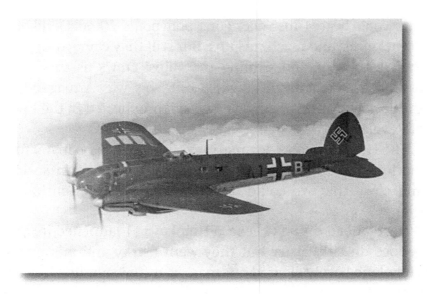

Heinkel 111 Torpedo Bomber

The AA cruisers and destroyers steamed at flank speed to position themselves ahead of the convoy, and then turned broadside to the enemy aircraft. Suddenly, the enemy formation altered course and started flying down the columns of merchant ships. The escort vessels unleashed a furious barrage of AA fire at the attackers, which were in turn spitting machine-gun fire at the merchantmen.

We identified the attacking aircraft as Heinkel 111 torpedo-bombers. They approached the convoy line-abreast, and then separated into groups that flew comb-like down the columns of merchant ships. Flames erupted, first from the guns of the destroyers in the starboard, outer ring of escorts, and then from the warships of the inner ring of defense and from the merchant vessels. Every naval and merchant vessel in the convoy opened up on the attacking planes with every weapon that would bear: 4-inch deck guns, pom poms, 20mm Oerlikons, Bofors guns, and machine guns. But still they came, dropping their torpedoes and strafing the ships' crews as they flew overhead at masthead height. God! This was Armageddon, the decisive battle of good versus evil prophesied in the Book of Revelation.

The Heinkels were decimating our side of the convoy formation, the starboard flank. They were coming in so low and close that we could have thrown our ammunition at them!

Dead ahead of the *Greene*, a Heinkel 111 launched its torpedoes directly at us, but they went astray and missed us. The plane barely cleared our mast as it flew overhead. Every gun on the ship concentrated its fire on this plane: our Oerlikons, 50-caliber Brownings, and 30-caliber Marlin machine guns poured thousands of rounds of ammunition into him and tore him to pieces before he plunged into the water. None of the crew emerged from the wreckage. All that could be seen where it hit the water on our starboard quarter was its rudder and part of its fuselage with a large swastika.

We were expending ammunition much faster than we had anticipated we would, and it had to be replenished. The magazine was three decks below our stern gun stations, well below the water line, and crammed with tons of shells and machine-gun bullets. It was not a place any sane person wanted to be while under enemy attack. Nevertheless, I got three of the crew to go down there with me to clip rounds into belts. We alternated tracer and armor-piercing shells. A red one...two black ones...or a black one...two red ones...We laughed and joked like crazy men about how nice it would be if a torpedo hit the magazine, as we would never know what happened. To calm ourselves, we sang "Praise the Lord and Pass the Ammunition!," "Hallelujah, Here We Come, Right Back Where We Started From!" and "The Battle Hymn of the Republic." The tension was nearly unbearable, and our emotions were at the breaking point. Our odd behavior reflected our state of near-insanity.

Suddenly, the vessel lurched and we were thrown over the ammunition cases and sent sprawling over the deck. Assuming we had been torpedoed, we jumped to our feet and ran up the three sets of ladders to our gun stations. The men in the gun nests pointed to starboard, where we could see a patch of flames on the water's surface.

I immediately thought of the English vessel that had been abeam of us, four ship lengths distant, and asked where she was. No one said a word. The vessel had been loaded with ammunition, and a torpedo-bomber had flown over her, dropped her "fish," and then *PHTTT*! Plane and ship blew up together. Not a damned thing was to be seen of either ship or plane.

This devastating explosion was what had thrown us off our feet down in the magazine. I stood there for a moment, stunned. There was nothing to see but the dust of death settling on the water. I was shocked that a 10,000 ton ship and an airplane had just disappeared into thin air. Then, I turned and looked at the havoc that was being wreaked in and over the sea all around me. What destruction! Vessels ablaze and sinking all around us. Those damned Heinkels, still roaring in to attack us! I thought for sure this was the end. My God, those bastards! All our guns were blazing, but still they came at us, attacking again and again! This was Hell. I can't say just how I felt, but I thought I would never live to see another day.

To be alive at this moment was an indescribably intense

experience. I had no hope of surviving this Hell. To hope that there would be another tomorrow would be asking the impossible. In England, I went to church for what I thought would be the last time. I wanted to be on the right side of God if I was to go through Hell on this voyage. I must have had a presentiment of some kind, although I surely did not have the imaginative powers to conjure up the Hellish scenario that I was now a part of.

Before leaving home and embarking on this fateful voyage, I had exuded confidence that I would return, and assured Mary, my betrothed, that all was well and that I would be home before Christmas. Never did I think that I would be sailing to Russia on a virtual time bomb! *Facere pax pro deus, familia, et alia*. Make peace with God, one's family, and with all. This thought was foremost in my mind before we departed Loch Ewe. I wrote to Mary, her mother, my parents and siblings, and my friends, to tell them that I loved them dearly and wished that I was back home with them. None of them knew where I was, where I was going, what perils I would confront, or whether we would ever meet again in this world. My house was in order, so let come what may. Not only was I fighting for my ship and my country, but for my very life as well. I had so much to live for. I would never give up!

What nerve the Nazi pilots had! They flew so low over our ship that we could clearly see their faces. Time after time, I was certain a Heinkel passing overhead was going to strike our mast or stack and come crashing down onto the *Nathanael Greene's* deck. As close as they were, no more than fifty feet at times, we couldn't miss them with our gunfire, although most of our 50-caliber machine gun bullets just bounced off their thick armor. But our 20mm Oerlikons were tearing huge chunks right out of their wings and fuselages. When a bullet-riddled Heinkel crashed into the frigid sea, there were rarely any survivors.

After sustaining heavy losses from the withering combined gunfire of the escorts and merchant ships, the torpedo-bombers flew off, re-grouped, and started circling the convoy, as though gathering their strength before delivering the final blow.

The temperature had dropped steadily throughout the day, and it was now well below freezing. None of us was dressed appropriately for the bitter cold weather, but we didn't dare leave our gun stations to fetch warm clothing. Heavy snow clouds hung over the convoy, and we prayed for a blizzard to hide us from the enemy and bring an end to the fighting for that day.

Ju 88s Take a Swipe at Us

Suddenly, through a break in the dense cloud cover, we saw a formation of high-level bombers flying directly overhead. Instantly, all our guns swung around and trained skyward. These aircraft were Junkers 88 bombers. The cruisers and destroyers quickly maneuvered into firing position and released a deafening barrage of AA fire at the bomber formation.

The *Greene's* forward three-inch AA gun was within firing range of the high-level bombers, but our other guns were not. Bombs started to drop on the convoy, all apparently missing, but casting up mountainous geysers when they struck the sea and exploded.

We could see the bombs coming down on us in groups of three, emitting a spine-chilling whistle as they fell. We could only watch with dread and a feeling of complete and utter helplessness as they grew larger and larger, wondering which bomb was meant for us.

One of the Ju 88s seemed to have selected the *Nathanael Greene* for destruction. It dropped its bomb load directly above us, and we waited and waited for the bombs to hit us and send us to Kingdom Come. But the bombs cleared our ship and now were on a path to hit the S.S. *John Penn*, the vessel four ship lengths astern of us. The first two bombs hit the sea just forward of the *Penn*, but the third bomb went right down the smokestack! There was a thunderous explosion as the ship's boilers erupted and sent a geyser of steam hundreds of feet into the air. The *Penn* slowly fell astern of the convoy and started to sink. This was the vessel that we had switched positions with two days previously. But for that switch, it would be the *Greene* and not the *Penn* that would be gliding down to her watery grave in the frigid waters of the Arctic Ocean.

One of the AA cruisers was so intensely engaged in evasive maneuvering that it appeared to be completely inundated as bombs exploded in the water around it. We thought this ship had had it, but it came back into view again, its guns blazing away.

The 20mm Oerlikon on the flying bridge deck immediately above me opened fire towards the stern, and the shells were whizzing by just inches from my body. Vessels all around us were firing all of their guns, and our vessel was caught in the crossfire. It was too dangerous to risk running across the afterdeck to my gun station, so I fell to the deck for cover. Looking astern, I could see the target of the gunfire, a lone Heinkel 111. It had absorbed thousands of rounds of AA, but somehow remained airborne. The gunfire subsided for a few moments, and I took this opportunity to rush to my gun station. Since this gun station was in an elevated position on the poop deck, well above the main deck, it was very exposed to the continuing crossfire. We were forced to seek cover until the gunfire subsided.

The Heinkel 111 was trying to escape by flying to the rear of the convoy. I could not understand how it managed to stay aloft. It seemed to be moving at 30 knots or less, just gliding along a few feet over the surface of the water, apparently oblivious to its inevitable fate. Escape was impossible. Finally, its fuel tanks were hit by gunfire, she exploded into flames, and disintegrated after plowing into the sea. Her crew was caught in the flames and could not escape.

Junkers 88 Bomber

When the gunfire stopped, a vigilant watch was maintained for a brief period, and then dismissal from gun stations was sounded on the ship's whistle. Before turning in, I joined my shipmates for some hot coffee and a cigarette. We discussed the action we had just been through. Of the men who had been in combat before, none could say that they had ever seen such intense action as they had witnessed this day. Some of the men had been torpedoed or bombed before, but none of their previous experiences were as nerve-wracking as this. It was something they would never forget.

Morale was high, but every one of us was fully alert and prepared for whatever Hell the enemy might bring next. That evening, German radio claimed that the day's battle in the Arctic Ocean was the beginning of another convoy catastrophe for the Allies. But the Germans had another thought coming, for there was plenty of fighting spirit left in the men of the convoy, despite having lost today's battle. The Navy and merchant crews had displayed plenty of courage in the face of an enemy Hell-bent on dealing death and destruction to the convoy. Despite being repeatedly strafed by machine gun and cannon fire, our naval armed guard and merchant crew remained in their gun stations and fought like demons.

In order for the Heinkel 111s to launch their torpedoes, they had to fly close to the surface of the water and directly at their targets. At that height, they were level with the ships' decks, so the raking of our crossfire across each other's decks was unavoidable.

Monday, September 14, 1942

At about 1:10 a.m., the general alarm sounded for submarine attack, and I ran like Hell to my gun station. With the ship in complete blackout, I was unable to see in the dark alleyways. As I started to pass through a doorway to the open deck, a heavy blackout curtain hindered my progress. I tore down the curtain and raced to my station.

We searched the water for submarines for an hour or so, and then were dismissed from our gun stations. Around 2:30 a.m., the alarm for submarine attack was again sounded. When we reached our stations, we heard an explosion on our port quarter. A U-boat had torpedoed an oil tanker. Vessels astern of us sighted the submarine and fired at it, but the machine-gun bullets just ricocheted off the surface of the water like ping pong balls. The U-boat vanished and the gunfire stopped. Once more, those of us off watch made our way back to our quarters to get some well-deserved sleep. We were worn out. The enemy would just not leave us alone; he attacked relentlessly.

Hell from the Heavens

I reported for duty on the bridge at 4:30 a.m. It was bitterly cold, with occasional snow flurries. The darkness yielded to the first rays of the rising sun around 5:00 a.m. To the north, I could make out the loom of the land--Spitsbergen. It looked like a giant iceberg, and certainly no place to be shipwrecked. The day before we had passed Bear Island to the south. Spitsbergen was the last land we would see until we arrived at the entrance to the White Sea. If we survived that long.

At 6:17, the commodore sent up a flag hoist to warn us of approaching enemy planes. The crew mustered to our gun stations, but no enemy planes materialized. We were dismissed from gun stations and I returned to the bridge. When I was relieved at 8:00 a.m., I went to my cabin and, without bothering to undress, quickly fell into a deep sleep.

At noon, I was jolted awake by the general alarm. I jumped out of bed and joined the frantic rush to gun stations to fend off an attack by high- and low-altitude bombers. I had thought heavy cloud cover would afford us protection from bombers, but I was disabused of this notion by the sight of bombs falling in the openings between clouds. The only indication we had that there were bombers overhead was the hum of their engines and the whistle of the falling bombs. Occasionally, we would see a plane in the openings between clouds.

The naval escorts opened up on the raiders with all of their guns. HMS *Avenger*, our aircraft carrier, steered into the wind and sent six of her Sea Hurricane fighters aloft. As the fighters took off, they dipped their wings in salute to the convoy before flying off to engage the enemy.

None of *Avenger's* aircraft participated in yesterday's battle and, so far, had only flown scouting missions. But now that they were airborne and in hot pursuit of the enemy, we cheered them wildly from the decks of our merchant ships. The AA fire from the Royal Navy cruisers and destroyers forced the Ju-88s above cloud level, and the Sea Hurricanes forced them back down into the naval gunfire, or drove them away from the convoy. After the last enemy bomber disappeared, we were dismissed from our action stations and returned to our amidships quarters.

But only briefly. No sooner had we started to unwind than the general alarm sounded again for another air attack! Back in our gun stations, we spotted the enemy planes on the starboard side of the convoy. "My God!" I said. "Look at them come! There's no use trying to count them." They were torpedo-bombers, squadrons of Heinkel 111s that from a distance looked like swarms of attacking hornets. All of our guns trained on them as they flew in tight formation ahead of the convoy.

We wondered whether they would attempt to split the convoy in two, as they had tried to do yesterday. The cruisers and destroyers had turned broadside to the enemy formation and were starting to hammer them with every gun they had. As the enemy formation flew over the first line of escort vessels, it split into two separate formations. One attacked the escort ships, and the other started to fly at low altitude down the columns of merchant ships and launch torpedoes.

The *Nathanael Greene's* forward 3.5-inch gun fired the first shot by a merchantman at the oncoming torpedo-bombers. It made a direct hit on the squadron leader, blowing his fuselage in two. The other merchantmen then opened fire on the attackers.

Perhaps provoked by our destruction of their squadron

leader, seven Heinkel 111s attacked the *Greene*. But we threw up a wall of lead with our 3.5-inch AA guns, our 20mm Oerlikons, our .50-caliber Brownings, and our .30-caliber Marlins. We gave them everything we had. What a blaze of gunfire! Our guns tore the Hell out of them, and every Heinkel that flew over our ship passed by us in flames.

S.S. *Mary Luckenbach* Explodes

I was in the port side machine gun nest with Blackie. He manned the gun as I directed the gun laying. I would find a target for Blackie, he would fire on it, and I would find the next target. There were many to choose from. But we had to move fast. There was no time for indecision. The Heinkels were spraying us with machine gunfire, and were just as determined to kill us as we were to kill them.

The *Greene* was zigzagging now, as bombs were dropping all around us. Captain Vickers sighted two torpedoes coming right at us off our port bow. "Hard left wheel!" he ordered. The quartermaster responded instantly, and the ship's bow

The SS *Mary Luckenbach* explodes

swung sharply to port to dodge the torpedoes. As the ship swung into the turn, her stern turned toward the S.S. *Mary Luckenbach*, which was falling back from abeam of us to our starboard quarter. I was looking at the *Luckenbach* directly astern of us when a sudden giant ball of fire erupted from her. As the shock wave of the explosion hit me, I yelled "Duck!" at the top of my lungs and we both fell to the deck of the gun nest.

The force of the *Mary Luckenbach* explosion was terrifying. Our vessel was lifted from the sea and shook violently as the obliterated ammunition ship rained down on us in the form of shrapnel. We were enshrouded in a dense cloud of black smoke. The air was saturated with dust and fouled by the acrid smell of gunpowder. We didn't know whether the *Nathanael Greene* was going to remain afloat or plunge to the bottom of the Barents Sea.

We climbed over the gun nest wall onto the poop deck, and then dove over the rail to the main deck below and crawled under cover. Ten thousand tons of ship and cargo had been pulverized and blown sky high in an instant and were now falling from the heavens, covering our ship and the sea around it with what had once been the S.S. *Mary Luckenbach*. Tons and tons of shrapnel continued to fall about us in every size and in cruel and grotesque shapes and patterns.

The smoke around our gun nest gradually cleared, but the bridge and midship housing were still invisible. The afterdeck rigging was in ribbons. The crates encasing the fighter planes, which had been chained to the cargo hatches, had disintegrated, and the tanks destined for Stalingrad were adrift of their anchor chains. Everything within sight was battered by the concussion and vacuum created by the explosion. Our clothing was ripped and torn by the blast, and saturated with shrapnel. The forward part of the ship must have been blown to bits.

I looked over the ship's side and saw the propeller slowly turning. Not knowing whether we were going to sink or remain afloat, I didn't know what we should do: dive overboard and swim clear of the sinking ship's suction, or hang on and wait for rescue by a destroyer. The latter seemed unlikely, considering how quickly the enemy pounced on and destroyed crippled merchant ships during yesterday's combat action.

As I pondered our fate, the dense black smoke started to dissipate and the rain of shrapnel subsided. Looking forward, I could make out the outline of the bridge. I was surprised that it was still there. Then, I heard the ship's whistle signaling us to report to boat stations. I made sure that all the men in the after gun stations were accounted for and on their way to the lifeboats.

Looking aft from my gun station, I was stunned to see the mate lying prone on the afterdeck, sobbing hysterically and trying to claw through the steel plating to escape the shells, bullets and falling shrapnel. Captain Vickers looked down at the man from the bridge and shouted at him to get up and return to his post. When the mate failed to respond to his command, Vickers ran into the wheelhouse and emerged with a Colt .45 pistol. He ran down the ladder, rushed over to the prostate figure, pushed the barrel into the back of the mate's head, and cocked the trigger. Seeing what Captain Vickers was about to do, I ran over, pushed his arm away, and gave the hysterical man a mighty kick in the ass. That did the trick. The mate rose to his feet, rubbed the backs of his hands over his cheeks, and walked quickly away without looking in our direction.

I returned to my gun station and Captain Vickers returned to the bridge. Thinking the *Greene* herself had been torpedoed, he ordered ABANDON SHIP, and the crew manned the lifeboats. Before leaving the gun station for the lifeboats, I remembered one last thing I had to do. When I was on watch the night before, Captain Vickers said to me, "Mr. Gill, during today's battles I noticed that none of our American ships, or those of our allies, flew their ensign. Now, if we had our Stars and Stripes flying from the gaff..."

I replied, "Aye, aye, Sir!" and promised that when we went into battle again I would make sure the Stars and Stripes were flying. In the chaos of today's combat, I completely overlooked my commitment to the captain. Now that the ABANDON SHIP alarm had been sounded, and the crew was manning the lifeboats, I remembered my orders and made my way to the mainmast. I removed the ensign from its locker, bent it on its halyard, and aloft she went! When the men saw the Stars and Stripes flying from the gaff of the mainmast they broke out in cheers. I felt a lump in my throat and was overwhelmed with emotion. I thought, *What heroes! We have so much to fight for!*

Captain Vickers gave orders to the chief engineer to stop the ship's engines and make a quick survey of the mechanical equipment and the integrity of the watertight compartments. I mustered the men assigned to my lifeboat, made sure they were all there, and awaited further orders from the captain, whom I could see on the wing of the bridge.

Some of the men were seriously injured. One member of my aft gun station had a huge piece of shrapnel embedded in his back and another had an arm that had been shredded by enemy machine-gun bullets. But there was no time to fully survey and document all of the crew's injuries.

"SS *Nathanael Greene* Rejoins the Convoy." Painting by Herb Hewitt.

Several of the injured men had made it to their lifeboats and collapsed to the deck. The two ship's cooks suffered severe head injuries, and two of the naval armed guard sailors were all shot up by enemy machine gun fire. When I looked around, I could see even more casualties. Someone reported seeing Willy, one of our messmen, being blown off the foredeck into the sea by the explosion. Many men had had their helmets torn from their heads by the violent concussion, and all that remained was the chin straps and cotton padding. Helmets worn by crewmen in the interior of the vessel were rippled like washboards, stark evidence of the violence with which the explosion had tossed these men around inside the steel confines of the ship.

We did our best to control bleeding from the most grievous wounds and to splint fractured limbs. We gave morphine to the most seriously wounded men, and were amazed to see that many men with serious injuries had no idea they were injured. Meanwhile, we still didn't know whether or not we had been torpedoed. The ship's engines were still working, the propeller was turning, and the steering gear was working. Maybe there was hope for the *Nathanael Greene*!

Captain Vickers sounded the ship's whistle for dismissal from boat stations, and then he rang up FULL SPEED AHEAD on the engine room telegraph. We were going to attempt to catch up to the convoy. Those who were capable of standing watch were ordered back to their gun stations. The air was heavy with suspense. Would the *Greene* make it back to her position in the convoy, or would enemy aircraft circle back to administer the *coup de grace*, as we had seen them do repeatedly in yesterday's fighting?

The men on the other ships in the convoy cheered and cheered as we caught up with them! The Stars and Stripes were still flying over this Yankee, so horribly scarred from battle with the enemy, with rigging hanging from the masts in threads, portholes blown in, heavy exterior oak doors blown off, life rafts blown away, and its decks strewn with debris from its shattered deck cargo and the shattered remains of the *Mary Luckenbach*. All that mattered to us now was that we were still alive and afloat, and that we were going to make it!

The surviving Nazi aircraft flew back to their base in Norway. On this day, victory was ours. We lost two vessels in today's fighting, but the enemy was made to pay dearly for his victories of the day before. The Heinkel 111 pilots had displayed unbelievable courage when they flew their planes straight down the columns of armed merchantmen, through blistering AA fire, sometimes releasing their torpedoes mere yards from the vessels they were attacking. No less heroic were the Heinkel pilots who flew headlong into the ferocious gunfire of our naval escorts. Some of these torpedo-bombers disintegrated in mid-air after being struck by 4-inch shells, while others were torn to shreds by a steady stream of 20mm Oerlikon shells and plunged head-first or cartwheeled into the cold waters of the Barents Sea.

When the ship's alarm signaled DISMISSED FROM GUN STATIONS, the men off watch returned to their quarters to find them completely devastated. Compartment doors were blown off their hinges, furniture and equipment were wrecked, and clothing and furnishings were in shreds. I was lucky. My cabin was the least damaged of the officers' quarters. When the British destroyer HMS *Onslaught* came alongside to take off casualties, her men were stunned at the devastation caused by the explosion of the *Mary Luckenbach*. They marveled that we were still alive and our ship was still afloat.

After regaining our station in the convoy, we realized that nearly all of the vessels in the column on our starboard side had been destroyed. But for Captain Vickers' skillful maneuvering to dodge the torpedoes launched by avenging Heinkel 111s, we would have been among the missing merchant vessels. After the ship's head swung to port, the four torpedoes passed beneath our bow and went on to strike the TNT-laden *Mary Luckenbach*.

Before we departed Loch Ewe, I went aboard the *Mary Luckenbach* to visit her second mate and bosun, both of whom were good friends and former shipmates with me on her sister ship, the S.S. *J.L. Luckenbach*. The thought that they had been atomized shocked me. I couldn't believe it, despite having seen the catastrophic explosion with my own eyes. I was numb. Would the *Nathanael Greene* meet the same fate?

The Royal Navy escort that protected the convoy consisted of anti-aircraft cruisers, an aircraft carrier, destroyers, submarines, minesweepers, and rescue trawlers. The British sailors on these escorts were a fighting breed, men Nelson would have been proud to number among his crew on H.M.S. *Victory*. We held them in the highest regard. No less formidable were the Royal Navy pilots who flew Sea Hurricanes off the deck of the *Avenger* to defend the convoy. Again and again they flew headlong into formations of Heinkel 111s, causing them to take evasive action and blocking their attack lanes. When the Nazis sent Ju 88 bombers to attack the convoy, the Sea Hurricanes' gunfire forced these high-altitude bombers beneath the clouds, where many of them were destroyed by naval gunfire.

One of these Sea Hurricane pilots radioed to the *Avenger* that he was out of ammunition. He had the choice of either being shot down by a squadron of approaching Heinkel 111s or flying directly into the formation to break up their attack on the merchant vessels. He chose the latter option. The Heinkel 111s, no doubt shocked and caught off guard by his seemingly suicidal maneuver, were forced to take evasive action and regroup. Against all odds, the dauntless pilot returned safely to the carrier.

I reported to the bridge at 4:30 p.m.. The only thing that was not smashed was the ship's wheel. The magnetic and gyrocompasses were useless. If we lost sight of the convoy, navigation would be impossible. Continuing heavy overcast made it impossible to take sun and star sightings for celestial navigation, so we had no way to correct for compass error.

I climbed up to the "monkey bridge" above the wheelhouse and saw "Sparks," John McNally, our radio operator and one of my closest friends on the ship. We embraced warmly. We were so fortunate to be alive. John was so convinced that we had been torpedoed that he had sent out a radio message to that effect immediately after the blast wave hit our ship.

During that watch, the convoy altered course and headed due south, having rounded the North Cape of Norway. The crew was elated, as this meant that we would be entering the submarine-sheltered waters of the White Sea, and would soon arrive in Archangel, our port of destination in the U.S.S.R.

After I was relieved of my watch, I returned to my gun station with my gun crew to survey the damage done by the *Luckenbach* explosion. A large section of our 4-inch surface gun base had been blown off. We got quite a surprise when we checked the ammunition ready box for this gun, which was full of 4-inch shells. A piece of shrapnel about six inches long and two and half inches wide had penetrated the armor plating of the box and the casing of one of the shells, but had failed to explode! What a miracle! There were over seventy of these 4-inch shells in the box, live and ready for action, powerful enough to have blown the stern of the ship to Hell and all of us in the crew with it. Someone "Up There" had been watching over us, of that we had no doubt. We had all been at Death's Door the past few days, yet had survived. When I turned in that night, I thanked God for protecting me, my ship and my shipmates. I know that I was not the only one communing with the Almighty that night.

Tuesday, September 15, 1942

When I reported for duty at 4:00 a.m., there had been little change in the weather. It was overcast, sea and swells were confused and moderate, and visibility was excellent. About 5:00 a.m., the commodore blinkered to us AA--AA--AA, the general call in Morse code to visually communicate messages between vessels at sea. I acknowledged his call with an Aldis lamp, and he asked how badly we were damaged and the number of injured men. Captain Vickers, who was at my side with Jones, the Chief Mate, wrote out his reply. The commodore answered with the message: "Reverence at your gun laying. You are at the top of the class."

The commodore had to send the message a couple of times, because I could not believe that our ship and crew were being cited by a British admiral for our performance in enemy action! I was overwhelmed with emotion thinking of the Hell we had gone through to earn this compliment. Captain Vickers was just as excited as I was, and he had me relay his appreciation to the commodore for his recognition of the ship's fierce fighting performance in battle with the enemy. The ship's crew and naval armed guard sailors were very excited and extremely proud of the admiral's battle citation. To be singled out as being at "the top of the class" for our fighting performance was a great honor.

There were a couple of alerts that morning for submarine attack, but depth charges scared the U-boats away from the convoy. Around 2:00 p.m., we went to our stations to fight off an attack by high- and low-level bombers. A low-level bomber flew over us pretty low and I emptied the ammunition box in him, but he just flew on.

The enemy dropped quite a few mines on parachutes, and the men tried to detonate them by shooting at them. As the bombers flew over us, the fellow assisting me at the gun would get excited and yell, "Shoot! Shoot! Let him have it, he's coming right at us!" But I couldn't, for he was a little out of range. I didn't want to waste ammunition. Then, another plane flew right over us, and I let him have it. I could see the stream of tracer bullets disappear right into his nose. I was excited, and yelled, "I got him! Dammit, I got him!" I emptied a lot of ammunition into him, 180 rounds at least, and then he disappeared in the heavy overcast.

That raid lasted for three hours, and we were frozen by that time. We were called out several times that night for a submarine attack. Too tense to sleep, some of us spent the night in the magazine clipping shells in ammunition belts in preparation for the next enemy attack. "A red one...two black ones...red...black...red...black...." On and on it went until, unable to keep our eyes open any longer, we returned to our quarters amidships and dropped off to sleep in our filthy bed sacks.

Wednesday, September 16, 1942

We were now passing through heavily-mined waters, and we had to navigate with extreme caution. As if the mines weren't enough of a threat, we regularly came under attack by enemy planes and submarines as well. Heavy rain squalls and low visibility made it difficult to maintain a sharp lookout for U-boats. I was so exhausted from lack of sleep that I was in a daze most of the day.

Thursday, September 17, 1942

Submarine alerts and harassing attacks on the convoy continued throughout the day. Russian planes are constantly patrolling for enemy submarines. The weather is stable, with air temperatures around 40 degrees. We have passed so many mines lately that every man has the jitters.

Friday, September 18, 1942

We entered the White Sea early this morning and now are

within sight of land. We should arrive at our destination within a few days.

The enemy staged another all-out attack on the convoy. It was Hell all over again. The Nazis were doing their damnedest to destroy the convoy. The Russian naval escort can't be compared to the superb Royal Navy escort that protected the convoy until a couple of days ago. When I saw the barrage of gunfire they put up, I felt sick. The Russians refused to open fire until the Heinkel 111s practically flew down the barrels of their guns! I was afraid that, after the Hell we had gone through to deliver our cargoes to the Russians, they were going to let the German aircraft destroy what was left of the convoy right under their Bolshevik noses! Whenever a Russian destroyer did shoot down an enemy plane, it would steam over to it and remain there until it disappeared beneath the surface of the sea.

Saturday, September 19, 1942

The convoy's merchant ships formed two columns during the morning, as instructed by the commodore. The wind increased to gale force, with a heavy fall of snow and sleet. We arrived at the Dvina Bar approaches at 7:00 p.m. We were close to our destination port, but our troubles were far from over. There was a whole gale blowing; the sleet was blinding, and the visibility was poor. Not ideal conditions for crossing the treacherous river bar.

In view of the adverse weather conditions, Captain Vickers decided that it was useless to try and anchor, as the anchors would not hold in gale conditions with rough and heavy seas and swells. For the safety of the ship and cargo, he ordered the quartermaster to heave to the wind and sea, with the ship's engines at full speed ahead.

As we hove to, three other vessels closed in on us, putting all four vessels in dangerous proximity. Each of the merchant ships carried ammunition in their bottoms, and a collision between any two vessels would trigger a chain detonation, blowing all four vessels to Eternity! When I turned in that night, I was more nervous than during any of the enemy attacks.

Sunday, September 20, 1942

There was little change in the weather overnight, although visibility was improved. Three merchant ships had gone aground during the night, vessels that had attempted to anchor but lost one or both anchors. The heavy sea and swell abated, so Captain Vickers ordered both anchors lowered and the engines SLOW AHEAD.

That afternoon the convoy was attacked by both high-level and dive-bombers. The high-level bombers dropped their bomb loads all around us, and we were completely helpless, as they were beyond the range of our guns and were hidden in the clouds. The JU 87 Stuka dive bombers, however, were repulsed by convoy gunfire and Russian AA batteries. The grounded vessels were sitting ducks and their crews wisely abandoned them and sought cover beyond the river banks. After what seemed like an eternity, the enemy bombers flew back to their bases in Norway.

Monday, September 21, 1942

At daybreak, the weather had improved enough for us to start the final leg of our long journey. The Russian pilot boat came alongside and the pilot came aboard. We weighed anchors and proceeded up the Dvina River to Molotovsk, where we docked and prepared to discharge our cargo.

The docking facilities were unlike anything I had ever seen. Bleak and primitive were the words that came to mind as I surveyed the scene from the bridge of the *Nathanael Greene*. All of the piers, docks, warehouses, streets, and administrative buildings were constructed of logs. Swarms of women cargo handlers descended on the ship. Their clothing, too, was primitive, at least to my Western eyes. Their heads were covered with scarves; their outer garments appeared to be of quilted burlap; and their feet were clad in padded cloth, rather than proper shoes or boots.

The commissars were easily recognizable, with their better-quality dress and the red star insignia emblazoned on their tunics and hats. Red Army soldiers seemed to have everyone under surveillance, especially the slave-labor political prisoners they were guarding with rifles and machine guns. The heavy overcast only added to the gloom of the Molotovsk waterfront.

It was a great feeling to have arrived safely at our destination after having run a gauntlet of fire and fury in the Arctic Ocean. But foremost in all of our minds was the question, "When will we leave for home?"

TWELVE

LAYOVER IN ARCHANGEL

Monday, September 21, 1942

W E STARTED READYING THE HATCHES for discharge as soon as we secured the docking lines, and teams of Red Army soldiers swarmed up the gangway and began unloading the holds the moment the hatch covers were removed.

Tuesday, September 22, 1942

We were anxious to complete the unloading as quickly as possible because the S.S. *Virginia Dare*, loaded with 3,000 tons of TNT, was tied up directly astern of us, and S.S. *Essex Hopkins*, carrying 1,500 tons of TNT, was docked directly in front of us. And we had several hundred tons of bombs in our hold!

That afternoon, I was standing on the afterdeck supervising the unloading of hold #5 when the *Greene's* cook emerged from the galley with a bucket of kitchen waste. He carried it to the stern, tossed its contents into the water, and returned to the galley. Suddenly, one of the political prisoners who was a member of the work crew jumped into the water, swam over to the floating garbage, and started devouring it.

The Mongolian guard at the gangway heard the splash and went over to investigate. When he saw the prisoner in the water, he didn't say a word, but simply raised his rifle, took aim, and shot the man through the head.

John McNally went ashore with Captain Vickers to attend a meeting, and got to look around town a little bit. He said the living conditions for the Russians made Tobacco Road look rich!

Saturday, September 26, 1942

Today we got six merchant crew replacements, survivors of the Liberty Ship S.S. *Christopher Newport*, which was sunk on July 4 while en route to Archangel in Convoy PQ17.

Captain Vickers came to the officer's salon in a very friendly mood and chatted for a while. This was not like him. He always had the German steward, Karl, serve him his meals in his quarters. He dared not leave the bridge at sea.

Monday, September 28, 1942

Three political prisoners were shot near the ship. Their offense is unknown, but could have been something as trivial as talking to their neighbors, or giving the guards a little lip. Life is cheap in Stalin's Soviet Union.

Enemy aircraft flew over Molotovsk tonight and dropped manganese flares which lit up the night sky. They then proceeded to heavily bomb the dock area, as they did almost every Monday night. Why Mondays, no one can say.

Wednesday, September 30, 1942

The Red Army longshoremen completed unloading our cargo. Now we are waiting for "volunteer" women workers to load a cargo of pulp wood.

Women from a local settlement came down to the river frequently to do laundry. They got down on their knees on the snow-covered banks and used rocks as washboards to thrash the clothing with wooden paddles to remove dirt. They did not appear to have any kind of soap.

Friday, October 2, 1942

Willy Parks, our mess boy who had been blown overboard when the *Mary Luckenbach* blew up, had been picked up by a rescue ship and was returned to us today. He had injuries to both feet after being catapulted into the sea, but was otherwise in good shape.

Saturday, October 3, 1942

A rumor was circulating that the ships would have to leave soon, so another 500 Red Army soldiers were added to the workforce to help finish unloading all the other vessels. We were told that cargo from PQ18 was being used on the front lines in Stalingrad within two days of its unloading.

We found a local cinema, where ships' crews, cargo handlers, and local people could watch newsreels of the fighting on the various Russian fronts.

Monday, October 5, 1942

The *Nathanael Greene* left Molotovsk, sailed up the Dvina River, and docked at Salombra, just downriver from Archangel, to load pulpwood. Mountains of pulpwood logs were stacked on the river banks, and there were several sawmills near the docks. The sawmills were manned by political slave laborers.

Wednesday, October 7, 1942

The S.S. *Charles McCormack* and the S.S. *Essex Hopkins*

docked at adjoining piers to load pulpwood. The logs were loaded onto horse-drawn sleighs at the river banks and hauled alongside the ships. They were then strapped in wire cables and hauled up ramps and into the cargo holds.

The Russian women cargo handlers were very efficient. They worked long hours without rest, unloading cargo, and then started loading pulpwood.

The crew took a special interest in the loading of the pulpwood cargo because, if the ship was attacked and started to sink, the pulpwood would provide extra buoyancy, and perhaps keep the vessel afloat long enough to allow rescue vessels to save the survivors of the attack.

Salombra was reasonably close to Archangel, and most of us were anxious to see the city. To get there, we had to take a ferry across the Dvina and then hang onto the sides of a very crowded trolley into downtown Archangel. The ferry was loaded with caskets and orphaned children.

Archangel was badly damaged by the almost daily Nazi air raids. The streets and shops were crowded with women, old men and children. The only young men I saw were Red Army soldiers or political prisoners, who were detained in barbed-wire cages when they were not hard at work loading or unloading cargo from the many ships in the port.

Mink and sable fur clothing was available for purchase, but the supplies had been picked over by the sailors from visiting ships, and what remained was pretty mangy. Reindeer-skin, fur-lined parkas, on the other hand, were in plentiful supply.

There was no shortage of liquor for sale on the English merchant vessels, especially Scotch whisky. And vodka could be purchased at the Russian Intourist store, or on the black market in exchange for American cigarettes, chewing gum, chocolates and candy. Crewmen brought copious supplies of vodka back to the ship to celebrate our survival.

Friday, October 16, 1942

Today, Russian carpenters and shipfitters came onboard to repair damage caused by enemy action. They repaired the crew quarters, replaced blown-out bulkheads and cabin partitions, and repaired the splintered oak doors as well as they could.

Sunday, October 18, 1942

Members of the crew of the S.S. *Ironclad*, from Convoy PQ17, were walking ship to ship, seeking food and clothing. A couple of days later, the skipper of the *Ironclad* approached our gangway, looking for food. He was pulling a sled behind him through the snow. Their ship is in very bad condition, a real derelict.

Tex, one of the Navy sailors, helped John put his radio antenna back up. It had been knocked down when we were under air attack.

Wednesday, October 21, 1942

We had had heavy snowfall for several days, and I found a Russian man who agreed to swap six pairs of skis for six packs of cigarettes. The skis were made of spruce and had leather bindings. I lent John a pair of my new skis, and we took the ferry across the river and skied into Archangel. We attended a performance of Russian ballet at the Archangel Opera House with two other ships' officers. The ballet, which was excellent, was put on in recognition of the convoy's delivery of much-needed war supplies to the Soviet Union.

On the way back to the trolley, we came across a puddle of

blood in the snow. Another political prisoner liberated from his earthly Hell by a trigger-happy guard, no doubt.

I discovered the Russian children loved to ski, and I spent endless hours skiing with the local kids. I became a sort of pied piper to them. I always brought treats to give them, such as pieces of fruits, candy, cake, bread, or whatever I thought they would like. They followed me everywhere on skis, through the town, across farm fields, around barns and other outbuildings. Once or twice I got lost, and the kids led me back to the dock where the *Greene* was berthed. It was not the hilly and mountainous terrain I had skied on in Vermont, but it was exhilarating and good exercise.

Thursday, October 22, 1942

Today was not a good news day: three seamen from the *Virginia Dare* had their clothing stolen by street hoodlums, and a member of the S.S. *Exford's* crew committed suicide. Looking on the bright side, the weather cleared and the women volunteer workers resumed loading our holds with pulpwood.

Sunday, October 25, 1942

The *Greene* had taken on a list to port when the *Luckenbach* explosion caused her cargo to shift. Today, she finally righted herself when the last of the cargo was loaded. Her cargo ramps were removed and she took on ballast for the return voyage to Iceland.

Today, we found out that we could send telegrams to our families from Archangel at the U.S. Naval Attaché's office. Unfortunately, bad weather made it impossible for any of us to travel to Archangel to wire our families before we departed on our homeward journey.

Thursday, October 29, 1942

Today we moved upriver past Archangel to have our gyro-compasses adjusted. The pilot said his brother had been Second Mate on the *Stalingrad*, which was sunk by a U-boat on September 13. He also said that ten U-boats had been sunk by our escorts on the voyage to Archangel. I found this hard to credit.

Friday, October 30, 1942

The *Greene* ran through a degaussing range today, and then returned to Salombra and berthed alongside S.S. *Charles R. McCormack* and S.S. *White Clover*. The degaussing range made the ship's hull non-magnetic, and made us immune to magnetic mines.

Sunday, November 1, 1942

The ship was covered with a four-inch blanket of snow. We fear that we will be frozen in if we do not leave Russia soon. We have only a two-month food supply remaining.

Friday, November 13, 1942

The Dvina River is frozen over in places. Our Russian passports were retrieved by a Soviet official, which means no more shore leave. Admiral Boddam-Whetham sent his regrets that he would not be able to return with the convoy to Britain.

Saturday, November 14, 1942

There was a Commodore's conference today. There is no official word yet, but the crew is confident that we will be leaving on our homeward voyage any day now.

Sunday, November 15, 1942

The *Greene* proceeded downriver today and changed berth position. The ice was piling up on the river banks, and we learned that the S.S. *Campfire's* steering gear was frozen and that she would have to stay behind. Our Russian pilot came aboard.

Monday, November 16, 1942

As other Liberty Ships came down the river today, they saluted the *Nathanael Greene* with catcalls, whistles, hoots and howls, paying their respects to the dreadnought S.S. *Nathanael Greene*!

Tuesday, November 17, 1942

We have been in the U.S.S.R. for two months, and at last sailing day has arrived, so today we will start the long journey home to America.

When we first arrived in Russia, we thought that we would find peace and rest, but we were badly mistaken. Enemy bombers flew over Archangel almost nightly to rain death and destruction on the docks, ships and people below. The manganese flares they dropped over the city made it easier for them to locate the docks where the ships of the convoy were berthed, while powerful Russian searchlights probed the skies for invading aircraft. It was a wonderful thing to see, but a Hell of a scene to be a part of. The ceaseless blasting of the Russian anti-aircraft guns and the continuous whine of falling enemy bombs were nerve-wracking.

After we had been in Russia for a month, German radio broadcasts declared that they had demolished the city of Archangel. This was pure propaganda. They never eased up on their bombing attacks on the city or the docks where our merchant ships were berthed. The Russian people were as steadfast in their defense of Archangel as they were in the defense of Leningrad and Stalingrad. They may have lagged behind America in terms of their standard of living, but they displayed fearsome courage in defending their homeland!

The Dvina River started freezing over at the beginning of November. Snow storms were becoming more frequent and more intense, and temperatures continued to drop. We knew that if we remained in Russia much longer we would be trapped in the Dvina River ice until spring.

Now that sailing day had arrived, we were all in high spirits. We even entertained the hope that we would be home in America in time for Christmas!

Icebreakers opened up a channel to the White Sea. It felt so good to be underway again, homeward bound! God, I prayed that I would not have to go through the same hellish combat that we had experienced on our outbound voyage. The thought of those enemy U-boats, JU 88 high-level bombers, Stuka dive bombers, and Heinkel 111 torpedo bombers attacking us again sent chills down my spine!

THIRTEEN

RETURN TO ICELAND

Tuesday, November 17, 1942

A T 9:30 A.M., THE SS *Nathanael Greene* cast off her docking lines and steamed seaward as part of Convoy QP 15. We had a very light escort for such a large convoy (thirty ships), just four Russian minesweepers, but we were to pick up additional escorts in the days ahead. The wind was from astern as we crossed the Dvina River Bar and steamed into the White Sea.

Wednesday, November 18, 1942

The convoy steamed north through the White Sea throughout the day and by early the next morning we had entered the Barents Sea. There were continuous snow squalls, which we counted in our favor, as they concealed us from enemy aircraft. By evening, the wind had freshened to gale force from the southeast.

Friday, November 20, 1942

The howling gale showed no signs of abating, and it became

impossible to maintain convoy formation in such conditions. We came within fifty feet of colliding with two other cargo ships, one of which was the S.S. *Charles R. McCormack.*

Saturday, November 21, 1942

There were very few ships within sight today. At 8:00 a.m., a corvette came alongside and asked if we had seen any other ships in our vicinity. The mercury continued to drop over the course of the day. The vessel pitched and rolled, laboring and straining in a very high, rough sea and heavy swell. The ship was covered with a heavy coat of ice and, from the bridge, the *Nat Greene* looked like a ghost ship! There was a whole gale blowing by noon. We commenced shipping seas over the decks and hatches, and efforts to sight the convoy were futile.

That night, with no improvement in the weather, we hove to wind and seas. We were in a tough position, for it was in these same waters that we had been so severely attacked by the enemy on our outward-bound voyage. We had entered the Arctic Ocean, and the next day we expected to pass north of Bear Island. It was quite risky sailing alone because our compasses were not very reliable. There was the possibility of running into the ice field or into Bear Island in the low visibility.

Sunday, November 22, 1942

After heaving to for several hours, Captain Vickers decided to take a chance and proceed west. We haven't seen the sun for many days now, and the thick cloud cover makes it impossible to take a star sighting to compute our longitude. We are well and truly lost in the Arctic Ocean!

We briefly caught sight of another vessel. They are also

lost. The horrible weather has kept the Luftwaffe grounded, but we still have U-boats to worry about, so we have commenced zig-zagging.

Monday, November 23, 1942

Today John McNally received a radio transmission from the Orkney Islands requesting all ships to rendezvous at a given point so we can reform the convoy. We have no hope of making the rendezvous since we don't know where we are. We are running continuously through ice fields now, and the odds are against us. It will be almost impossible to extricate ourselves from the maze we have become lost in. The crew was not aware of our predicament.

Tuesday, November 24, 1942

The gale shifted to the north today, and the temperature is 13 degrees Fahrenheit. The icy wind blowing down from the ice fields is making the cold almost unbearable. Captain Vickers decided to steer south today. He made an educated guess that we are too far west to be vulnerable to attack from Nazi aircraft flying from Norwegian airfields. We continued zig-zagging.

Wednesday, November 25, 1942

There were still no other ships in sight. The air was dead, and the only sound came from the ship cutting through the ice. The bow would slide up onto the ice, then plop down through it. A blue wake trailed behind the ship for miles. We have finally gotten used to the perpetual darkness.

Thursday, November 26, 1942

Today is Thanksgiving Day, and we have much to be

thankful for, as we were now in sight of Iceland! Our 4-inch gun went off accidentally during a test.

Friday, November 27, 1942

We arrived in Akureyri and anchored in the Eyjafjord. There was no blackout ashore and the lights of the town were beaming. Several stragglers from the convoy joined us in the anchorage: S.S. *Esek Hopkins*, S.S. *Lafayette*, S.S. *Temple Arch,* S.S. *Charles R. McCormack*, and S.S. *William Moultrie.*

Saturday, November 28, 1942

Captain Vickers attended a Commodore's Conference today. The crew hopes against hope that he received orders for the *Greene* to return to the United States. He remained mum, but we were soon back at sea again, headed for Loch Ewe, Scotland. We sailed in company with *Lafayette* and two tankers.

Wednesday, December 2, 1942

A destroyer came alongside today and gave us orders to proceed to Loch Ewe at full speed in company with V*irginia Dare, Patrick Henry, Esek Hopkins*, and a Russian freighter. We were not going to the States!

Thursday, December 3, 1942

We arrived in Loch Ewe and received orders to go to the United States. The orders were changed several times, but the last order was for us to proceed to Loch Long. This news had a devastating effect on the crew's morale. The next day, *Virginia Dare* and *Esek Hopkins* received orders to return to the United States!

Saturday, December 5, 1942

We arrived in Loch Long at 11:00 a.m. and dropped the hook. Captain Vickers sent Christmas greetings to the captain of the *Esek Hopkins*. There were more ships in Loch Long than ever before.

Sunday, December 6, 1942

We moved over to the Holy Loch anchorage today. Lighters came alongside and stevedores came aboard to commence discharging our pulpwood cargo. The change from Loch Long to Holy Loch made it a little tougher to make trips ashore. Now, we had to take a bus to Dunoon, then a ferry across the River Clyde to Gourock, then a bus to Greenock, where we would catch a train to Glasgow.

Today, the SS *Charles R. McCormack* arrived in Holy Loch to take on some of our cargo for the United States!?!?

Friday, December 11, 1942

I went to Gourock and sent Maura a telegram today:

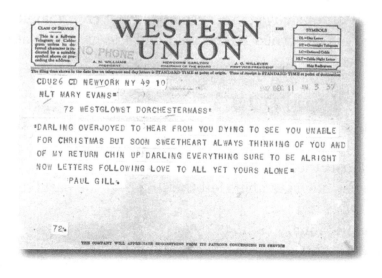

Thursday, December 24, 1942

On Christmas Eve, John McNally, Joe O'Neill (3rd Assistant Engineer) and I went on a drinking/crying jag in Gourock, bemoaning our misfortune in not being home for the holidays.

Tuesday, January 5, 1943

We tied up at a pier and huge cranes started loading Sherman tanks in the holds. There were a lot of ships taking on cargo at the docks. They would load cargo and then anchor in the loch.

Sunday, January 10, 1943

Captain Vickers told John that the ship needed to prepare for another four months at sea. The men were fed up, and only a skeleton crew remained aboard. We received replacement crew from Estonia, Latvia, Poland, and Norway from the large merchant seaman replacement pool in Glasgow.

The ship underwent extensive repairs of the damage sustained on our voyage to Archangel. The chronometer was tuned and returned to the ship and the gyrocompass was repaired.

Sunday, January 17, 1943

Captain Vickers left the ship a couple of days ago and left Chief Mate Jones in charge. We started referring to the captain as the Sea Phantom!

Eleven crew members left the ship over the past few days.

Monday, January 18, 1943

Captain Vickers returned today, and the gangway was

hauled up at 11:30 a.m. Chief Steward Harry Smith threw himself down the stairs at the Princess Hotel in Glasgow and was paid off.

Tuesday, January 19, 1943

The ship pulled out into the stream today and headed for Loch Long, where she dropped anchor. Captain Rawles, U.S. Army, is aboard with tank crews.

Wednesday, January 20, 1943

Two more Oerlikon AA cannons were installed amidships above the boat deck, so that we now have six of these terrific guns. Captain Vickers attended a Commodore's Conference, while John went to Gourock to attend a radio operators' conference.

Thursday, January 21, 1943

We departed in two-column convoy formation early this morning, bound for Mostagenem, Algeria. Dick Colin, our 2nd Assistant Engineer, treated John to a slug of Scotch.

FOURTEEN

TO THE MEDITERRANEAN

Sunday, January 24, 1943

W E ENTERED THE BAY OF BISCAY this morning and the convoy shifted into full broadside formation, with a Royal Navy escort. We had bright sunshine for two days in a row, and then the wind picked up and the ship commenced heavy rolling, pitching, hogging and sagging in a troubled sea. The rough sea conditions held the convoy's speed to 8 knots. Chief Mate Jones was very unhappy with the station-keeping performance of the ship ahead of us in column.

Monday, January 25, 1943

There was a roaring head wind today as we slogged across the Bay of Biscay. We made a measly twenty-five miles in twenty-four hours! S.S. *Panama* lost a man overboard today.

Tuesday, January 26, 1943

Convoy columns 11 and 12 on the starboard flank drifted away in the storm and were lost for a while, but rejoined the convoy by day's end.

Thursday, January 28, 1943

We are going through one of the roughest stretches of weather in the brief history of the S.S. *Nathanael Greene*! We are off Saint-Nazaire, France, and are halfway to the Strait of Gibraltar.

Friday, January 29, 1943

It snowed heavily all day today. St. Elmo's fire raced through the ship's radio antenna! We are making slow headway to the south.

Sunday, January 31, 1943

The gale appeared to have blown itself out, but then it returned with a vengeance and broke up the convoy formation. The convoy reconstituted itself before nightfall. We are now off the coast of Portugal.

Monday, February 1, 1943

The ships of the convoy have heaved to wind and sea at 6 knots.

Wednesday, February 3, 1943

At last, we have left the gale behind and are now enjoying warmer weather and sunshine. The Army soldiers are sleeping on hatch #4 while they air out their bedding.

Thursday, February 4, 1943

We are approaching the Strait of Gibraltar and have moved into two-column formation. The convoy is moving slowly, biding our time before we make our dash through the narrow strait under cover of darkness. Captain Rawles split a bottle of White Horse Scotch with John and knocked off John Barleycorn!

Friday, February 5, 1943

The convoy left the Rock of Gibraltar well astern of us by mid-morning. The ships maneuvered from two-column formation back into broadside column formation. After entering the Mediterranean, the convoy split in two as ships were directed to different destinations. The *Greene* has received orders to proceed to Mostaganem, Algeria.

Saturday, February 6, 1943

Land has come up on the starboard beam. Some vessels peel off toward Oran, and we continue on into the port of Mostaganem. Another large convoy passes us to the westward heading to the Strait of Gibraltar. We arrive in Mostaganem mid-morning, secure to the dock, and prepare to unload our cargo. The waterfront is a beehive of activity. Ship unloading operations are performed by U.S. Army Stevedore Battalions, and Jeeps, trucks, and Sherman tanks are driven off the docks as quickly as they are unloaded.

Sunday, February 7, 1943

Army stevedores boarded the ship, opened the hatches, set boom rigs, and commenced discharging cargo from our holds.

Tuesday, February 9, 1943

Today, we discharged the last of the Sherman tanks and Captain Rawles left with his equipment and troops to join the American forces at the front. Godspeed, tankers!

Arabs pillaged our cargo and that of all the discharging

vessels along the waterfront. Their baggy pants certainly provided ample storage capacity for stolen ship's property. But there was little we could do. As infidels, you could not lay a hand on them without putting your life in jeopardy. On the other hand, Arabs bought soap, clothing, linen, and anything else the crews could get their hands on to sell them.

The fighting at the front in Tunisia to the east of us was fierce, and we felt most fortunate that we were not unloading cargo at this time in Bizerte or at Cape Bon.

Friday, February 12, 1943

Army stevedores supervised the Arab longshoremen who were unloading our cargo of bombs destined for the Royal Air Force, along with other weapons and supplies. Luftwaffe air raids were heavy but intermittent. Our AA fire was deadly and accurate, and took a heavy toll on enemy aircraft.

Saturday, February 13, 1943

Today, Arab longshoremen buckled a cargo boom. The boom had to be taken down and dismantled, which delayed unloading operations.

Sunday, February 14, 1943

The *Nathanael Greene's* cargo for Mostaganem is completely discharged. We are ready to go to sea.

Thursday, February 18, 1943

A gale swept through the port this afternoon, and the ship tied up next to us, the S.S. *Ethan Allen*, lost two booms and some of its cargo rigging. Arab sabotage is suspected.

Friday, February 19, 1943

Captain Vickers attended a Commodore's Conference today, and John McNally attended a radio operators conference.

Tuesday, February 23, 1943

A British corvette escort vessel tied up alongside us. Captain Vickers threw a party, but served no liquor!

Wednesday, February 24, 1943

Today is Maura's birthday. I would give anything to be home with her in Boston today, rather than many thousands of miles away, in a remote corner of the world called Mostaganem, on the Arzew Gulf, in Algeria, North Africa.

We departed at noon today to deliver the balance of our cargo of bombs and heavy artillery to Algiers for use by the Allied forces who are pursuing Field Marshall Rommel's Afrika Korps across the deserts of North Africa.

The crew spent the morning securing the cargo hatches, cargo booms, rigging and winches and clearing the decks for sea. The loading of the ship's stores, provisions, water, fuel oil, and ammunition for the Armed Guard were completed, and the captain's sailing orders were finalized. The mail was sent ashore for dispatch, the rat guards were removed from the mooring lines, and the ship's gangway was raised and secured for sea.

When the ship was ready for departure, I reported to Captain Vickers on the bridge. The Second Mate, who was the Navigation Officer, had assumed bridge duty for the 12:00-4:00 p.m. watch, and the quartermaster was standing by the ship's wheel and awaiting orders. The Chief Mate and the Third Mate were directing the deck hands as they prepared to release the bow lines, stern lines, spring lines, and breast lines from the dock. On the captain's command, all mooring lines were released from the mooring bitts and hauled aboard, using the capstan forward and the winch drums aft.

The captain issued engine orders that were relayed to the Engine Room via the Engine Room telegraph, and the ship was maneuvered from the dock and seaward, into the Arzew Gulf

The Engine Room was manned at this time by the Second Assistant Engineer, Irwine Colin, who was the duty officer in charge of the 12:00-4:00 watch, the Cadet-Midshipman, John Robert Gordon, Jr., Wiper Charles Anderson, and Fireman Thomas Mullins.

We were joined at the breakwater by the Royal Navy minesweeper HMS *Brixham,* and proceeded at slow speed while we waited for another merchant ship to come out from Mostaganem and join us. Then, the three vessels proceeded on a course of 19 degrees to rendezvous with eastbound Convoy MKS-8, which was seen hull down on the northern horizon.

After we had steamed across the Arzew Gulf and into the broad Mediterranean Sea, the captain released me from duty on the bridge. I was exhilarated to be underway once again, ultimately homeward bound on what seemed to me and the other crew members to be a never-ending voyage.

Before going to my cabin, I walked the boat deck with other members of the crew, relaxing and engaging in light conversation. The weather was excellent, with nary a cloud in the sky, a welcome contrast to the harsh, brutally-cold, dark, and gloomy Arctic weather we had experienced on the runs to and from Russia. We felt as though we were basking in a sea of tranquility in comparison to our experiences in the Arctic Ocean, the Barents Sea and the White Sea.

Mostaganem was dropping below the horizon astern of us, and I went to my cabin to nap on the settee for a couple of hours before I reported for duty on the 4:00 to 8:00 p.m. watch. My thoughts were of returning home to Mary as I drifted off into a sound sleep.

Suddenly, I was awakened by a thunderous explosion! I was lifted bodily off the settee and slammed into the cabin ceiling and dropped back down onto the settee with a thud. In a state of shock, I sensed that the explosion had come from forward of my cabin.

Before I could get my wits about me, there was another explosion, this one even more massive and more deafening than the first! This second blast came from the Engine Room, which was immediately beneath my cabin. The force of the explosion blew me up against the ceiling and dropped me onto the steel deck, where I struck my head and blacked out.

I have no idea how long I lay unconscious on the deck, but I was awakened by live steam flowing into my cabin from the Engine Room. The steam smelled of cordite, and was saturated with fine dust which blinded me. As I looked about me in a daze, I quickly realized what had happened. We had been torpedoed! I crawled across the deck, which was knee-deep in debris from the explosion and my scattered belongings. I felt my way to the doorway and discovered that the door was gone!

As I struggled through the debris strewn across the floor of my cabin, searching for essential belongings that I had to salvage, I saw that the cabin was tilted, and realized that the ship was going down by the head, sinking bow first! I quickly grabbed my indispensable belongings: my sextant, my seaman's credentials, and Mary's letters! That was it! It was time to abandon ship!

Crawling to my feet in the alleyway outside of my cabin, I could not see or hear anyone, and I cursed at the top of my lungs to attract attention. But there was no one there to hear me! There was only one way to go, aft toward the stern, where I hoped the rest of the crew had gone. I quickly scrambled up the sloping deck of the alleyway to the watertight doorway and swept the blackout curtains aside so I could climb out onto the boat deck. I looked aft and saw, to my great relief, that I was not alone on the ship! The merchant crew and Armed Guard were gathering on the stern deck. I joined the stragglers who were abandoning their amidships quarters. Haggard, and still in a state of shock from the explosions, the survivors warmly embraced each other and shook hands, grateful to still be alive.

Then I learned what had happened. We had been attacked by a U-boat and torpedoed on the starboard side. One torpedo hit forward between #1 and #2 holds, and the other hit amidships in the dead center of the Engine Room compartment and killed Colin, Gordon, Anderson, and Thomas Mullins. David Galley, the Chief Cook, later died of injuries he sustained in the explosions. The ABANDON SHIP order had been sounded by the ship's whistle, and #2 and #4 lifeboats were launched on the starboard side. The boats rowed off some distance from the ship, but when the men saw that she was remaining afloat, they returned and gathered on the poop deck aft.

We were deeply distressed at the loss of our shipmates after all that we had gone through together: air attacks in Britain, U-boat attacks in the Atlantic, and U-boat and air attacks on our voyage to Archangel.

John McNally transmitted SOS signals immediately after we were hit, and the HMS *Brixham* came alongside to render assistance. We fed an insurance cable to her, and she started towing the ship to the beach at Salamandra, a few miles west of Mostaganem. At 9:00 p.m., the Royal Navy tug HMRT *Restive* took over towing duties, and beached the *Greene* at 6:30 the next morning. The injured crew members were taken off the ship by a U.S. Navy destroyer, and the rest of the crew climbed down Jacob's ladders onto the deck of the *Brixham*. I fell asleep on the trip back to Mostaganem.

February 25-April 6, 1943

We arrived back in Mostaganem, and Captain Vickers rented an apartment to accommodate him, Chief Engineer Iverson, and me until we had finished drafting the ship-loss reports and forwarded them to the War Assets Administration. The merchant crew was lodged in an Army stevedore battalion barracks. Over the next two weeks, they were put on a number of different ships and repatriated to the United States. The Naval Armed Guard returned to the United States on the transport U.S.S. *Anne Arundel* in mid-March.

After the *Greene* was beached, the crew recovered their belongings and selected cargo was removed from Hold #3. I was issued a Colt .45 automatic sidearm and ordered to stay aboard the vessel for two nights to guard the ship against Arab pilferage of chocolates and other food remaining in Holds #4 and #5 as well as armament and other ship's equipment. In the meanwhile, I was assigned to the U.S.S. *Redwing,* a Navy salvage and repair vessel, to assist in the dismantling of the *Nathanael Greene's* armament.

The armaments may not have been the most coveted items remaining on the beached *Nathanael Greene*. While the Navy salvage crew was busy dismantling the four-inch and three-inch guns, the .50-caliber machine guns, and the

Oerlikons, an Army barge secured alongside the ship and stevedores went aboard and started unloading case after case of rum from Hold #3. When the barge returned to the dock at Mostaganem, it was placed under heavy armed guard. Despite this precaution, the rum disappeared.

Lieutenant Billing stated in his official report that he believed that the U-boat (later determined to be *U-565*, under the command of Korvettenkapitän Wilhelm Franken) had advance knowledge of the *Nathanael Greene's* movements and had been lying in wait near the 100-fathom curve.

According to the Summary of the Statements of Survivors of the S.S. *Nathanael Greene* issued by the Navy Department on May 5, 1943, the submarine-launched torpedoes struck the *Greene* at 1:51 p.m. Although there were multiple lookouts posted at the time, neither the U-boat nor the wakes of the torpedoes were seen. A few minutes later, a formation of Heinkel 111s approached from the east. Five of the German torpedo-bombers were shot down by AA fire from HMS *Scylla*, a Royal Navy cruiser escorting Convoy MSK-8, and RAF Hurricane fighters broke up the formation.

German submarine *U-565*

A shell from one of the *Greene's* guns hit one of the planes in the tail, and it crashed into the sea. However, one of the Heinkels was able to get close enough to the *Greene* to release three torpedoes, one of which hit her amidships. The report went on to say:

> The midship section was engulfed in smoke and could not be seen. The deck cargo of tanks and trucks was littered with debris. Holes were blown in hull at #2 hold and the engine room, causing immediate flooding of both sections and disabling the engines. The crow's nest was blown off, the midship deckhouse smashed, all doors and blackout equipment destroyed...#3 lifeboat was demolished...pipes were broken and water was in the rooms...and she settled with the bow just awash...The vessel's complement consisted of 61 men, including 16 Armed Guard. There were 57 survivors, seven of whom were injured. Four merchant crew members were killed in the torpedo explosion.

Chief Cook David Galley later died of his wounds.

Unwinding

During my off-duty hours, I cavorted with U.S. Army Air Force P-38 Lightning fighter pilots and other airmen drinking the long, meaningless hours away, recounting our exploits and lamenting our current predicament. These men escorted B-17 bomber formations that flew over Italian mainland targets every day, softening them up for the impending invasion. They recounted a gruesome story about an American soldier who had raped an Arab girl. Men from her family caught the guy, cut off his genitals, sewed them inside his mouth, cut his throat, and left his body on the street as a warning to the other Allied servicemen in Mostaganem.

On one of my hitchhiking missions to Oran, I was picked up by a U.S. Navy captain driving a Jeep. His name was Robert Davis, and he was a Navy Seabee (Construction Battalion) commander. We had the misfortune of hitting and killing a German Shepherd owned by a beautiful young French mademoiselle. After conveying our sincere apologies, we proceeded to a bar and tied one on.

I had a lot of free time during my post-torpedoing days in Mostaganem, and I occupied myself making the rounds of the cafes, ogling the beautiful French girls, sampling the wines, savoring the choice horse-meat steaks, and wishing that I would soon get the Hell out of there and return home!

On March 25, 1943, I boarded a troopship in Oran, the SS *Shawnee*, and arrived in New York on April 6, 1943. I had plenty of time on the long voyage home to meditate on all I had seen and done since joining the S.S. *Nathanael Greene* that April morning in New York a year ago.

We had made fourteen war-zone runs on an eleven-month voyage, making ports-of-call in Nova Scotia, Scotland, England, Iceland, Russia, and North Africa. The *Greene* sailed over 20,000 miles through the U-boat-infested waters of the North Atlantic and Arctic Oceans, and the North, Norwegian, Barents, White, and Mediterranean Seas. We had taken part in the biggest convoy battle of World War II en route to Archangel, U.S.S.R., and had been singled out for praise by the commodore of the convoy after destroying eight enemy aircraft. We had been battered by powerful polar gales in the White Sea, and hopelessly lost in the ice fields of the Arctic Ocean. Finally, our luck ran out when we crossed paths with *U-565* one sunny afternoon off the coast of North Africa. But the *Greene* went down fighting, as our Armed Guard destroyed one last enemy torpedo-bomber even as she was in her death throes, pierced by three enemy torpedoes. Dreadnaught *Nathanael Greene* indeed!

As the ongoing life-and-death struggle continued on the long voyage, I underwent a metamorphosis in my thinking. I had become a born-again American, with an overwhelming sense of patriotism and pride in my flag and my country. The bitterness borne of years of emptiness, of denied opportunities in my youth, had been replaced by an appreciation of America's overwhelming economic strength and the opportunities she offered her citizens.

FIFTEEN

FORT TRUMBULL AND
THE U.S NAVY

Repatriation and Wedding Bells

I EXPERIENCED A FLOOD OF emotions—relief, sadness and, above all, pride—as the hospital ship that brought me home from the war steamed past the Statue of Liberty on the afternoon of April 6, 1943. I could scarcely believe that a mere year had passed since the *Nathanael Greene* had slipped her mooring and set out from this very port on the first leg of her long voyage to north Russia and the Mediterranean. I never could have imagined the sights I would see on that voyage, the horror and excitement of combat, and the grief I would experience at the loss of my ship and six heroic shipmates.

But these emotions were replaced by feelings of intense joy and anticipation as the ship nosed into her North River slip and I gathered my belongings and prepared to step foot on American soil again for the first time in over a year. I wished with all my heart that I could have gone directly to Grand Central Station and boarded the next train to Boston and my beloved Maura. But first, I had to visit the offices of the United States Lines, the owners of the *Nathanael Greene*, and obtain a formal release from their employment.

On the morning of April 8, I boarded a New Haven Railroad train at Grand Central Station, and my heart was pounding out of my chest as the train glided into South Station four and a half hours later and I spotted Maura waiting for me on the platform. I bounded off the train and we flew into each other's arms. I cannot say how long we stood there, locked in a tight embrace, tears streaming down our cheeks, oblivious to the people around us or the passage of time.

Mary and I were married in St. Anne's Church in Dorchester, Massachusetts, on April 17, 1943. We had a small reception at the Fairmont Copley Plaza Hotel in Boston's fashionable Back Bay, and then traveled by train to the Pinehurst Resort in North Carolina for our honeymoon.

I Return to Fort Trumbull

When Maura and I returned to Boston, I started to give serious consideration to my future. The war was far from over, and I wanted to return to sea duty. However, the long voyage had had a deleterious effect on my health. Repeated exposure to the deafening roar of anti-aircraft guns in the run to Archangel had taken a toll on my hearing, and I was left almost deaf by the blast of the three torpedoes that slammed into the *Greene* off Mostaganem. Additionally, I learned that I had contracted malaria, and poor nutrition and stress produced severe chronic gingivitis and loss of most of my teeth. The most perplexing health issue was repeated bouts of severe abdominal pain that started shortly after the explosion of the *Mary Luckenbach* in the Barents Sea. I underwent a battery of tests to determine the origin of the pain. The results were all "negative." The doctors told me the problem was psychosomatic, and I was referred to a psychiatrist for counseling.

I had a difficult time reintegrating into society when I returned to America. I was shocked at the many people who hardly seemed to be aware that there was a war on. They complained about the rationing of gasoline and other commodities, and were worried about getting enough ration coupons to buy fuel, clothing, food, etc. There was full employment, wages were high, and many workers were able to fatten their paychecks by working overtime. It seemed everyone was making a lot of money, women as well as men, and had never had it so good. I felt that talk of the "Home Front" was ridiculous. There were many fronts in this war, where men were dying in huge numbers, but there was no front in America. The civilian populations of Germany, Britain, France, Russia, Norway, Denmark, Belgium, Holland, Japan, China, the Phillipines, and many other countries had suffered grievously from repeated air raids and the invasion of enemy armies, but the American mainland had been spared. Americans didn't know how good they had it.

Wanting to contribute to the war effort, but disqualified from sea duty by my hearing loss, I applied for a teaching position at the Fort Trumbull Maritime Officers Training School and was offered a faculty position. Starting May 3, 1943, I taught a class in Seamanship and Cargo Handling. After four months, I was asked to organize a new Department of Defense of Merchant Shipping. I supervised six instructors and was responsible for drawing up course outlines, introducing new training materials, and integrating the training schedules of the various departments.

I Join the Navy

The teaching post at Fort Trumbull was a fine gig, and I knew I was contributing in a meaningful way to the war effort. I could have remained in this draft-deferred position for the balance of the war. And yet, I was haunted by memories of shipmates who never returned from the war-torn waters of the Arctic Ocean and the Mediterranean Sea. I was overcome with guilt at the thought of all those merchant seamen and servicemen who would not come home until the war had ended. I hated the thought that servicemen home on leave from the fighting front would look upon me as a shirker, a man who was hiding out the war in a safe stateside position. That was intolerable to me.

I resigned from my U.S.M.S.Officer Training School position on September 29, 1944, and accepted a commission as an ensign in the United States Navy Reserve the next day. I knew that by volunteering for the Navy I was jumping from the frying pan into the fire. On convoy duty, I was riding a cargo of weapons and ammunition, and watching ships all around me being blown to Kingdom Come. After that terrifying experience, I was getting right back into the midst of the action, as a Stevedore Officer unloading ammunition ships somewhere in the vast Pacific Theater of Operations. The Naval Procurement Officers who processed me into the Navy questioned why I felt compelled to go out there again. Without giving voice to the thought, they must have thought I was crazy. My friends in the Maritime Service certainly thought I was, and my friends in Boston also thought I was daft.

On the other hand, my practical experience as a deckhand on cargo ships, longshoreman, stevedore, shipyard worker, ship's officer, department head at the U.S.M.S. Officer Training School teaching seamanship, cargo handling, ship construction and operations would qualify me for duty as a Stevedore Officer in a Construction Battalion. The Naval Civil Engineer Corps assigned me to the 37th Naval Construction Battalion in Pearl Harbor, Hawaii.

Mary and I were very grateful to the Navy for allowing her to join me in Hawaii after I had been there for a few months. We had a small apartment on the base at Pearl Harbor, and had access to all the amenities the Navy provided to its commissioned officers and their families. One day, I went for a swim at the Officers' Beach and had climbed up onto the raft that was anchored some distance from the beach.

Lieutenant Paul and Mary Gill

An older gentleman swam out to the raft, climbed up the ladder onto the raft, and sat down across from me. He had a foul anchor tattooed on his right shoulder, similar to the one I sported on my left arm. I introduced myself as Lt. (j.g.) Paul Gill, and I almost fell off the raft when he reached out, shook my hand, and told me he was Bill Halsey. I couldn't believe I was sitting on a swimming raft at Pearl Harbor with Admiral William F. "Bull" Halsey!

After Japan surrendered on August 14, 1945, I was reassigned to the 14th Naval District and made assistant to the Automotive Superintendent. I was office manager and supervised a staff of ten officers and non-commissioned officers. My job was to develop a system of control and record-keeping for a fleet of 22,000 vehicles. One of the perks that went with this new position was that I was allowed to use any vehicle that was not otherwise in use. Many afternoons after work, Mary and I would sign out a Jeep, and she would take me for a driving lesson. I had received my Second Mate license before I left the Merchant Marine, and it granted me the privilege of navigating any vessel of any tonnage on any ocean. Under Mary's expert tutelage, I qualified to operate a motor vehicle (of limited tonnage) on the roads and highways of the Territory of Hawaii!

One evening, on a lark, we signed out an Admiral's limousine. We knew that none of the flag officers were going to need this vehicle on this particular evening, so we jumped into the back seat and were chauffeured around by an enlisted man. The limousine, a very impressive, shiny black Cadillac with gleaming chrome trim and bumpers, had flags affixed to its front fenders that sported two stars, representing the two-star rank of the Admiral who was the usual occupant of the vehicle. When we drove through the gate, the sentry on duty came smartly to attention and snapped us a respectful salute. Mary and I and our driver did our best to conceal our huge smiles as we drove through the streets of Honolulu, receiving crisp military salutes from sailors of all ranks as we proceeded down the main boulevard in our borrowed VIP conveyance. It was a lot of fun, but looking back now, I realize that I probably could have been busted to the enlisted ranks for the crime of impersonating a flag officer! Mary and I still laugh when we recall how much fun we had that evening skylarking in an Admiral's limousine.

During my time in Hawaii, I was introduced to local businessmen at various social affairs. Some of these men were impressed by my "up the hawse pipe" story, ascending from hobo to Merchant Marine and Naval officer at a young age, and offered me jobs in their organizations. Mary and I were sorely tempted to take them up on their offers. We loved Hawaii, and could easily envision becoming permanent residents. But we knew that we would miss our families back in Boston too much to ever seriously contemplate putting down roots there. And I was determined to continue my education, and felt that my native Massachusetts was the best place to do that. I informed the Navy of my desire to leave the service, and received an honorable discharge on June 12, 1946.

SIXTEEN

BACK TO SCHOOL

Suffolk University

MARY AND I RETURNED TO Boston in June, 1946 and I enrolled at Suffolk University, a school that was willing to overlook the fact that I had completed only one year of high school. I made the case to the admissions officer at Suffolk that, although I lacked a high school diploma, I had proven my ability to do college-level work when I graduated from the Fort Trumbull Officer Training School. I had taught myself algebra, geometry and trigonometry during my offwatch hours at sea, and had no difficulty learning celestial navigation, which requires proficiency in all of these mathematical disciplines. I hadn't taken any English or history courses at Fort Trumbull, but I was a voracious reader, and so I had a good fund of knowledge and good writing skills. My performance on the IQ tests they administered to all prospective students bolstered my case, and I was accepted into the freshman class entering in September, 1946.

As a Navy veteran, I qualified for GI Bill benefits, which covered my tuition bills and some, but not all, of our living expenses. To make ends meet, I took a job at the Post Office sorting mail on the night shift. After many years at sea working all hours of the day and night, sometimes under very trying conditions, I did not find the night shift onerous. However, after our first child, Judith, was born in January, 1947, I found that I wasn't able to get much studying done in our cramped South Boston apartment. I needed to find a better study environment.

The solution to this problem came in the person of my brother-in-law, Emmett Evans. Emmett was also attending college on the GI Bill, and needed to supplement his income. I suggested that he get a job working nights at the post office with me so that he and I could divide up the work and carve out some hours for studying. He got the job, and we devised a system to get all of our mail-sorting work done in half the allotted time. Emmett would then find a quiet corner in the post office to do his homework, while I generally went across the street to South Station and sat in one of the wooden pew-like benches in a corner of the cavernous waiting area and dove into my German, economics, and accounting textbooks,

I completed my undergraduate work in three years and applied for admission to Harvard Business School, where I hoped to earn a Master of Business Administration degree. I was accepted, and I was told that I was the first non-high school graduate to be tendered admission to the B school.

However, before I started at Harvard, I had a medical issue that had to be resolved. I had continued to suffer from the bouts of agonizing abdominal pain that started soon after the to voyage Archangel. I would double up with pain, turn white, sweat profusely, and vomit repeatedly. These attacks could last anywhere from thirty minutes to several hours. Sometimes, the pain was so unbearable that I would go to the corner bar and toss off boilermakers, shots of whisky with beer chasers, to take the edge off it. I had seen several physicians about this problem over the years, but the tests they ran were inconclusive, and none of the doctors had been able to come up with a definitive diagnosis. Finally, I was referred to a psychiatrist, who concluded that my symptoms were psychosomatic in origin. That diagnosis didn't sit well with me. I knew that there was an organic problem, and insisted on exploratory surgery to get to the bottom of the problem.

The surgery was revelatory. When they opened my abdomen, the surgeons discovered a piece of shrapnel embedded in my small intestine. The shrapnel had been causing intermittent bowel obstructions and all the attendant pain and other symptoms. They were so amazed at this finding that my case was the subject of a Surgical Case Presentation at the Brookline Veterans Administration Hospital, and it was written up in a prominent medical journal.

Having put paid to my health problems, my next challenge was to find suitable housing for my growing family for the next two years while I was in graduate school. My son, Paul Junior, was born in May, 1948, and he was a howler. Our one-bedroom apartment in South Boston was no longer adequate to our needs. However, the flood of servicemen returning from Europe and the Pacific had created a huge housing shortage in the post-war years, and we had no idea where we were going to find a larger apartment.

The solution to this problem came in the form of a favor returned. I was walking through a residential neighborhood near the Harvard Business School campus one day in July, a few weeks before classes were scheduled to start, and came upon an elderly man shoveling topsoil from a pile on his front lawn into a wheelbarrow. It was an oppressively hot day, and I got the distinct impression that the gentleman was not used to such strenuous labor. Beads of sweat peppered his brow, his cheeks were pale, and his shirt was drenched. I said hello to him, took the shovel out of his hands, and finished shoveling the dirt into the wheelbarrow. I asked him where he wanted me to deposit the contents of the wheelbarrow, and he led me into his backyard and indicated a flower bed where I should dump the topsoil. Then he invited me into his house for a glass of ice-cold lemonade.

We introduced ourselves and sat at his kitchen table and chatted for a few minutes. He told me his name was Wallace Donham, but said little more about himself. He seemed more interested in learning about me. I told him that I would be attending the B school in the fall, and had been in the neighborhood scouting out apartments. He wrote the name "Florence Glynn" and a phone number down on a slip of paper and asked me to give her a call that afternoon.

When I got home, I dialed the number on the paper. A woman answered the phone and said, "Hello, Dean David's office, this is Florence Glynn, how can I help you?"

I identified myself, and told Miss Glynn that Mr. Wallace Donham had asked me to call her. "Yes, Mr. Gill, I'm Dean David's secretary, and I was Dean Donham's secretary until he retired a few years ago. I have been expecting your call. Mr. Donham thinks he can help you find an apartment. If you come over this afternoon, we can talk about some possibilities."

"That's wonderful," I said. "But where is your office?"

"Why, at the Business School, of course!""

I was stunned! The man I had stopped to help that morning turned out to be the former dean of Harvard Business School! There had been times in the past when I almost believed in guardian angels. Now I was convinced of the reality of such supernatural beings!

Harvard had a list of housing that it reserved for visiting faculty, and Florence put my name at the top of the waiting list for a two-bedroom apartment. We moved in before the start of classes in September, and Mary and I became good friends with Florence. We stayed in touch for many years, and never forgot the kindness that she, and Dean Donham, extended to us in our hour of need.

The B School was an exhilarating experience for both Mary and me. Harvard attracted talented people from around the world, from every imaginable background and ethnic group, with sometimes astonishing personal histories. My background was certainly unconventional, but the B school seemed to seek out students who not only had exotic resumes, but who also possessed the drive and imagination to succeed in the most challenging business environments. Although I regret not having had the time to participate, there was a full slate of extracurricular activities for students to get involved in. However, I almost always made room in my busy schedule for the Dean's teas, which Dean David and his wife held at their house once a month. Mary loved these affairs, and was not at all shy about hob-nobbing with men and women from the far corners of the world. The lass from Monaghan, Ireland, felt that she had arrived in her adopted country when she found herself drinking tea and chatting with Harvard professors and future captains of industry. These teas helped erase memories of the "IRISH NEED NOT APPLY" signs she saw everywhere in Boston as a young girl. Both she and Boston had come a long way. And so had I.

I received my MBA from Harvard University on June 21, 1951, sixteen years, almost to the day, since the day I wiped away my tears, said goodbye to my parents, and walked out of my family home and into a future that promised nothing but challenges, hardship, and uncertainty. I wasn't a scared young boy anymore, but I shed a private tear or two that day in Harvard Yard, as I stood with my family, posing for photographs with my diploma in hand. Not tears of sadness, but tears of gratitude that I lived in a country that afforded me the opportunity to rise up out of poverty, to become a naval officer, and to gain an education. And tears of gratitude to God for guiding me safely through so many perilous situations, in ocean storms, in foreign ports, on scaffolding high up on the walls of skyscrapers, in boxcars roaring across the continent, and in deadly combat in the Barents Sea and the Mediterranean. And above all, for my wonderful Maura, and our children.

Top: Paul G. Gill,
M.B.A., with Judith
and Mary Gill.

Left: Paul G. Gill's
Harvard Diploma

EPILOGUE

By Paul G. Gill, Jr., M.D.

B Y THE TIME MY FATHER sat down to write his memoirs in 1982, he had long since lost contact with his former shipmates. The internet and search engines were still figments of futurists' imaginations, and few of the written inquiries he sent out to the United States Lines, the U.S. Coast Guard, and the U.S. Navy yielded useful information. Since I took over the project in 2020, I have made extensive use of the internet to gather information not only about Convoy PQ18 and the *Nathanael Greene*, but also about the CCC, the other ships Dad sailed on, the ports he visited, riding the rails in the late 1930s, the Dust Bowl, and Fort Trumbull. I was curious to know what became of the men and ships Dad knew and this is what I have learned:

William F. Gill, Jr, Dad's oldest brother, served as mate on a number of ships during the war. I haven't been able to uncover many details of his service, but Dad told me the following incredible story: On D-Day, June 6, 1944, Bill was Chief Mate on a merchant vessel, the SS *Robert Battey*, that was carrying supplies across the English Channel to one of the landing beaches. Halfway across the channel, Captain Richard Hunt lost his nerve and ordered the helmsman to turn the ship around and head back to England. Bill, who had a master's license, was having none of it. He took over command of the ship and had Captain Hunt confined to his cabin. The ship continued on to the invasion beaches and discharged the desperately-needed cargo.

Several months later, Dad's twin brother, **Philip**, reported for duty on the SS *Richard V. Oulahan*, in Baltimore. The vessel was taking on munitions for delivery to the war zone in the western Pacific, and Phil was to be her Chief Mate. When the captain greeted Phil at the head of the gangway, he gave him a queer look and said, "Philip Gill? Do you have a brother Bill?" Phil acknowledged that he had an older brother, Bill, who was a Chief Mate in the Merchant Marine.

The captain looked at Phil for a moment or two, and said, "I know. He took my ship from me on D-Day." Captain Hunt made life miserable for Phil throughout his term of service on the *Oulahan*.

Synchronicity? I would think that the odds of one captain, in a war involving thousands of ships over all the oceans of the world, having two brothers serve serially as his Chief Mate must be vanishingly small. And in such embarrassing circumstances? The captain could have been forgiven for believing that he had been cursed by the sea gods.

Phil made a career of the Merchant Marine. He earned his Master's license before the end of the war, and served as Master of a series of merchant vessels until he swallowed the anchor in 1971. He then worked as a ship surveyor until he retired in 1985. He died in 1996. Bill returned to New York after the war and resumed his steeplejacking career. He died in 1972 from injuries he suffered in a fall.

Dad's brother **John** also served in the Merchant Marine before and during the war. He made numerous war zone runs from late 1941 until March, 1945. He sailed to Murmansk in late 1942 on SS *Yorkmar* in Convoy JW51b, and participated in the Battle of the Barents Sea.

Steven Gill served on many of the same ships Paul Gill sailed on, before and throughout the war years.

Captain George Vickers was awarded the Merchant Marine Distinguished Service Medal for his performance as Master of the S.S. *Nathanael Greene*. This is the citation:

> The President of the United States takes Pleasure in Presenting the Merchant Marine Distinguished Service Medal to
>
> George A. Vickers
> Master of SS *Nathanael Greene* (GSA) 03/42 to 02/24/43
> For distinguished service in the line of duty.
>
> In the early spring of 1942, SS *Nathanael Greene* sailed with a full cargo bound for Russia. Eleven months later, with all housing above deck either demolished or damaged, and with her bow blown away, she was beached by her crew on the North African coast. But in those eleven months she had delivered an urgently needed cargo to our Russian ally; returned to the United Kingdom and repaired and loaded there; and had delivered an equally vital cargo to our own forces in North Africa. On the Russian voyage, the ship survived ten torpedo plane bomber attacks, was twice attacked by submarines, and had dodged four torpedoes by clever maneuvering. In a sustained attack, over three days, the ship's guns were credited with the possible destruction of eight enemy planes.
>
> On the succeeding voyage, she had discharged nearly

all of her military cargo at Algerian ports and was en route to her final port of call when struck by two torpedoes. In a sinking condition, she was further attacked by enemy aircraft. The planes hit her with three aerial torpedoes but during the fight a shell from one of her guns tore off the tail of one of the attacking planes. With bow underwater; below decks bulkheads ripped out; deck houses wrecked; and steam pipes broken, she was towed in stern first and successfully beached.

Captain Vickers, Master of a gallant ship and a gallant crew, exhibited qualities of leadership and high courage in keeping with the finest traditions of the United States Merchant Marine.

For the President

Admiral Emory Scott Land

Dad reconnected with his old shipmate, radio operator John McNally, in the late 1980s. John lived in Connecticut for many years after the war, and then retired to the McNally family home in his native Swanton, Vermont, in the mid-1980s. He and Dad spent many hours on my front porch in Middlebury, Vermont, reminiscing about their old captain and their other shipmates; their escapades in various pubs in Scotland and England; the long layover in Archangel; their experiences in Mostaganem, Algeria; and the final attack and destruction of the *Nathanael Greene* by *U-565* and a Heinkel 111.

U-565 was scuttled in Skaramanga Bay, off the coast of Greece, on September 24, 1944, after being severely damaged by U.S. Army Air Force bombers. Her captain, Korvettenkapitän Wilhelm Franken, died in a fire on a ship in Kiel harbor on January 13, 1945.

Captain George Vickers (*right*) receives the United States
Lines Distinguished Service Medal

S.S. *Halo* was struck by two torpedoes fifty miles from the
Southwest Pass of the Mississippi River on May 20, 1942.
She broke in half and went to the bottom in less than three
minutes. Of her crew of thirty-four crewmen and eight
officers, only one officer and two crewmen survived. *U-506*
was credited with the kill.

S.S. *Manhattan* continued in service as a passenger liner
until the United States entered the war. Before Dad made
his two passages on her in 1937, she carried the U.S. Olympic
team to Europe in 1936 to compete in the Berlin Olympics,
and Joseph Kennedy and his family to England in 1938 after
he was appointed Ambassador to the Court of St. James.
After the U.S. entered the war, *Manhattan* was purchased by
the U.S. Navy, converted into a troop ship, and renamed the

U.S.S. *Wakefield*. Between April 1944 and February 1946, the *Wakefield* transported 110,563 troops to Europe and brought 106,674 troops back to America. She was struck from the Navy list in 1959 and scrapped in 1964.

S.S. *President Roosevelt* was taken over by the War Department in October, 1940, converted to a troopship, and re-named the *Joseph T. Dickman*. She transported troops to invasion beaches in North Africa, Sicily, and Normandy, and was preparing to participate in the invasion of the Japanese Home Islands when the war ended. She was scrapped in 1948.

S.S. *Gulfwave* was torpedoed by Imperial Japanese Navy submarine I-10 south of Tonga in the South Pacific Ocean on March 1, 1943. However, she was not seriously damaged, and made it into port under her own power and without injury to any of her crew. She was scrapped in 1959.

S.S. *William Luckenbach* hauled cargo for the Luckenbach Steamship Company throughout World War II. She was sold to an Italian shipping company and converted to a passenger liner in 1946. She was scrapped in 1952.

U.S.A.T. *Republic* continued transporting troops from San Francisco to Honolulu and the South West Pacific Area until early 1945. She was then used to transport troops back to the United States from the Far East. She was scrapped in 1952.

S.S. *Uruguay* was converted to a troopship and carried over 200,000 troops to virtually every theater of war from 1942-5. She was converted back to a passenger liner after the war, and made regular runs to Rio de Janeiro, Buenos Aires, and other South American ports until 1954. She was scrapped in 1964.

S.S. *J.L.Luckenbach* continued in service as a cargo carrier throughout the war and was sold for scrap in 1959.

S.S. *Nathanael Greene* lay on the beach at Salamandra until 1948, when she was purchased by an Italian firm and scrapped. Her mortal bones, and those of the brave men who sailed her into battle, are no more, but their fighting spirit will live forever.

* * * *

On October 10, 1991, Dad and other merchant marine survivors of the Russian Arctic convoys gathered at the Soviet Embassy in Washington, D.C., where they were awarded the Commemorative Medal "The 40th Anniversary of the Victory in the Great Patriotic War."

My father, **Paul George Gill, Sr.**, died on February 23, 2000. He had made it known that he wished to have his ashes spread on the waters of Boston Harbor. The family wanted to comply with his wishes, but we were uncertain how to do it. My son, Paul G. Gill III, provided the answer. Keeping with Gill family tradition, Paul joined the crew of the "Baltimore Clipper" topsail schooner *Pride of Baltimore II* that spring. The *Pride* was part of an international fleet of Tall Ships that sailed up the United States East Coast that summer, stopping at ports along the way and participating in glorious parades of sail. My wife and I watched from a Staten Island ferry as the *Pride* entered New York Harbor on July 4, sailed past an armada of welcoming pleasure craft, fireboats, and ships, and secured alongside a dock on the Hudson River. We met Paul at the dock and gave him a container with my father's ashes.

The Tall Ships' next port of call was Boston. On the morning of the fleet's departure from Boston Harbor, Paul asked the captain if he might discreetly pour his grandfather's ashes over the side of the *Pride of Baltimore II* as they put to sea. The captain not only granted permission for Paul to do so, but

Top: Mariner's Medal
Bottom: Soviet Commemorative Medal

Pride of Baltimore II (Photo courtesy of Matthew Abbot)

ordered the ship's cannon to fire a salute as well. I know Dad was looking on from Fiddler's Green and beaming with pride as the beautiful War of 1812 privateer heaved to in Boston Harbor and his beloved grandson and namesake returned his mortal remains to the waters that lapped the beaches where he and his twin brother once scavenged for driftwood.

Day is done, gone the sun,
From the lake, from the hills, from the sky;
All is well, safely rest, God is nigh.

~ "Taps" ~

ABOUT THE AUTHOR

P AUL GILL, SR., a native of South Boston, Massachusetts, was the twenty-two-year-old Third Mate on the Liberty Ship SS *Nathanael Greene* (one of just nine merchant ships to be recognized as a Gallant Ship of World War II), which sailed to Archangel, Russia, with Convoy PQ18 in September 1942. He enrolled in the Civilian Conservation Corp at age fifteen, joined the Merchant Marine and made eight passages to European ports as a sixteen-year old, rode the rails across the United States in search of work in 1938; returned to the Merchant Marine and ascended "up the hawse pipe" to become a licensed Merchant Marine officer, participated in the biggest convoy battle of World War II, and received an MBA from Harvard in 1951. Paul George Gill, Sr., died on February 23, 2000.

ABOUT THE EDITOR

P AUL G. GILL, JR., M.D. is a fifth-generation South Boston-
ian. He grew up in Stony Brook, New York, and attended
the University of Notre Dame and the University of Alabama
School of Medicine. He practiced emergency medicine for
thirty-five years and was a freelance medical writer for many
of those years. His articles appeared in many outdoor magazines, and his books, *The Ragged Mountain Press Guide to
Wilderness Medicine & First Aid* and *The Onboard Medical
Handbook* were published by McGraw-Hill. He retired from
medical practice in 2013, and now spends his time building
boats and furniture, sailing, and hiking in the United States
and Europe with his wife, Mary.

WWW.HELLGATEPRESS.COM

Made in the USA
Middletown, DE
26 February 2023

25693793R00225